DANNY MURTAUGH AND MICKEY VERNON

ORDINARY HEROES

FOREWORD BY RAY DIDINGER

ROBERT N. MCLAUGHLIN

RNMcLaughlin 2016

CLOUD9 PUBLISHING COMPANY
PHILADELPHIA, PA
9

Danny and Mickey, Ordinary Heroes

Dedication

From my heart

To Dorothy Donnelly, who smiled at me so long ago, and stole my heart

From my soul

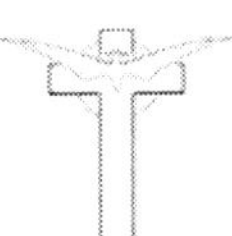

To James William Reese, Chester HS graduate and Congressional Medal of Honor recipient, who gave his life while saving his fellow soldiers on Sicily in 1943

Danny and Mickey, Ordinary Heroes

Library of Congress Cataloging-in-Publication Data.
McLaughlin, Robert N.
Danny and Mickey, Ordinary Heroes/ by Robert N. McLaughlin
ISBN 978-0-692-76518-0

Cover design by Helene McKelvey-McLaughlin

Cloud9 Publishing Company
Philadelphia, PA

Visit www.dannyandmickey.com

Acknowledgements

I want to begin my acknowledgements for this book by thanking all of the sports writers in Chester, Delaware County, and Philadelphia who have kept alive for fifty years the valid position that the two subjects of this book deserve a place in Major League Baseball's Hall of Fame in Cooperstown, NY. Without their persistence, and without the loyalty of local county baseball fans, especially Jim Vankoski, President of the Mickey Vernon Sports Museum, I might not have read my 'one-hundredth and something' sports article questioning MLB's omission of Danny and Mickey from the Baseball HOF. I saw the latest plea for our local stars in March or April 2012. On that day, only months after I retired to pursue my life-long dream to write my own, great American novel, I chose to put that dream aside, and climb on the bandwagon for Danny and Mickey. I figured wrongly that this task wouldn't take very long. I believe they belong in the Hall and I am convinced baseball fans around America lack an awareness of their baseball achievements and of their lives in general. Thus, this book was born. It was conceived as a screenplay, and once the screenplay was completed, it evolved into a book.

There are many people that contribute to any major project. I want to express my thanks first to my son, Stephen, who purchased the first books on the subject for me; for Chris West, John and Nancy Schmidt, my son-in-law, Mike Taddei, my oldest son, Bobby, and my fifth brother, Mike Blair, for all taking the time to look at the early beginnings of this work, and for being immediately enthusiastic for the project, and for me. Thanks also to Bill Smeck who reviewed the military chapters to ensure I didn't confuse Army and Navy jargon. All of their faith and excitement were contagious, and so I continued.

My earliest fan and cheerleader was my daughter, Laura. That is Dr. Laura, I'm proud to add. Her constant and sincere interest wouldn't allow me to be sidetracked from this good work. The combination of her skill with headers and footers, and my wife, Dorothy's final 'eagle-eyes on the prize', confirmed the book was ready for show time.

Additionally, and most importantly, were the various readers, my diverse team of editors, who seriously read the book, one chapter at a time. John Mooney, my former high school teacher, was kind and diligent in reviewing every page of the transcript, as was my high school friend, Frank Wujick, a Villanova grad who was available only when the 'Nova basketball games were not on television or radio. Pat Brough, my wife's godson, baseball fan and strategist, provided important feedback on content, and questioned passages and phrases that seemed clouded and needed clarification.

Certainly, I welcomed the support and participation of the Murtaugh family. The Murtaugh family was engaged early in the project. My first interview was with Tim Murtaugh in May 2013, followed shortly thereafter by an interview with Ben Wilson, Danny's nephew who lived in the Murtaugh household for several years after his own father, Captain Bennie Dale Wilson, was killed in an Air Force crash in 1953. Gay Vernon, Mickey's daughter, responded to requests for information and provided her support for my interest in her father's life. Such family communications and occasional clarifications on facts continued intermittently throughout 2016.

I learned gradually how research is endless on every project. One fact can lead to many other facts. The previous books written solely about Danny and Mickey were very valuable to me. Colleen Hronrich's biography of her grandfather, 'The Whistling Irishman. Danny Murtaugh Remembered' gave me an insight into the many facets of Danny's personality and life achievements. Rich Westcott's biography, 'Mickey Vernon. The Gentleman First Baseman' is an enjoyable history of a man who is still revered in his home town, Marcus Hook, and throughout Delaware County. These books allowed me to see both the measure of these men and their accomplishments so that I could understand their place in time, and speak for them in this book. Other books listed in the bibliography such as those written by Rick Cushing and Jim Reisler, and numerous articles and internet searches provided helpful and innumerable bits of information, especially two online baseball search sites - baseballalmanc.com, and baseballreference.com.

Jim Vankoski who is mentioned earlier provided a firm foundation for this book because he preserved the baseball facts and the essence of these two men through his caring stewardship of the history of all sports in Delaware County. He is a modern Homer who keeps us connected to these and many other priceless memories of our community.

My high school lab partner, published author, accomplished Educator, and quizzical writing consultant, Mike Milone, offered stark advice at key moments of this journey, and kept me on the forward path, challenging me to always do better with such scholarly instruction as, 'Just write the damn thing.'

I was fortunate to have my grandson, Kevin, create my website, dannyandmickey.com, which allowed me to introduce Danny and Mickey to the world via the internet, an audience I'm told that reaches well beyond Pennsylvania. My daughter-in-law, Helene McKelvey-McLaughlin, applied her professional graphic arts talent to make the selection of a cover design a non-event for me. The quality of the cover designs was simply a matter of selecting a best from among the best. Thanks also to the many persons who voted on the website for the book cover they liked best. The cover design that received the most votes now graces the front of this book.

I am grateful to Ray Didinger, a worthy member of the Philadelphia Sportswriters Hall of Fame, columnist, author, TV and radio sports analyst, and playwright, for providing a foreword that dignifies the simple grace and exemplary character of Danny and Mickey in words that capture their impact on those who knew them.

Danny and Mickey, Ordinary Heroes
I wish to soulfully acknowledge the sacrifices that men and women in our armed forces make daily to enable us to pursue life, liberty, and happiness in our daily lives. Likewise, I acknowledge our veterans, past and present, and especially Congressional Medal of Honor recipient, PVC. James William Reese, Chester High Class of '38, whose short life and sacrifice is an integral part of the spirit behind this book.

Joyfully, I thank my wife, Dorothy, who supported her 'Ernest' during the uncountable hours he was selfishly sequestered within his home office. The book was always her only competition for his attention, and it was certainly a poor second. 'Earnest' needed her love and her patience.

Foreword

Every time I receive Holy Communion, I think of Danny Murtaugh. If you are a Baby Boomer who belonged to Our Lady of Peace Catholic Church in Milmont Park, Pa., you may have the same memories.

Even though Danny, Sr., managed the Pittsburgh Pirates, the Murtaugh family kept their home in Delaware County. When the baseball season ended Danny returned to the area and his usual seat at the eight o'clock Mass. He was there almost every day. As kids, we all knew him. We saw him when we went to Connie Mack Stadium to see the Phillies play the Pirates. When he reappeared at Our Lady of Peace in the fall, it was a big deal. As a young baseball fan, I couldn't take my eyes off him.

I'll always remember the sight of him walking up the aisle to receive Communion. He held his hands just so: his palms together, his fingers pointed upward. This did not go unnoticed by the Sisters of St. Joseph who taught at the school. They knew the older boys -- even the altar boys -- weren't real comfortable holding their hands like that. We didn't think it looked, well, manly.

One morning after watching a long line of boys shuffle up the aisle, their hands drooping below their belts -- and, yes, I was one of them -- Sister Irenaeus, the Mother Superior, pulled us aside. She pointed at Danny, Sr., who was putting on his coat and heading for the door.

"You boys see Mr. Murtaugh go to Communion every morning," she said. "You see how he holds his hands? If Mr. Murtaugh can hold his hands like that so can you."

Sister Irenaeus had delivered the same message before but this time she put it in terms a fifth grade boy could understand. Yeah, if the manager of the Pittsburgh Pirates can do that, why can't I? The following Sunday we all had our palms clasped at our chests and our fingers pointing to heaven. That was 60 years ago and I still receive Communion that way. When I do, I always think of Danny Murtaugh.

It was impossible to be a boy growing up in Delaware County in those days and not know the stories of Danny Murtaugh and Mickey Vernon. Danny was from Chester and Mickey was from Marcus Hook and they left a sizeable footprint. We saw them on television, we collected their baseball cards and we enjoyed their success because there was nothing to celebrate with the Phillies. It was a bleak time at 21st and Lehigh but Danny and Mickey were doing Delco proud.

It seemed as though every man coaching Little League in the area had a connection to either Danny or Mickey. They were teammates in high school or they played against them on the sandlots. They may have worked alongside them in a factory during the off-season. They all shared the blue collar roots of Delaware County and were proud of it. I heard dozens of those stories and they always ended with someone saying, "What a great guy."

In 1960, with the Phillies going nowhere, the Pirates became my team. Danny, Sr., was the manager and Mickey was a player-coach. When they went to the World Series against the mighty New York Yankees, I convinced several teachers to let us listen to the games on the radio. Yes, the World Series games were played during the day back then. When Bill Mazeroski hit the home run to win Game Seven, I jumped as high and cheered as loud as any kid in Pittsburgh.

A couple weeks later, Danny, Sr., was back at Our Lady of Peace. He was going to Communion -- and his hands were perfect.

- Ray Didinger

DANNY & MICKEY, ORDINARY HEROES
TABLE OF CONTENTS

INTRODUCTION

"Play ball!"

I always got excited whenever I heard the two words, "Play ball!" Whether I was standing on a dusty neighborhood sandlot, or on a neatly-groomed ballfield, whether I was playing as a young boy, or watching as a twenty-something adult, or sitting in the leftfield grandstand with my own kids, or even much later in life wallowing in the luxury of field level seats eight rows behind home plate, I always welcomed the umpire's official command to begin a game of baseball.

This loud call to action, boldly directed to all players on both teams, always preceded the game of baseball everywhere. It seemed most powerful to me because it immediately followed the singing of America's National Anthem by the crowd of baseball fans surrounding the field of play. I recall many times even as a kid when I would sing a few lines as I ran onto the makeshift fields in our old neighborhood.

This call still echoes across America's vast landscape and baseball is still affectionately referred to as 'America's Favorite Pastime'. Undoubtedly, swimming and fishing are America's most popular summer activities but baseball has been the king of American sports since the first ball was thrown in an informal neighborhood contest. Today football is being touted by many people as America's most popular sport. I don't think so, not by a long-shot.

Baseball most likely had its roots on an early summer day more than one-hundred and fifty years ago when that first inventive and spirited young man whittled a three foot piece of wood into a slender caveman-like club and setup nine men to a side. Then he positioned them on a sun-coated, green, grassy field and fashioned the first rules of the game that evolved and held fast over the many years that followed. Thus began this game of baseball that was believed to have been first formally played in the northeastern states in the mid-nineteenth century.

It is a simple game and it is reasonable to believe that its popularity spread during the American Civil War when weary, homesick, soldiers sought some relief from both the horror and the boredom of war. Between battles and after marches to other battles, soldiers would gather in any open field to play, run, laugh, and jump with abandonment before the next dreaded call to battle. When the war mercifully ended, these ex-soldiers from every state, both Union and Confederate, took the game home with them to their own towns and cities. This is how baseball came to Chester, Pennsylvania, my hometown.

Chester is a medium-sized city nestled on the Delaware River in the farthest southeastern corner of Pennsylvania. It is so far south and east in the corner of Pennsylvania that it is said if it fell into the river, it would float and attach itself to either the New Jersey or the Delaware shoreline before you could yell 'city overboard'. Here the river is neither picturesque nor countrified. There isn't much fishing or weekend boating here, and I wouldn't expect that Tom Sawyer and his buddy Huckleberry Finn would ever take a raft out onto this part of the Delaware River. Chester is an old shipbuilding city and the river has served the city and an armful of industrial riverside communities since Pennsylvania's founding in 1682 by a prosperous English Quaker named William Penn.

Situated only 12 miles south of Philadelphia, Chester is equidistant between New York and Washington, DC. As a northeastern city with river access to the ocean it was highly industrialized prior to and during the two world wars. Many weapons manufacturing plants were built here as well as several ship building companies and large oil refineries. Natural fuels (oil, gas, water), access to transportation (rivers, railroads, highways), and available skilled labor all contributed to the city's early prosperity. The city of Chester and the towns and boroughs nearby share a common membership and together comprise the regional and political district of Delaware County.

Surprisingly though, once you stray westward from the river, the county has a predominantly rural landscape. As you travel inland, its rolling hills, lush valleys, and flat farmlands are numerous and inviting. The fields not yet plowed or built-upon soon become picnic and play areas. The new game of baseball instantly found a home here in the county.

Baseball fever grew rapidly and by the beginning of the 20th century, the nation and its citizens found relaxation and relief from hard work in this sporting game that its Civil War veterans created and embraced. Soon, Pennsylvania had two cities with their own professional teams, Philadelphia on the far eastern end of the state, and Pittsburgh a short distance from the Ohio border, on the far western end of the state. Other large urban cities also formed professional teams and chief among the competing teams were the New York Yankees, the New York Giants, and the Boston Braves. The rival Yankees and Giants were always the top-ranked teams in the baseball leagues. As the game's popularity increased, Philadelphia could proudly boast it had two professional baseball teams, the Philadelphia Phillies and the Philadelphia Athletics.

Baseball was 'king' and its roots became more firmly planted in Chester in 1908 when the Delco Baseball League was formally organized. This local league sought to be competitive with the two larger professional leagues and appeared to have some success in the first decade of the twentieth century when it began signing major league players such as "Frank "Home Run" Baker, pitcher Charles "Chief" Bender, and boldly offered a formal contract to baseball's newest pitching and hitting sensation, Babe Ruth. However, the owners of the more-established and more-profitable National and American League teams led by Ruth's contract-holder, the New York Yankees, branded the Delco League as an 'outlaw league' and successfully defended their monopoly of baseball. Though the Delco League was unable to compete with the larger rival professional leagues, it has remained continuously active since its formation in 1908. The league celebrated its 108th season in 2016.

The other Pennsylvania team, the Pittsburgh Pirates had some early success, winning several pennants before 1927. However, they soon suffered a long drought, rarely winning more games than they lost. It would be thirty-plus years before the Pirates would regain a respectable place among the leaders in baseball. When they did, they were led by two boyhood friends who grew up in Delaware County during the golden years of baseball. One boy was born and raised in the city of Chester and the second boy was born and raised in Marcus Hook*, a river community six miles below Chester. Though their boyhood loyalty belonged to the baseball teams in Philadelphia, their destiny took them and Pittsburgh to baseball's version of Mt. Olympus.

---

* **Marcus Hook is a neighboring town on the Delaware River just a few miles below Chester. It was settled as waterfront community in 1892 just as the oil boom began in the beginning of the twentieth century. Like Chester, its location on the river and its access to the Chesapeake Bay and the Atlantic Ocean made it a suitable place to establish oil refineries where raw petroleum could be received and processed into finished products such as the gasoline that was shipped to other US coastal cities and overseas. Marcus Hook is also known as a favorite port of call for the English pirate, Edward Teach, infamously known as Blackbeard the Pirate. It is still believed his pirate treasure is buried somewhere along the shores that meet the water's edge along the Delaware River and the Chesapeake Bay.**

PREFACE

October 14, 1960 "Dear God…"

It seemed too good to be true. But it wasn't a dream. Danny was definitely awake. He awoke with a sudden jolt in a large bed after sleeping soundly for the first time in the last few months. Actually, it had been longer than a few months. He hadn't slept soundly since the long season began. The deep rest felt good, but now his head was hazy and he was trying to remember some of the facts from the day before. He knew he wasn't home and he recalled that his wife, Kate, was with him. But she wasn't next to him now. He panicked at first, then he shuffled the plush bedcovers a bit and called out to Kate. There was no answer. He was alone now. He feared that he overslept. Then he realized his fear of oversleeping wasn't so much that he missed a meeting, or that he failed to run a timely errand. He was beginning to recall some events from last night. He feared that he overslept and lost precious minutes on the very first day after the most unforgettable day of his life. He overslept on a day in which he wanted to spend every minute wide awake. He was beginning to remember it all. He whispered under his breath, "Dear God, how did all this happen?"

PROLOGUE

August 1950 Forbes Field

The summer sun was sitting high over the industrial city of Pittsburgh in the far western part of Pennsylvania. A large number of fans that only an hour ago had filed into the Forbes Field baseball stadium to watch the hometown Pittsburgh Pirates hopefully defeat the league-leading New York Giants were now trying to find some way to cool themselves. The streets surrounding the stadium were becoming less congested as the final group of spectators entered the ballpark. A visitor from another planet or a time traveler stepping this moment into this Oakland neighborhood near Schenley Park might think the entire 'Steel City' was abandoned.

This was because everyone within several blocks of the stadium was off the street. They were either inside the large ballpark being attentive to the activities occurring on the bright green, pasture-perfect playing field, or they were working the grandstands hawking hot dogs, peanuts and sodas to the crowd.

The Giants were currently in first place in the National League and the Pirates were experiencing another rare winning season, and hoping to mount a late winning streak to get back into the league's pennant race. It was rare when the Pirates were winning more than they were losing and were ranked among the teams in the top half of the league standings. But in the past two years they actually finished in or near the top of the National League standings. Certainly, winning barely half of their games in three years isn't a notable streak but it was a comparative dynasty for the perennial bottom-dragging Bucs who more commonly finished last or next to last. Lately though, they were playing good baseball, surprising everyone, maybe including themselves.

Danny and Mickey, Ordinary Heroes

Down on the field the game had already advanced into the bottom half of the fifth inning when Danny Murtaugh, Pittsburgh's feisty second baseman, stepped up to home plate. Danny walked earlier in the game but he was stranded on base when a teammate made the final out of the second inning. Now he was the lead-off batter in this inning and would be facing Giants' pitcher Sal Maglie again. Maglie was an aggressive pitcher who was recently reinstated back into the major leagues after being banned by baseball commissioner, Happy Chandler. Barber's crime* was daring to participate in a rival league in Mexico. After a period of banishment and after begging forgiveness from the major league owners, Sal was admitted back into major league baseball. As normal baseball business practices would sometimes arrange things, he was signed back into the league by the New York Giants, a National League power team in a major market. He was a slightly above-average fast ball slinger when he originally played in the majors but after several years in Mexico under the tutelage of Dolf Luque, a Cuban pitcher/Manager, he developed into a no conscience, aggressive, brush-back pitcher, possessive of the area surrounding home plate. This added talent of throwing his fastball high and inside to all batters, both left and right-handed batters, produced pitches that were often near the head, and sometimes just under the chin, and they were referred to as "close shaves." This unique approach kept batters away from the plate and always had the batters on their toes. It was effective for him and he became a feared and winning hurler for the pennant-contending Giants. Upon his return from Mexico, his steady use of these 'close shave' pitches led to his newly acquired nickname, Sal the Barber.

Danny Murtaugh was an aggressive singles hitter who crowded the plate. His journey to the big leagues was arduous and marked by excellent infield play, an ability to get on base any way possible, and his speed on the base paths. Danny now cocked his bat behind his right shoulder and was concentrating on Maglie's first pitch.

The Giants' catcher, Wes Westrum, squatted immediately behind home plate. Looking over the catcher's shoulder was the final arbiter of all baseball decisions, the home plate umpire. Just as Danny positioned himself into the batter's box, a Pittsburgh teammate leaned over the dugout railing along the first base side of the playing field and yelled encouragement. "C'mon, Danny. Let's start it off".

Up in the broadcast booth, the Pirates announcer was speaking to his listeners, providing them with play by play coverage and the constant update and sundry pieces of information that allowed the listener to know what is going on at every moment so they could visualize and feel as excited as the fans who were sitting in the stands.

"Well, fans," the announcer began. "The Pirates are trailing 2-0 here in the fifth inning. They have managed only two hits so far. Giant's pitcher Sal Maglie is pitching as effective as ever and his double in the third inning plated the Giants' second run." The announcer paused for a breath and swallowed a short sip of water, then he began speaking again. "OK, Murtaugh is ready. He is the Pirates leadoff batter this inning. Let's see if Danny can get something started for the Bucs." The announcer hesitated for a moment, then continued. "With the top of the Pirates lineup to follow, Maglie will want to keep Murtaugh and his speed off the base paths. Danny is having another good season this year. He is batting .294 coming into today's game."

The crowd noises, chants, and the fans screaming encouragement all combined to raise the volume, and these sounds filled the ballpark. Danny was in his batting stance. The catcher and the umpire were crouched directly behind him. Before the first pitch, the Giant's catcher looked up at Danny standing above him and said. "OK, Murtaugh. You're out number one".

Danny didn't take his eyes off of the pitcher on the mound but he sent his comment back over his shoulder and down toward Westrum, "It's too bad for me that you're not out in the field, Wes. I'd have a better chance to get on base if I hit anything to you".

"Yeh." answered Westrum. "Well, I ain't out there and you ain't gonna hit nothing anyway."

At that moment, the umpire chimed in forcibly, "Cut the crap, fellas. Just play ball."

Just before the pitch, a voice from the Pirates dugout called out to Danny, "C'mon Danny. A hit or a walk sets up a big inning."

Now the announcer leaned into the microphone and spoke in a normal voice. "Danny is digging in at home plate. But, he has to be careful. Everyone knows Maglie is aggressive. But I don't think Maglie wants to walk Danny again and put the lead-off runner on base. So it looks like Maglie will throw some strikes. McCullough, the Pirates catcher, is on deck."

The announcer cleared his throat. "Maglie is ready on the mound. He cradles the ball in his glove, and looks into Westrum for a signal for the next pitch. Now he's got the sign. He goes into his windup and launches a pitch towards home plate."

Danny tightened up his batting stance on the right side of the plate. His eyes were focused only on the ball coming out of Maglie's hand.

The pitch moved at 85 miles per hour and it was meant to drive Danny off of the plate. But it didn't break left and away from Danny. It didn't drop down, and it didn't slow down. Before Danny could fully react, the ball was in on him. He ducked and fell away to let the ball go by him. It was ball four when it reached home plate, then it smacked him on the head. **Whapp**! Danny fell instantly, and a huge, collective "Oohhhh" rose up from the crowd. Then the loud, noisy stadium was suddenly silent.

Danny was lying in a lifeless heap, face down beside home plate. The catcher and the ump were the first ones to reach out towards him. They left him lying face down. He wasn't making a sound. No moans, no groaning, not even air was coming from him. He was knocked out. The umpire turned Danny's head to the side so he could breathe and he instantly saw a nasty bruise and red swelling on the left-side of his forehead. There was still a hush over the stadium. Players and officials started running towards home plate to assist the fallen player.

A field attendant dressed in Pirate black and gold clothing approached the umpire and asked. "Oh my God. Is he breathing?" A second attendant with glasses told him. "Feel for his pulse."

The umpire's only words were solemn. "Don't move him."

All movements on the field were frantic yet carefully orchestrated. A doctor was hurriedly escorted to home plate. He checked Danny's breathing and noticed the large red welt on Danny's forehead and issued instructions to others even as he continued to examine Danny. He gently rolled Danny over and examined him and took his pulse. An emergency cot from the locker room appeared on the field and Danny was placed on it. He was laid on his back, still motionless and his eyes were closed. He wasn't making a sound. Now a single ambulance siren was heard faintly in the distance.

Out near the pitcher's mound, Sal Maglie and a few Giant teammates were huddling. They were worrisome and stunned.

A view from the upper stands presented a panorama of thousands of people focused intently on a single patch of grass and dirt inside the diamond-shaped infield far below them. The mood was doleful and from that distance everything seemed to move in slow motion. The large crowd continued to watch breathlessly and waited to hear an announcement that would provide them with information about the activities on the field, or someone would announce to them that the game would continue or be suspended. They were all trapped in this singular place and time. The minutes continued to stretch out longer and longer. Soon, the only sound across the stadium was an ambulance's siren getting louder as it approached the ballpark. The bright sun lessened and a grey tint attached itself to the increasingly cloudy sky.

***Players, responding to a lack of positive action from the baseball owners to the players' request for higher salaries and improved benefits, left the major leagues in 1946 to sign on with a new professional Mexican League begun with an investment of fifty million dollars from Jorge Pasqual, a Mexican customs broker, and his four brothers. When the players jumped to the Mexican League, Happy Chandler, MLB Baseball Commissioner, banned the players from returning to the major leagues for five years.**

CHAPTER ONE
CHESTER, PA

1917 The Midwife

October is a transitional month in the seasonal weather pattern in the Northeastern United States. Not only are the trees and birds adjusting to the changing seasonal climate but people are doing the same. The red, brown, and yellowing leaves overtly signal that the warmer days of early October are soon be replaced by cooler and overcast days later in the same month.

This day was one of those cool, dreary October days in Chester, PA, a gritty, industrial city located on the Delaware River just twelve miles south of Philadelphia. The wind blowing from the northwest was light but the morning temperature was fifteen degrees lower than yesterday. It was a normal working weekday so there was above-average activity on the city's downtown streets as people moved busily to and fro in the midst of completing their daily routines. A remnant of a newspaper blew across the street. It was yesterday's news, already mostly forgotten and quickly replaced by a pile of today's newspapers that lay on top of a wooden crate in Roder's newsstand, a small triangular piece of real estate located at 7th Street and Edgemont Avenue in the center of downtown.

The largest headlines on the front page of the newspaper announced the latest triumphs and defeats of the seemingly deadlocked war in Europe. The war encompassed all of Europe and it had been repeating its death and destruction there and elsewhere for more than three years. But now in October 1917, the war news had a new urgency for Chester and for all its neighboring towns and boroughs in Delaware County. This stale, bloody war included a new combatant, the United States of America.

A newsboy downtown could be heard shouting at the top of his lungs snippets of today's major stories pertaining to business, crime, entertainment and sports. The majority of the sports news these past two weeks focused on professional baseball's World Series. Today's sports section featured an article and a photo of the Boston Red Sox star pitcher George Ruth who just completed his third full season as the Red Sox newest pitching sensation. In the past two seasons, Ruth won 47 games and lost 25. His combined ERA for both years was under 2.00. He was going to be a star pitcher for Boston for a long time.

Baseball news would soon fade as the college football season began to receive the maximum attention. The sports readers would soon hear the newsboys noisily shouting the scores from the public's favorite football teams. Also buried today in a lower corner of the sports section was another small matter of interest. A small headline announced that a group of 'footballers' in Canton, Ohio were planning to start a professional football league.

The war had finally come into America's homes. It did not surprise everyone in Chester. As early as 1914, America's political and business leaders had anticipated America's entry into the World War. Chester's shipyards, docks, and related weapons industries were already busy manufacturing products to support the country's entry into the war. Employment was always welcomed but now there were mixed emotions as America's young men began to ship out from its cities and towns to fight in a war far from home. This war, touted by many as the war to end all wars, was soon labeled 'the Great World War'. Later, however, in only 25 years it will be succeeded by an even larger global war and thereafter this Great War will be unceremoniously remembered and referred to by its abbreviated identity, WWI, the first of two world wars fought in the first half of the twentieth century. Its short, bland title did not lessen its ravages even when compared to the larger conflict that would follow.

Chester and its neighboring towns and boroughs along the riverfront were not postcard communities. The Delaware River was a backbone of commerce for this Tri-State area where three states bordered one another: Delaware, Pennsylvania, and New Jersey. Situated on the river, Chester transported merchant goods, food supplies, coal and oil to ports overseas in Europe and South America and throughout America via ships and trains. Chester's commercial center of town was in the northeast end of the city, four blocks east from the waterfront piers along the Delaware River; the state of New Jersey was a quick boat ride across the river*.

The city's commercial area took the shape of a slightly irregular rectangle, approximately nine blocks long (east to west) and five blocks wide (north to south). All of the remaining land around the edges of the business area were built-up with a collection of family residences for low income and modest income wage earners. The majority of the houses were arranged in neat rows, some attached in groups of four or six residences. This mixed business/residential part of the city included many small businesses such as grocery stores, carriage repair and car repair shops, and metal shops that shared the street and community with its neighbors.

Barclay Street was one such street. Only a few blocks south from the center of town, Barclay Street ran west from Front Street on the Delaware River to Ninth Street, skirting the business area. A string of small row houses lined both sides of Barclay Street between Fifth and Seventh Streets.

Looking down from the sky on this part of the city, a woman in a light cloth coat and soft hat could be seen walking briskly from downtown Chester south towards Barclay Street. The house that she was walking towards sat amid this cluster of homes on Barclay Street.

The woman was a midwife**. She was experienced in the timeless manner and ages-old skills that assist and comfort a woman in delivering her child. Although the early decades of the twentieth century brought advances in technology such as telephone, electricity, and automobiles, bringing babies into the world was still primarily a woman's task and triumph. Even in urban cities and towns, medical doctors were not plentiful, and were not readily available to attend to women during childbirth. The skills and compassion of a good midwife were treasured.

The woman continued walking toward the house. Just as she reached the outside step to the house, the door opened. A young girl who appeared to be waiting for her greeted the woman nervously.

***There was no bridge access between Chester and southern New Jersey until 1973 when the Commodore Barry Bridge was built to connect the two shores. The Chester-Bridgeport Ferry line did run a regular schedule between PA and NJ for pedestrians, and horse-drawn and engine-powered vehicles for nearly a century.**

****A midwife is a medieval term that originated in England circa 1250AD. It was used to identify a woman who is experienced assisting women with the birth of a child.**

Chester, PA

The Murtaugh Family

Betty Murtaugh was nine years old. She had straight dark shoulder-length hair, and she was the oldest of Nellie Murtaugh's daughters and she was trying hard to be helpful and brave for her Mom and for her Grandmother and her aunts. After all, she was barely a toddler when her sister Eunice was born so all this commotion was new and uncomfortably exciting to her. She managed to smile politely at the women standing at the door.

"Hello, Mrs. Cassidy. Mom is upstairs in the front bedroom."

The woman stepped inside the house and immediately felt the warmth of the coal-fired heater that was working noisily in the basement to push hot air upward into the living spaces.

"Betty dear, how is your Mother today?" Mrs. Cassidy inquired.

"She's doing fine." Betty replied. "She said she's ready. Her water broke and she's been waiting for you." The young girl was only repeating what she heard while sitting among her aunts. She wasn't sure what the words meant.

With a smile and a nod of her head, Mrs. Cassidy greeted the several women who were seated in the downstairs front parlor. She knew all of them and they all knew why Maggie Cassidy was there. Now they could all breathe a little easier. Mrs. Cassidy went directly upstairs and entered the bedroom as if it were her own private delivery room. She smiled and nodded towards Nellie's sister and mother, then smiled warmly at Nellie. Betty's mom exhaled but she didn't exchange any words with the midwife. After all, this was Nellie's third baby. Birthing one or ten babies didn't mean that it ever got safer or less difficult, but it did mean that she knew what to expect. She was prepared for the long wait and the hard work that would come.

Turning to Betty, Mrs. Cassidy said softly but firmly, "Betty dear, have someone find your Dad and your Uncle Tim and let them know I'm here."

Betty glanced worriedly at her mother, then quietly left the room, closing the door softly behind her.

"Maybe a baby brother for me."

Several hours later most of the women in the family were gathered downstairs in the front parlor and in the dining room. Nellie's Mom, sisters, and two young daughters, Betty and Eunice, were all waiting for the arrival of the new baby.

As the women shared cups of tea, Mrs. Cassidy and two neighborhood friends tended to Nellie and prepared her for the baby's arrival. There was not much that anyone upstairs or downstairs could do to speed up the baby's arrival. So the time was filled with stories and gossip that made the tea even tastier. Every so often one of the upstairs ladies came to the top steps and offered an update to everyone downstairs. Nellie's husband, Danny, was still at work at the shipyard. It's where he was most of the time and where he must be to provide for his young family. But Uncle Tim, Nellie's brother, sent word that he would come as soon as he could. He had always been there for his sister, Nellie. Uncle Tim Mc Carey had a good job with the city and he was generally able to fit his personal schedule comfortably into his work schedule. It was a perk of the job and the job was a product of being many things for many people who had a lot of influence in the city's affairs, especially the city's jobs. Abruptly, there was festive whistling heard outside on Barclay Street and the sound was rising toward the front door. The door opened and a big man walked lively into the front parlor. It was Uncle Tim and he was smiling. He was lovingly referred to as Unkie by his two nieces and when Eunice, Betty's little sister, heard the whistling, she dashed from the dining room and ran out to Unkie and gave him a big hug around his big leg, for that was the only part of Unkie that her little arms could reach.

"Hi, Unkie." She squealed brightly. "Mom's gonna have a baby today. Maybe a baby brother for me."

"And for me!' Uncle Tim responded loudly.

Unkie loved his precious nieces but he had waited and wished a long time for a boy, his own nephew. Once inside the parlor, Uncle Tim looked around the room. He addressed all the ladies at once. "Hello, everyone. Is everything fine? Has the baby come yet? Then he added, "Is Dan here?"

Nellie's younger sister lifted her head from her tea cup and replied just as neatly as possible. "Everything is fine, Tim. But, no, the baby's not here yet. And Dan is still at work."

Nellie's older sister addressed her brother curtly, "He's not likely to be here 'til after his shift is done."

Uncle Tim nodded and stepped out of the parlor and walked through the dining room and into the kitchen. He joined in the waiting but not in the gossip or stories. He'd brought the day's newspaper with him and sat at the table. Soon, everyone returned to their quiet watch and settled down for a longer wait. There was very little discussion as time passed and evening neared. Just as everything quieted there was a shout from upstairs that was heard by everyone.
"It's time. Boil the water, bring it up." This command was delivered by one of the neighborhood friends who was assisting Mrs. Cassidy. Immediately there was activity and excitement as some women rushed in to the kitchen and others to the stairs. Betty and Eunice remained downstairs with Uncle Tim. Slowly, another thirty minutes passed. Then a baby's tiny cry was audible.

Betty was the first person downstairs to hear the baby's cry and she jumped up from her chair in the parlor. "Oh, my Gosh! The baby's here."

Eunice almost fell over her own feet as she ran to the steps. "Is it a boy or another girl?" she called up the stairs to anyone who would answer her.

Walking to the bottom of the stairs, and looking up, Uncle Tim asked excitedly. "Is the baby fine? What can you tell us, will it be bonnets or boxing gloves?"

Nellie's oldest sister stood at the top of the stairs, looked down, smiled, and said to her brother. "It won't be bonnets this baby will be wearing, but he won't be wearing boxing gloves either if I can help it. He is a fine looking boy and I want him to stay that way."

"He's a boy! Hooray! Hooray! Praise St. Patrick, and all his saints. A boy." Uncle Tim shouted gleefully.

Shrieks of joy and laughter filled the parlor as Uncle Tim and the girls danced around the room, accompanied by more sounds of a crying baby boy coming from upstairs.

Uncle Tim was overjoyed. "He sounds feisty." He yelled. "What name will he have? Daniel, after his father? Maybe Timothy" he added with a hearty laugh.

Nellie's youngest sister then spoke for Nellie who was breathless and a bit weary now. "Yes. It's Daniel. Nellie always had that name picked out for him. It's a fine name."

The house was filled with laughing, shrieks of joy, and wonderment. The long vigil was ended with the best outcome. A new, healthy, baby had arrived to brighten the Murtaugh's modest household. Then, amidst the joy, there was a sudden scream from Nellie's bedroom. Everyone turned and looked anxiously up the stairs.

Chester, PA

"He's Turning Blue."

"Help! Help! The baby is choking. He can't cry or make a sound." The neighborhood friend whose eyes betrayed her fear was shouting for help and holding the soundless baby. She handed the baby to Mrs. Cassidy.

"It must be his windpipe that's clogged.' Added another woman.

Uncle Tim reacted instantly and swiftly moved his large body, and in a frantic, yet controlled rush, he bounded up the stairs and into the bedroom. He reached out to Mrs. Cassidy.

"Hand me the boy! Tell me what you need me to do. O my God! He's turning blue."

Amid shouts and screams and shrieks of prayer coming from those inside the suddenly crowded room, Mrs. Cassidy turned the baby upside down and handed the baby to Uncle Tim, instructing him to hold the baby's legs in one hand and carefully insert one finger of his other hand down into the baby's mouth and gently clear the baby's throat of any material.

Unkie did as he was told and pulled out a soft mass that was blocking the baby's air passage. The baby began to cry, low and intermittent at first. Mrs. Cassidy's face lightened when she saw the mass in Tim's hand, then she breathed a sigh of relief. "There. There it is. You've cleared something. Do it again until we hear him cry. Shake him just a wee bit and smack his bottom lightly. Crying will force him to push air through his windpipes."

In what seemed like minutes, but what was only a few seconds, the baby cried more, and soon he was shrieking loudly and confidently announcing himself to the world.

Nellie who helplessly witnessed the scary scene was still crying as she reached for her baby boy. "Give me my baby. Let me see him. Oh, God save my baby boy."

Mrs. Cassidy took the crying baby from Uncle Tim, checked the baby's mouth and throat and breathing, then she handed the baby boy to his mother. The baby's crying lessened as he was cuddled in his Mother's arms.

"He's breathing fine now, Nellie," Mrs. Cassidy assured her. "It must've been birthing residue that he inhaled and he couldn't expel. His breathing is good now. We'll keep a watch on him." Turning to Unkie, she gave him one final instruction. "Tim, would you notify the doctor as a precaution?"

Mrs. Cassidy was back in control. She spoke to everyone. "Now let's empty the room. Please go downstairs. I'll sit with Nellie to keep a watch on her and baby Daniel. He will be fine. He's already shown a feisty side that will serve him well in his years to come."

A loud "Amen" was hurled across the room by Uncle Tim.

Nellie was holding Daniel but still crying softly, and motioned her brother to her side of the bed. "Tim, you saved Daniel's life. I wouldn't expect less from you. You're his angel, his archangel."

"Sis, I've never been so scared in my life. God has a mighty hand in these things."

A few more hours of the long day passed and in the downstairs parlor Uncle Tim and his sisters were recovering from the events of the day. Dan came home after working two shifts at the shipyard and Uncle Tim shared the frightening moments with his brother-in-law. Dan went upstairs immediately to be with Nellie and his newborn son.

Now with the midnight hour gone, Uncle Tim rose from his chair to leave. He stood in the parlor and looked up the stairs. "Good night all." He said.

Then as if speaking to his new nephew, he added. "Little Daniel, I'm going to buy you your first set of boxing gloves. I'll bring them around tomorrow. I expected that you would've really needed them if your Mom had named you Cornelius as she planned to do."

Tim's oldest sister would not let this pass unchallenged. "Now, Tim, I told you it won't be boxing gloves that he will be wearing. Not for a long time. And I'm hoping, maybe never."

"Well, dear sister, a boy can always use boxing gloves to learn how to fight, so he can protect himself and others."

"Oh. No. There is already too much fighting, here and everywhere." Gathering her fullness of spirit, his sister whispered lowly but emphatically. "I'm most hopeful to believe those who ought to know about such things when they say that after this war is ended there will be no more wars. I pray to God that they are right. Then this baby boy won't have to ever go off to war – not for anything, not for anyone. And I pray that he won't ever need to box his way through life either."

Uncle Tim, remained silent for a moment and standing with his head bowed, replied. "Yep. I pray for the same."

Then he lifted his head and motioned upward again towards the stairs, and under his breath he promised mischievously to his nephew. "Daniel, my boy, what can it be if not good Irish boxing gloves? There's baseball. But there's not enough fisticuffs and body slamming for a young fellow in baseball. Ah, Football! Now there's a game of sport with some life and force in it. OK, football it is. We can slip a pair of boxing gloves on you when you're older and your aunties aren't watching. But baseball? Never! You might as well wear a kilt, and play golf."

Uncle Tim walked out the front door, stepped down onto the sidewalk, and breathed in the clean coolness of the beginning of a new day. He put his hands into his coat pockets and began briskly walking home, whistling happily all the way.

CHAPTER TWO
"YOU HAVE TO GO AND GET IT"

1924 The Roar before the Crash.

The Great War (later to be renamed World War I) ended on November 11, 1918, Armistice Day. America survived the war with less personal and economic losses than Europe. When the armistice was signed the total of military personnel and civilians dead from both sides of the battlefield between August 1914 to November 1918 was 17 million people. Eleven million were military personnel and seven million were civilians. An additional 20 million were wounded. America's casualties through 18 months of engagement were 53,000 persons killed, and 62,000 wounded, a regrettable amount, but much less than the number Europe suffered.

The primary reason that America's number was lower was because America entered the war nearly three years after the conflict began. Peace arrived after a great cost to many nations, soldiers and citizens. It ended not so much with a victor as it ended from exhaustion and economic bankruptcy. However, even as the armistice brought peace and a welcomed end to death, an equally fatal blow was soon to strike the suffering nations in the fading shadow of the war.

With the interaction of nations and peoples at war in an increasing rate of numbers and speed, health risks increased during World War I. Subsequently, after the first three years of war, an epidemic of great tragedy began to envelop the world in 1917. The Great Swine Flu, also known as the Spanish Flu pandemic (later identified as H1N1), rained suffering and death on the already devastated nations and quickly the entire world. It is estimated that world-wide at least 50 million and as many as 100 million people died from the Spanish Flu between 1917 and December 1920. The most virulent strain of this flu later struck in 1918 and Boston's outbreak in August 1918 was recorded as the most lethal in the United States.

By October 25th, 350,000 people died in Pennsylvania including 150,000 in the Philadelphia area. The commonalities between Boston and Philadelphia were that they were both major port cities where both commerce and military personnel exited and entered the United States. Overall, within a year, more than a half million people in the United States were killed by the Flu. The world was in the throes of a great pandemic. There was not a community on earth that was not victim to this calamity. Strangely, the flu was most fatal to young adults, between 20 and 39 years old. This the most likely reason why all of the members of the Murtaugh family in Chester survived the pandemic. Fortunately, they were all on either end of this perilous age range.

Gradually, the war's damage to America faded and prosperity began to benefit everyone in America. This was certainly so in Chester and the surrounding communities along the river. Jobs were plentiful and money seemed to grow on trees. If not trees then it seemingly sprouted from tomato plants. The economy was booming. America embraced its leisure time with picnics on Sundays, day trips to public beaches and amusement parks. Attendance at movie theatres skyrocketed, the Charleston and the Lindy were putting people on the dance floor, and a frenzy arose for all sporting activities overnight: horse racing, boxing, and especially 'America's Favorite Pastime', baseball. The country was headed for unlimited prosperity. There was even a label for these hectic times, the Roaring Twenties.

The old adages didn't seem to apply, certainly not the one that says what goes up must come down. Certainly not in the closing years of the 1920's. The only thing lacking in America was the ability to buy a legal glass of beer, wine, or whisky at a corner taproom or anywhere in public as the public consumption of alcohol was illegal when the Prohibition Law was passed and strictly enforced from 1920 to 1933. Nevertheless, this nearly decades-long party continued unabated and baseball was in the middle of its golden age. Every boy wanted to be a baseball player and every small field was commandeered by boys and transformed into a miniature baseball diamond. Yes, horse racing was still the sport of Kings, but baseball was the sport of the people in the Roaring Twenties. This baseball fever did not skip the men and boys in and around Chester, PA, especially youngsters like Danny Murtaugh and Mickey Vernon.

1924 "You have to go and get it."

Danny was seven years old now. There didn't ever seem to be a single day that he was unable to fill his day with plenty of activity. He now had two younger sisters, Mary and Peggy. As the only boy among four sisters, he was overtly his Mother's favorite. Actually, he was his four sisters' favorite too. They all loved him, and inside the Murtaugh home, he was as close to royalty that any of them would ever see. Betty and Eunice were in charge of him whenever his Mom was working on the different jobs she did to bring in much-needed money for the family. Laundry and ironing were steady work and often-times the older girls would help their Mom with these tasks.

Though Danny was smaller than most boys his age and was certainly cuddled and sheltered by all the attention that he received, he was surprisingly independent and able to defend himself, often defending himself against those who were bigger and older than him. Many times he was defending his friends from bullies. That inner strength and self-confidence was no doubt inherited from his father. Danny's father still worked long hours at the shipyard but he provided Danny with quiet instruction and advice so that Danny would know what is required from a young boy like himself. Though he was not tall, he was fast and fearless. If he was knocked over, he got up quickly.

To Danny's advantage and to his Uncle Tim's delight, Unkie spent as much time with Danny as his city job allowed. Unkie still hadn't been successful in putting boxing gloves on Danny as he had hoped to do, but he knew that boxing, 'the manly art', could be best introduced to him when Danny got a few years older and time filled out his sturdy frame.

After all, Danny's father was shorter than average but he was strong and had been a formidable soccer player when he was young.

A favorite place in the summer for Danny and Unkie was the Murtaugh's small fenced-in backyard at the rear of their house on Barclay Street. Their yard was just one of several at the rear of a string of houses all connected to one another. Row homes was the official name for them. The yards all ran perpendicular to a grassy field behind the houses. This open field was a perfect size for the younger kids to play ball and the grass plot was referred to by the neighborhood kids as Barclay Field. The field was adopted by each new generation of kids as an all-purpose sports complex for each seasonal sport. In the summer, it was a makeshift baseball diamond. In the fall, it served as a football field.

The field's dimensions were restricted by the backyards that lined three sides, and the railroad track that ran across the back, or as the neighborhood kids called it, across the outfield. Standing inside Danny's backyard and looking out onto Barclay Field, the far narrow right end of the field abutted four backyards and was approximately sixty feet wide, then the long side of the flat field stretched one hundred feet to the left and just up to the base of a small hill that gradually ran ten feet to the crest where train tracks ran parallel to the field. The surface along the rail line was filled–in with small ballast stone used to prevent grass and weeds from growing over the steel rails. Everyone wisely agreed that the games would be paused whenever a freight train passed by the field.

The neighborhood kids also all agreed, especially the power hitters (these were usually the oldest and biggest kids) that any ball hit to the crest of the hill just before the railroad tracks was an automatic homerun. This was a safety feature and it was made to ensure that no one climbed the hill to make a catch on the tracks. Because there was no official umpire or ground marker, many boyhood hours were spent arguing whether a hit ball was a homerun, or whether a ball caught on the hill was an out or a homerun. This was a problem that generations of boys wrestled with for the many decades that games were played there. It might still be a problem when games are played even now on Barclay Field.

On this morning, Danny and Unkie were inside the Murtaugh family's backyard tossing a ball back and forth. Unkie was always bare-handed but Danny was wearing a new baseball glove. It was a surprise gift today from Unkie, and it replaced an old bruised glove Unkie had given to Danny last year.

"Let's get your new glove in shape." Unkie said.

With an instructive tone, Unkie tossed a ball to his nephew and said, "Here's another grounder."
Danny caught the slow roller.

"OK, that's good." Unkie remarked. "But don't just reach for it Danny. Move your feet to catch it."

After missing the next ground ball, Danny threw the ball back, directly into Unkie's glove, and said, ""OK, Unkie. Throw me another one. I'll get it this time. I promise."

"Yep. Well, I'm going to throw plenty more, and if it ain't coming right to you, I want you to move your feet and body to get the ball. Don't be afraid to get dirty. Get the ball!"

Unkie tossed another ball on the ground, a little faster this time, and away from Danny. Danny moved quickly but clumsily to the ball. He bobbled it, but he held on to it.

"There you are. That's swell." Unkie was pleased. "Catch it just like that. You'll be a major leaguer someday. That's for sure."

Putting his hands at his sides to signal that Danny should hold the ball, Unkie gave Danny what Unkie liked to think of as a tiny lesson-moment. "Danny, remember, the ball won't always come to you. If you really want the ball, or anything at all, you have to go get it. It won't always come to you." Danny nodded. At seven years old, that lesson-moment might not sink in today but that tiny lesson like many others to come would be one that he will hear again, a thousand times or more. Many times it will be his own voice that was repeating it.

Now Unkie raised his hands and motioned for Danny to toss the ball back to him. Unkie continued to hit slow ground balls to Danny.

The first one to get tired was always Unkie. He wasn't an athlete but he wouldn't trade these hours for anything else. He knew that Danny, Sr. worked many hours every week. That was tough on both his nephew and his brother-in-law but it worked out perfectly for Unkie.

"OK, Danny, now let's get that new glove dirty. Bend your knees, open your glove. Now, put the glove right on the grass. Yep, that's it. That way your glove is lower than the ball and the ball can't skip under the glove."

Danny bent his body over and reluctantly placed his brand new glove on the grass. Unkie was pleased. "OK. Keep the ball in front of you, and get that glove dirty. Stop the ball!" He straightened up to ease the soreness in his own back. "Remember the glove isn't supposed to stay clean, it was made to scuff the grass and the dirt, and catch the ball."

Whenever Danny made a good play, Unkie let out a piercing whistle as a congratulatory salute to Danny. Danny liked the loud whistle. It meant that he was fielding the ball the right way and he was getting better. Danny soon learned how to make the same whistle and it became a personal means of communication between them, and later, between Danny and his teammates on the baseball field. If you didn't see Danny, you could always find him by listening for his whistle.

The informal practice finally ended. The neighborhood kids were already on the open field outside the fenced–in yards, placing cardboard pieces, burlap sacks, and anything that would serve as a home plate and three bases. Danny was anxious to be out there with them.

"Unkie, before you go, can you throw me some pop-ups? I want to be like Babe Ruth."

"Danny, everybody wants to be like Babe Ruth. You can be Babe Ruth soon enough. Right now, let's work hard on being the best ballplayer in this backyard. Here's a pop fly for you."

Unkie tossed the ball about fifteen feet into the air to the boy's left. Danny moved as the ball climbed up. He darted left, then shifted right, then he lunged for the ball as the ball dropped in, and then out, of his glove. "Shoot! That was tricky."

Unkie looked more seriously at his nephew and corrected him. "Now Danny, watch your words." He didn't want his nephew repeating words that his sister Nellie, Danny's mom, would trace back to him.

"OK, let's try a few more pop-ups. Catch these and you can go and join your pals on the field."

Uncle Tim continued tossing pop-ups to Danny for another minute or so: some on the ground, some in the air, some were caught, some were missed. Babe Ruth's job in right field was safe for now.

"Bless us, O Lord."

The Barclay game ended just before evening arrived as darkness usually determined when a game was over. But this was one baseball league where neither the umpire nor nature were the final arbiter. Mom was. A call to dinner ended those games that lasted into the dinner hour.

Danny and Mickey, Ordinary Heroes

In the small kitchen, Danny's Mom was standing at the stove. Danny's older sisters, Betty and Eunice, were providing help and responding to their Mom's instructions. Mary and Peg were seated dutifully at the kitchen table.

"Mary, fetch the butter for the table. Eunice, pour a glass of water for everyone. Betty, come help me move the meat loaf from the pan onto the platter."

The girls moved to complete their assigned tasks and Peg the youngest sat quietly, waiting to be fed. Danny walked into the kitchen with his ball and his new glove. He didn't go anywhere without a ball and glove. He placed them on the table and sat next to his pal, Peggy.

"Can I help, Mom?" he asked.

Turning from the stove, Mrs. Murtaugh looked at her son and smiled. "Yes, you can. First go wash your hands. Wash them good. Come right back. Sit right there." She motioned to the seat next to her where he always sat.

Danny rushed upstairs to the bathroom to wash his hands, then ran down the steps and sat in his seat. The table was set and everyone was seated at their regular places except for their Dad who like so many other nights was working late hours at the shipyard. Mrs. Murtaugh folded her hands, and all five children did the same.

"Ok. Danny, now you can help. You can say grace so we can eat a thankful meal." Noticing the ball and glove on the table next to his plate, she added. "But, first young man, remove that dirty ball and glove from the table."

Danny quickly placed the ball and glove on the floor at his feet. He made the sign of the cross on his body and began the daily prayer of thanks from the family. "Bless us O Lord for these gifts that we are about to receive from your bounty. Amen."

"Danny, that was mostly right," said Mrs. Murtaugh. "And fine for God and for us but the priests and good sisters would want you to add, 'through Christ, our Lord. Amen'."

Proud of being selected to say grace for the family, and even happier that he did it so well, he smiled at his Mom. "OK, Mom. I keep forgetting that last part."

Then, Mrs. Murtaugh handed the bowl of vegetables to Betty. "Well, let's eat. She paused for a second, and simply added, "Your father won't be home for dinner. He's working late again."

Once the food was presented to everyone, the kitchen filled with conversation as fresh stories from today's adventures, and neighborhood news was exchanged. Everyone took what food they could reach and put it on their plates. They took turns passing their plates around to one another so they could help each other in getting food from the bowls that they couldn't reach. Soon the conversations slowed down and they ate and talked to one another randomly; often interrupting one another's sentences.

As dinner neared an end, little Peg directed a question to her Mom. "Mom, are we still going to the movies tomorrow, like Daddy promised?

"Yes, dear. You are. But only if you eat all your dinner."

Danny and Mickey, Ordinary Heroes
"..a better baseball player."

In the summer, bedtime for children came much later than during the school year primarily because there was no school in the summer and no need to wake up early in the morning. The bigger bonus was that the sun stayed higher in the sky longer, and the night sky didn't start to darken until eight or nine pm. Nevertheless, people went to sleep earlier then than they do now because electricity was new and home lighting in 1924 was much less than what we have now. In fact, many homes didn't have electric power and were still using oil lamps and candles. Television was not yet invented and even radio was hardly a fixture in many homes. Very few families owned a radio and radio entertainment was only beginning to be regularly broadcasted around the country.

Danny was in his upstairs bedroom. The only light in the room was from the moon shining through his small window. He knelt at his bed with his ball and held his new baseball glove closely beside him and finished his prayers in a whisper. "....and God bless everyone else, especially Unkie, and please help me be a better baseball player… like Babe Ruth. Amen." He climbed onto his bed, laid his ball and glove next to him, and fell promptly to sleep.

Danny's father came home much later. Everyone was sleeping when he entered the house. Tired and moving slowly after working two eight-hour shifts at the shipyard, and spending the last hour at a nearby corner taproom on Third and Franklin Streets, he never failed to perform his ritual night-watchman's tour of the kids' bedrooms. He checked the girls' rooms first and looked in on them, then he moved across the narrow hall into his son's room. Danny was sound asleep. He noticed the new baseball glove that lay beside his son. He noticed a baseball on the floor just a few feet from his son's dangling hand. He picked up the ball and turned it over in his own hand, almost dropping it back onto the floor. He gripped it tightly and smiled, then he placed the ball gently back into the shiny new glove with a single grass stain on it. He turned and left the room quietly. No one would ever know that he had been there, not even Danny.

Saturday Matinee

Even in 1924, Saturday morning was kid day at the movie house, or bijou as they were called in the earliest years of the film industry. So just before noon and just after Peggy's father completed his promise that she could go to the movies, she, Danny, and her sisters were standing outside the Washington Theatre in a long line with their friends and a bunch of neighborhood kids. This theater was the local neighborhood movie house that was closest to their home. It was on the edge of the downtown shopping area across the street from the post office, the largest public building in Chester. All of the kids were waiting in a long line for the box office to open. Betty was holding tightly onto the twenty-five cents that will get them all into the theatre. It cost each kid a nickel to get in to see a feature film, usually a western film or comedy, followed by a comic reel, a cartoon, and maybe a newsreel. These were all silent films because talking pictures hadn't been introduced to the world yet*. The silent newsreel wasn't a favorite for most kids. It showed highlights of the previous weeks' world events. But Danny like most boys his age was interested in the sports events because there was a good chance that he would see the mighty Yankees new star slugger, Babe Ruth. For Danny, this former all-star Boston pitcher-turned Yankee slugger was worth the nickel all by himself.

Betty was already feeling a little grumpy because she was responsible for her brothers and sisters. She knew that Danny was not the youngest but he's the one who required the most attention. He was itchy to do things that he shouldn't do while the girls were not going to move too far from her and were never going to make a fuss. Betty couldn't understand why Danny had to be so difficult but Betty's mother wasn't surprised. Betty thought that maybe that's the big difference between boys and girls.

Talking directly to Danny, she reminded him smartly. "Danny, listen. Mom said that you and Peg are to stay with me when we get inside. You both have to sit right next to me."

"Aw! Sis. Why can't I sit with Eunice and Mary?"

Betty answered quickly, "Because they always sit up-front and Mom doesn't want you to sit too close to the front. It isn't good for your eyes." Betty remembered to give Danny one more instruction. This one wasn't from Mom, it's a primary annoyance to Betty herself. "Oh, and no shooting back or yelling when the cowboys and the Indians start shooting. OK?"

"OK, but what's the big deal, the other kids do it."
He thought for a moment then looked at Betty. "OK. Then you got to promise not to talk to me or anyone else during the newsreel. I don't want to miss seeing Babe Ruth and the Yankees. And mom said that I don't have to leave until everything is over, even the newsreel. OK?"

Betty let out a long sigh. "OK. You and your dumb Babe Ruth."

The clock struck noon to signal the box office ticket window was opened and the line of excited kids quickly moved into the theatre. Betty dutifully secured seats in the back of the theatre for Danny, Peg, and herself.

A clip of the Yankees latest win was included in the newsreel and Babe Ruth hit another home run. He would hit 46 homeruns before the 1924 season ended. This newsreel clip also showed how the Babe knocked himself out when he ran into a fence while chasing a fly ball.** Danny was speechless when the film showed the Babe lying on the field surrounded by players and umpires. They finally woke him up when they poured a bucket of cold water on him. He brushed off his uniform, put on his cap and picked up his glove and stayed in the game.

"Danny whispered excitedly to Betty. "Wow, Sis! He hits home runs farther than Paul Bunyan would. He might hit 60 someday. Someday, I'm gonna be just like him."

"Uh Huh. Well, hitting 60 homers in one season is impossible. Ask Dad. Anyway if you want to be like Babe Ruth you better eat all your vegetables."

"Why? I never see Babe Ruth eating vegetables."

"I'm sure he does. Anyway, stop talking. Here comes the western. Remember, no shooting or yelling or I'm not bringing you the next time."

***It will be three more years, 1927, before Warner Brothers makes film history and releases "The Jazz Singer", the first full-length motion picture with sound, music and some dialogue.**

**** Babe Ruth switched from pitcher to the outfield so he could provide his hitting skill and power in every game.**

1927 – Meeting Mickey

Every summer ends just in time for the school year to begin. Moms, teachers, and kids know it. It's a biological rule of some kind.

Danny's grade school wasn't far from the Murtaugh house on Barclay Street. The Franklin Elementary school was on Fourth Street in the middle of the block between Franklin and Fulton Streets. The school building and school playground were one city block wide. It was one of the many public schools built to educate the city's children through grades one through eight. There was only one high school in the city and it was unimaginatively titled Chester High School. In this riverfront city of 45,000 people, education was not a priority. There was no premium on education for most parents and children in the city; there was only a premium on working hard and earning a living.

Danny, his sisters and their friends, attended Franklin school. There were no designated buses for transportation to and from school. The schools were community based so students generally attended schools that were within reasonable walking distance of their homes. Public buses and trolleys were available but they were neither plentiful nor convenient for elementary students. And they were not free. Automobile ownership was still an uncommon luxury for the average family so a car ride to and from school or anywhere else was not a likely option in 1927. Walking remained a necessary and effective means of travel if you wanted to get anywhere.

Franklin's school routine like most schools was enforced by its school bell. The bell rang three times a day. It rang at eight am to begin the school day, and it rang at noon for lunch, and at three pm to signal the end of the school day. Today, the bell rang for the third time and several boys, ten and eleven years old, quickly exited and were already walking on the sidewalk away from the school, tossing a football to each other as they headed toward the local park several blocks away.

One of the boys, Benny, grabbed the ball and asked everyone at once. "Hey, guys, how about that movie newsreel on Saturday showing the Babe hitting his 60th homerun?"

"Yeah, that was super." Will answered as he ran to keep up with the bigger kids. He always liked to get his answer in before anybody else because that was the only way he could ever be heard over the older guys. Speak first and fast, that was Will's motto. So he continued. "I liked that the Babe talked on the film, and you could even hear the sound of his bat on the ball. That was dandy."

Johnny who was the biggest Yankees fan after Danny looked directly at Benny who was a home town Athletics fan and taunted him. "Yeh! I liked it because they showed the Yankees winning the Series, again."

Benny struck back at Johnny with words that he hoped would come true. "That's OK. The A's will win it next year. The Yankees can't keep winning them all."

Joe heard enough. Holding a football under his arm, he changed the subject. "Forget baseball. This is football season now." He tossed the pigskin a short distance in the air, then caught it. "Hey!" He reminded everyone. It's my team's turn to be Notre Dame today, and we get the ball first."

Will twisted his face into an angry, child-like grimace. "No. We do. You guys got the kickoff the last time."

"Nah, you did." Joe answered. "We get the ball first this time." Joe was confident that he was correct and that his team should receive the first kickoff. After all, not only was he correct but he was one of the oldest and one of the biggest boys in the group.

"Nu Uh. You went first and you know it, Joe." Will shouted. Will was not big but he was brave. Sometimes those traits were not to his advantage.

Weakening a little, Joe shifted tactics. "Well, Will, we don't have the same sides this time."

This bickering about who goes on offense first was a normal negotiating technique and it always lasted longer than it should. This time it was halted when Johnny noticed an unfamiliar boy walking towards them. ""Hey, look. Who's that kid?'

Walking away from the park and towards them was a tall kid carrying a basketball under his arm. He didn't look familiar to them. "What about him? Do you know him?" Will asked.

Johnny continued to look closely at the kid. "No. I don't. I don't think he's from the neighborhood."

Joe hadn't seen him before either. "Maybe he's new on the block."

Johnny who could often be a jerk kept looking at the kid. Then sporting a mischievous smirk and speaking out of the side of his mouth, Johnny said. "So, let's spook him some."

"Why? He's just walking." Benny challenged Johnny. Benny didn't like it when Johnny acted like a jerk. It usually caused trouble for everybody. "Just because. Just for fun." Johnny slid further into the sour mood that he fell into every so often.

As the new boy approached, he seemed friendly but his smile faded as soon as he got near the group because none of the boys were smiling back at him. He stepped towards the outside of the sidewalk to move past the boys but Johnny stepped in front of him.

"Hey kid! Where you from? Are you lost?'

The tall kid who was bigger than all of the others responded to Johnny. "Nope, I'm visiting my Mom's friend. I'm just taking a walk. That's all."

Johnny looked back at his buddies and smiled. Then he lit the trouble lamp. "Does your Mommy know that you are out by yourself?"

The new kid began to feel uncomfortable and looked at the other boys, then back at Johnny. "Huh? Whaddya mean?"

"Well." Johnny continued. "Wouldn't she be mad if you hurt yourself or you lost that basketball?"

Now worried but getting ready for trouble, the tall kid answered defiantly. "I'm not gonna lose this ball."

Johnny stepped closer and started to crowd the kid. Though the new kid was taller than everyone else, he was still only one person. No one else said a word. Johnny started this as fun but now he was getting edgier with each exchange and the new kid wasn't backing down. It looked like trouble was unavoidable. This was just another example where one person's idea of fun sometimes leads to trouble.
Just then, there was a piercing whistle and two more boys came around the corner and headed towards them. Danny was the shorter of the two but he was the one who usually took charge. "Hey," Danny shouted as he got closer to the boys. "Do we have enough for a game?" Then he laughed as he always did before he delivered his own punch line, "If not, Joey and me will play against all of you."

Now all of the boys turned away from Johnny and the tall kid. They noisily greeted Danny and shouted different remarks at the same time. Noticing the tall kid, Danny smiled and said hello to him. Danny sensed something was wrong between Johnny and the new boy so he moved in between them. He stood in front of the tall kid and faced Johnny. "OK, Johnny, let's get to the field before someone else takes it." Then he turned and spoke to the new kid, "Do you want to play some football?"

"Nope. I can't. My Mom is waiting for me."

Though the boy was tall, he seemed younger than everyone else. Since Danny didn't recall seeing him before, he asked him. "Did you just move here?"

"No, I'm visiting my Mom's friend. I live in Marcus Hook*."

"OK, Hook," Danny added, "Maybe you can play some other time when you're visiting. We can always use another player."

The tall kid nodded his head affirmatively at Danny and walked away in the opposite direction. Then he turned and looked over his shoulder one last time at Johnny who he decided was a donkey's rear end. The tall kid and Danny exchanged waves and slight smiles. Neither Danny nor the tall kid knew then that they would become life-long friends and share one of the greatest thrills in sports.

1929 Franklin School

The world was at peace. The Roaring Twenties were still roaring. Although not many people in the city of Chester were wealthy, most people were content because work was plentiful and that allowed them to enjoy their lives. There was every reason to believe that this prosperity could last forever. No one, and certainly not the Murtaugh family, could know that forever will arrive several months from now, in October 1929, and that similar prosperity would become elusive for decades to come.

It was mid-June and neither the students nor the teachers were able to concentrate inside the warm, humid classrooms. But one look at the school calendar this morning released them all from their little miseries. Today was the last day of school for the boys and girls in Chester. It was three o'clock and summer officially began now for Danny, his sisters and his friends, even for the weary teachers, as they all anticipated the school bell's final ring announcing the joyous news that the school year had ended.

With the sound of the school bell, the doors flew open wide and there was much chatter, laughter, and activity as students charged the door and released all the energy that was forcibly held in check during the final weeks, and especially on this one last final day of classes. A group of seventh grade boys led the dash of students out the front door and onto the school's paved playground.

Once these boys got a few feet away from the front of the school, Joe stopped them in their tracks. "Fellas, did you see Kathleen Clarke's face when Miss Clarkson told her to remove the paper airplane from her hair. I couldn't stop laughing. The school bell rang just in time."

Johnny was laughing. "Boy that was the best. I got out of there before I busted a gut laughing."

Will, responding slower than usual, said. "She was fuming, and she was almost in tears."

Artie was next to speak. "Who? Kathleen Clarke or Miss Clarkson?"

Will replied, "Both of them."

Johnnie looked back to the school entrance. "Look. Miss Clarkson is talking to Kathleen now. Where is Danny?"

Will, regaining his knack for first responses, spoke first. "I watched him. He got out of the school like a jackrabbit: smooth, quiet, and fast."

They all looked around the school playground until they saw Danny standing in a far corner of the playground with Bennie and Jimmy. They all ran towards him. They were all laughing and trying to speak to him at the same time.

Joe was the loudest "Danny, how did you do that? Kathleen Clarke didn't even know it was in her hair."

"Shhh! Not so loud. I just used a little Houdini magic with a small piece of tape. I told her there was lint in her hair and then I pretended to brush it off while I taped the plane on the back of her hair. It was easy."

"Didn't she get mad when you touched her hair?" Will asked.

Danny smiled. "Nope. She likes me. Not like a boyfriend! She trusts me."

Joe ignored the boyfriend remark but the trust word got his attention. "Not any more she doesn't. She's gonna squeal on you."

Danny didn't seemed worried. "Nah. She won't because she really likes my sisters. They're all friends. She's a good egg. It was just a 'last day of school' joke. Miss Clarkson can't blame her. She knows no one would do that to themselves. Besides, Miss Clarkson wasn't supposed to see it."

Joe laughed and punched Danny lightly on the arm. "Teachers are never supposed to see it."

Johnny as usual was impressed with Danny's latest prank. "Danny, that was the best one yet. It was better than the glass of water with the fish in it that you left for Annie Reilly to drink last year."

"Oh, Yeh." Danny said as he laughed at that memory. "That was classic. But that was a close call. Annie almost swallowed the goldfish, and I had to get that fish back to my Aunt's house.'

They all laughed as they remembered Annie spitting out the goldfish onto the lunchroom floor.

Joe changed the subject quickly. "Hey! Forget all that now. No more school! Let's play ball. I'll see all you guys at the baseball field in an hour or so. OK?"

Danny heard him and all his buddies did too. But no one answered Joe because they all followed Danny's eyes as he looked across the playground to the school's front door. They heard Danny say in an ominously low voice, "Uh Oh, here comes Miss Clarkson. She sees me and she doesn't look happy to see me. I wish I was invisible."

1929 Sandlot baseball

A month later, Danny and his buddies were among fifteen or so pre-teen boys tossing baseballs to each other at an old storage yard that was once used for World War I surplus military equipment. The storage yard was converted into a baseball field by the neighborhood just a few years ago and now Danny and his pals were at the age where it fit them. It's like they inherited it and they played there almost every day. In a year or so, most of them, at least the better players like Danny, would outgrow this limited space with its short outfields and less than standard base paths.

Already, the late morning sun had begun its rise to its full height over the field. The boys were standing in a lazy circle. Naturally, Danny was standing in the center of the group and it was clear that he was in charge. Even though he was nearly the shortest in the group, he was definitely the leader. He was already recognized as the best ball player in his age group in the neighborhood.

They were all there to play sandlot baseball. These were the best kind of baseball games where everyone batted, there was no umpire, no coaches, and plenty of discussion regarding the rules, and who had the correct score of the game. Baseball was always more fun on the sandlot.

Danny stated the obvious. "OK. Joe, we need three more players to make up two full teams."

That was when Joe saw Johnny and Ray running across the outfield towards him and Danny. He motioned towards them and pointed them out to Danny. "There's two. Now we only need one more player."

Danny looked across the field and saw the two boys waving as they ran to the circle. Over their shoulders and about ten yards behind them, Danny saw a tall, lanky, kid walking onto the field. The kid had a glove in his hand and Danny called out to him, "Hey, kid, do you wanna play some baseball?"

The kid looked up and yelled, "Yeah, sure I do."

As the boy got closer to the circle of players, Danny recognized him as the kid with the basketball a year or so before, during football season. "Don't I know you? Aren't you from Marcus Hook?"

"Uh huh." He replied, surprised that Danny remembered him.

The kid joined the circle of players. Now they had the number of players needed to make two full teams. Danny sized him up. The boy was tall, thin, and he certainly looked comfortable with his glove on his hand. Danny noticed that he was left-handed. The first thing that Danny thought was that it was really a bonus that the boy has his own glove. That was a good thing because there are very few left-handed players in this neighborhood and even fewer left-handed gloves.

"Can you catch a fly ball?" Danny asked him.

"Sure, I can." The boy fidgeted as he replied. "I can catch anything. I usually play first base but I'll play anywhere you want me to play."

Danny looked closely at the taller kid. He didn't know if the kid was a good player or if he just looked and talked like a good player. Nevertheless, he was the eighteenth player and he made the sides even. That was enough to seal the deal.

"OK." Danny answered. "Both teams already have a first baseman. So, you're in right field."

This didn't really take much thought by Danny. He just did what he always did whenever a new kid showed up. He always sent new kids out to right field where little harm can be done since baseballs aren't often hit that way. After all, he was never sure if a new kid could play no matter what the kid told him. Danny's Mom always said that 'the proof is in the pudding'. Once you taste it, you'll know if it's any good or not. So, after a few balls were hit in that direction you would have certain proof if the kid was good or not.

As the kid ran out towards right field, Danny yelled out to him from the infield. "Hey, Hook, what's your first name?"

The boy kept running, turned halfway around, and yelled back. "James. But everybody calls me Mickey."

"OK, Mickey. My name is Danny. You'll be on my team."
Now the teams were set. There was a short, but loud, and traditional discussion about whose team would bat first. Joe was the self-appointed captain for the other team and he was pleading his case that his team should bat first. Players from both teams started speaking at the same time.

"We go first this time cause you…"
"No! You guys always go first."
"That's not fair…."

"Hold it." Danny interrupted the argument. "OK. Joe, you guys can bat first. Heck! If we don't start soon, it will be dark before we can even play three innings."

Art was on Danny's team but he wasn't happy with batting last. "Why let them bat first, Danny?"

"Artie, pipe down. We gotta get started. It ain't so bad to bat last. I think it's lucky."

There was more to Danny's thinking than that. Even at eleven, Danny knew that nothing was as valuable in sports as the home advantage, especially in baseball because you got the final at-bat. That's why playing in your home field was commonly referred to as the 'home field advantage'. Unkie always told him that having the last bat was the best advantage in all sports. Danny knew that the odds of winning with the last at bat were usually in your favor, whether you play three innings or fifteen.

The game finally began and there was plenty of action on the field, some good and some bad baseball. The new kid surprised everyone with his hitting and fielding. He got on base twice in his two turns at bat. But

Danny and Mickey, Ordinary Heroes

Danny's team was still losing and they were batting in the bottom of the fourth inning. With darkness coming, this would be the last bat of the shortened game. Danny started the inning grounding out to the second baseman, but now they had two guys on base. Mickey, the new kid, was batting.

"OK. Hook, let's bring 'em in. Then we can go home."

The ball was pitched to the new kid who swung and made hard contact and the ball took off on a long ride to right center field. The right fielder looked up at the ball coming towards him and saw that it was still rising. He turned his back to the infield and raced to get under the ball. After only three steps he stopped and watched as the ball landed out in the high grass beyond the outfield. Mickey was running quickly around the bases, almost catching up to the boys running in front of him.

"Holy cow! That was a rocket! How'd he do that?" Art was shocked. Most of the boys on both teams were still staring into the outfield waiting for the outfielder to catch up to the rolling ball. A few other boys watched as Mickey ran the bases. On the sidelines, Danny was among those watching the outfielder, and then, talking to no one in particular, he said. "Geez! He sure slugged that one." He yelled out to Mickey as he saw the kid race hard towards third base. "Hey Hook, you can slow down. That ball ain't coming back in here too soon.'

Mickey crossed the make-shift home plate and all the players on his team greeted him with smiles and patted him on the back and shoulders. It was a fun way to end a game just before the sun went down.

Even though that ended the game and Joe's team lost, Joe complimented him. "Hey, that was some hit. You can play with us anytime. But next time, you are on our team. You can even play first base."

Mickey, out of breath from running the four bases, simply said. "OK."

Danny approached him with a big grin on his face. He knew that this kid was a ballplayer. He asked him. "Hook, what's your full name, anyway? How old are you?"

Mickey answered him quickly, "My name is Mickey. Mickey Vernon. In school it's James Vernon, but my family always calls me Mickey. I'm ten."

"OK. Mickey. Well, you're a tall ten. My name is Danny. Come back again."

All the boys slowly gathered up their bats, balls, and gloves and they began the post-game calculation of their personal statistics; the number of hits they each made and their own runs scored and batted in. The final tally of hits, runs scored, and runs batted in among the players always exceeded the actual statistics in the game. An official scorer could keep a more exact track of who did what but none of the boys was brave enough to do that job. Close enough was good enough.

Now they headed home just as the field darkened and turned itself back into an old storage yard. Danny and his friends went one way. Mickey walked alone in the opposite direction.

Danny and Joe trailed behind the other kids.
"Joe, do you remember that kid now? He was the kid with the basketball that Johnny pestered. He's quiet. But even then I thought that he would've decked Johnny. Boy, can he hit a baseball."

Joe nodded affirmatively "... and he can run and field."

Danny laughed, "Yeah! And all that, too."

CHAPTER THREE
HARD TIMES

1931- Pennies on a Dollar

The Roaring Twenties and its seemingly endless prosperity came to a sudden halt in October 1929. Prices on the New York Stock Exchange began to fall lower in the late summer and tumbled out of control in the following months. The euphoric frenzy of the previous years of consistent upward growth in the nation's economy had resulted in the easy access to cash and loans for countless personal uses and increasingly ill-conceived business ventures. The rush to participate in this 'gold rush' economy blinded the country to the normal ebb and flow of commerce. The inevitable decline in commerce escalated into an economic disaster.

The October 26, 1929 Stock Market Crash severely shook the financial and manufacturing foundations in America. Within months, the powerful institutions of banks and brokerage firms bankrupted and investments valued at thousands of dollars only days before suddenly became worth only pennies on a dollar. In some cases, many became simply worthless. Quickly investors, businesses and banks could not pay their bills as their cash was depleted. Property values also fell sharply because there were no buyers with cash left to purchase properties for sale. How much is a dollar worth if no one even has a dime to purchase anything from you?

Within a year, full employment ended and working families lost their jobs and could not pay bills, buy clothes, keep a shelter over their heads, or even feed their families. The economy and the spirit of America was down lower than ever. The Great Depression was suffocating America's confidence and its hope. The only thing that was plentiful and free was the air you breathed. To make matters worse, all countries throughout the world were equally in dire economic straits.

Danny and Mickey, Ordinary Heroes

In the following decade, life changed drastically for everyone, everywhere, in America and abroad. The Great Depression worsened in the winter of 1931. Cash was scarce and bartering - exchanging one object or service for an equally-valued object or service - became the new cash in many communities, rural and city alike. Pride and timidity were cast aside as everyone sought to survive the scarcity of food and shelter amid the abundance of increasing despair. Men and boys who had previously never traveled beyond their town limits were leaving their hometowns and riding the highways and railroads to find any profitable work. Every member in a family contributed in any manner that they could, even down to simply eating less and sharing more with others. There were many lives changed for the worse in these difficult years. Danny's and Mickey's families and neighborhoods were equally impacted.

During this time, Danny rolled out his old red wagon several evenings a week and scavenged around his neighborhood seeking anything that he could use, sell, or trade. This was one way that he knew he could help his family. He usually scavenged alone so he could maximize the number and quality of the things he found. Other nights, he would invite a friend to join him. Everyone was in need.

Artie his younger friend had been asking for weeks to join Danny on his rounds. Tonight, Danny invited Artie to come along. He didn't really need his help but it was a free country. Besides, he liked him. Artie was never any trouble and he wanted to learn how to help his own family.

It was already nearly eight o' clock and they had been outside for an hour. Artie was glad to be included in the hunt.

"Danny, thanks for letting me come along with you. I wanna find some things and maybe sell them too like you do."

Artie walked as fast as he could to keep pace with the wooden wagon that Danny was pulling. After doing this for the past two months, this was routine for Danny. He took his wagon out several nights after he pretended to do his school work, and searched the area along the B&O tracks for any material or goods that could be sold or used by his family.

Some nights were better than others. Tonight, the bitter cold burned his face, hands and feet and made it more difficult to look for discarded metals, wood, and paper, or anything of value that can be taken to junkyards for cash or burned as fuel in a house furnace. Suddenly, junkyards became a better source of cash than banks. Tonight Danny and Artie were walking the railroad tracks to hunt for pieces of coal that might have dropped from trucks and trains that made deliveries earlier in the day to homes and businesses. The wagon that he once used to play in the neighborhood was now used to carry whatever discarded treasures he could find in the late evening.

Fortunately, Danny's father still had his job at the shipyard but many factories and businesses were closed now and many fathers no longer had jobs. It was the same all over America. Jobs were hard to find and even harder to keep. Those jobs that did remain paid lower wages, and those same wages were going to drop even lower. Although prices were lower, fewer people had any money to buy anything. The Roaring Twenties were gone – they came 'in like a lion, and went out like a gutted lamb'. In the space of two years, the whole country had moved backward into a darker era, and some darker images even recalled the Dark Ages in Europe. People, families, neighborhoods were focused only on survival.

Danny and Artie continued walking for another twenty minutes in the dark along the railroad tracks. The night air got even colder. Danny's small wagon was now half-full with the various objects they found along the tracks. It was a bountiful night. Every night's results were different.

Pulling the wagon along the street, Danny boasted. "Artie, last night I found pieces of wooden pallets and even some coal scattered near the bend just ahead. I think we are doing even better tonight."

Nodding, and shivering from the thick air, Artie spoke haltingly through his cold lips. "OK, good. So can we go home now? It's a lot colder now. How much stuff do we need?"

Pulling his coat collar tighter around his neck, Danny was cold too but this was the very reason why few people came out at night. Because he would suffer the cold, he gained the advantage in finding these reclaimed treasures. His truthful reply to Artie was simple.

"More. We always need more. We keep going and hope to find more stuff. Stuff we can sell, or burn for heat. Remember, you're gonna get almost half for helping me tonight."

"Yeh, but I think it's getting scary, here alone, at night."

"Sure it is." Danny agreed as he looked up and down the street. "But this is the best time to look. See, you got to get here at night. By nightfall most of the freight cars have passed. Up here at this bend in the track you can usually find coal because some of the loose coal laying on the top of a coal car falls onto the track when the train turns on the bend."

"I don't see any coal, Danny." The cold air and the darkening night made Artie less interested in finding more 'treasure'.

"Well, it isn't always easy to see and it isn't always there. You have to go slow and look hard. Look for anything. If it was too easy, everybody would be out here." Then he paraphrased Unkie's favorite advice. "If you want something, you gotta go get it." He smiled to himself, paused, then he added. "Keep looking."

Soon, Danny knew that Artie could go no farther and that was OK because they had to walk all the way back and it was now darker and certainly colder. He would check this one last bend in the track, hopefully they would find some coal and then head back home. As the boys approached the railroad bend they picked up other articles around the track and along the sides. At this moment, they saw another figure appear on the track about twenty yards ahead. It was a man. A big man.

"That ain't your wagon."

The man continued to walk towards them. He was starting to walk faster now that he saw the two boys.

Artie was frightened and asked a worrisome question. "Who's that?

"I don't know. Don't say anything. But do just what I say. OK?"

"OK." Artie was hardly able to speak.
As the man got closer, Danny didn't recognize him as anyone he knew from the neighborhood. Artie was now standing behind Danny and Danny whispered to him. "Don't run. Don't do nothing now. But when I say something to you, do exactly what I tell you to do."

The man was now in front of them. He was just as big as he looked from a distance and much bigger than the boys. He was dirty and disheveled and he was carrying a burlap sack. On his shabby trousers he had what looked like a sheath for a knife hanging from his belt but there was no knife in it. Walking slower and getting closer, he motioned toward the wagon, and asked in a low gravelly voice. "Whaddya boys got there?"

Danny didn't say anything at first. The man repeated his question and without waiting for a reply, he spit into the ground and looked directly at Danny.

"I asked you a question." The man snarled at Danny. "Whaddya doing out here? Ain't it kinda late for you boys?"

His legs shaking but his backbone stiffening, Danny answered the man bravely. "My dad sent us out to find some stuff. We found all this lying along the tracks, sir. It's for my dad." Danny was doing his best to sound steady but his fear was rising.

It's possible that the man could feel Danny's fear. He growled low and mean-like. "Oh yea. Well I'll bet that ain't your wagon, is it, boy? Why don't you just give me the wagon and the stuff and you boys can go home where you won't get in trouble with anyone bigger than you are."

Danny was trying to stay calm and he thought for a second and his words come out firm and clear. "It's my wagon. And my Dad is just behind us a bit. He'll be here in a minute. So you better move along. We aren't bothering you."

The man looked past the boys and down along the tracks from where they came. "I don't see nobody behind you." The man thought for a moment and spoke accusingly. "Boy, I think you're lying. And I know that wagon ain't yours, at least not anymore. Now, give me the wagon and the stuff in it. Then go along home."

Danny touched Artie on the arm and said loudly in a firm voice. "Artie, run back fast and get Dad. Hurry!"

Artie did as he was told and broke into a fast gallop just as the man stepped closer to Danny and reached for the handle of the wagon. Danny didn't let go of the wagon handle. The man raised his other hand towards Danny, but he stopped just as he heard yelling coming from behind Danny and from the same direction that Artie was running to for help. The man looked in the distance and saw several shapeless figures running towards Artie, Danny, the wagon, and him.

The man suddenly realized that Danny's father was on his way after all. He pulled his hands away from Danny and the wagon handle and he turned and started running in the same direction that he came from, away from Danny and from the approaching figures. He growled back over his shoulder to Danny. ""OK, kid. Keep the damn wagon."

In less than a minute, Artie, followed closely by Danny's friends Joe and Johnny, reached Danny and the wagon and watched in the distance as the man continued to run away with his burlap sack waving wildly at his side.
Joe spoke first, "Danny, are you OK?"

Johnny, huffing from running so fast asked. "Who's that? What happened?"

Danny's chest was heaving wildly now even though the man was gone. The fear of what had happened started to overwhelm him so Artie answered for Danny. "That man was going to take Danny's wagon, and everything we put in it."

Joe was concerned and placed his hands on Danny's shoulders. "Did he hit you?" he asked.

Catching his breath and trying to slow his mind and body down, Danny barely whispered a response. "No, Joe, he didn't hit me. But, I think he was going to hit me."

Johnny was alarmed. "Why?"

"I guess just like Artie said he wanted the wagon. I guess so he could take what we collected and then keep the wagon as his own, or sell it."

Artie put his arm around Danny. "Fellas, Danny pulled a great trick by telling the man that his dad was right behind us, around the bend. The man didn't believe Danny's dad was right behind us."

Feeling more at ease as he told his friends what happened, Danny explained what stopped the man from hitting him and stealing the wagon full of found goods. "No, he didn't believe me at first. But when he saw you guys coming, he thought you were my dad." Danny smiled for the first time that night. "I'm sure glad you guys showed up. You arrived just in the nick of time, just like the United States Calvary chasing away the Indians."

Joe liked the compliment but he was still puzzled. "But we're just kids, not adults."

"Yeh," Danny answered. "But he didn't know that. From here, in the dark and in the distance, you looked and sounded like men."

Artie was still very excited and repeated his praise. "Danny, that was smart thinking. He doesn't run if you don't trick him by telling him that your dad is right behind us, and then send me for help."

Danny looked at Joe and Johnny, then at Artie. "It was all I could think of to buy time. I was scared." He paused for a thought, then asked his good friends. "What made you two come out tonight anyway? I thought you were both grounded at home."

Johnny nodded toward Joe. "We are. But Joe and I thought that we'd spend a little time with our pals and get back before anyone missed us."

Joe wasn't smiling now. "Yeh. Only after everybody hears this story we'll be in trouble for being out here tonight."

As always, Danny had a solution. "We won't tell anyone. It'll be one more thing we pals keep to ourselves. OK?"

Standing together and facing Danny, the partially frozen younger, neighborhood version of the Three Musketeers (Athos, Aramis, Porthos) heartily answered their trusty d'Artagnan. They all replied loudly at the same time.

"OK! All for one and one for all."

Then they headed home. Artie forgot how cold he was until he got outside his own house. "Danny, I don't think I'll go out with you tomorrow night."

The four Musketeers all laughed heartily again.

1935, Chester High School

Over the next four years' the country's economic performance was more of the same as its preceding years. Jobs were scarce and money was even scarcer. Government programs were implemented to create employment and produce a measure of income to replace private industry that was almost non-existent. Banking institutions were bolstered and the general population's hopeful mood was resuscitated by an unprecedented federal mobilization of work programs and relief activities that stemmed the feeling of doom that had been haunting the masses of people.

Through all of this, Danny and his friends' high school years continued modestly unchanged. After all, there were not many options to school. Paying jobs were limited to older men with family responsibilities, and all of the branches of the military services had an age restriction of eighteen years of age. So secondary education became a buffer that softened the hard fact that there was no work for young persons. Schools at least provided some place to gather and it was expected that more schooling would inspire a wider choice of careers when jobs did arrive. Mostly, it was hoped that with the passage of time, jobs would become available later when the economy recovered from its calamitous fall.

So Danny and his boyhood friends saw each other regularly at school and in the neighborhood. He was a popular student and participated on several school sport teams (soccer, basketball, and baseball). Baseball was his first choice and most of his baseball experience was gained from playing in local community leagues throughout the summer. He was particularly fond of the competitive American Legion league. This is where he was reacquainted with Mickey Vernon, John Podgajny, and others, either as a teammate or as an opponent depending on which team and in which league he played.

Girls were the newest addition to his fuller circle of friends. The girls he knew were either friends of his older sisters or his classmates in school. He was starting to have a growing interest in one girl he had known the longest, and tormented the most, Kathleen Clarke, the girl with the paper airplane in her hair.

The school day routines from Monday through Thursday were primarily the same but when school let out on Friday the students gathered in small groups on the lawn outside the school, or sidewalks, and even on the street corner to plan their weekends.

Kathleen Clarke and three girlfriends were in front of the school planning for their weekend before heading home. The girls were a close knit group who shared secrets with one another so easily and so often that there really were no secrets between them. Anna McLaughlin was seventeen and as the most vocal and outspoken member of the troupe, she usually assumed the lead in planning their activities. Nicknames were common, even for girls, and Anna's nickname was Mickey, a short and cute substitute for McLaughlin.

The other girls, Doris, Joan, and Kate, were talking among themselves when Anna noticed several boys crossing the street and walking towards them. She had expected that if she and her friends stood here long enough, the boys would go out of their way to walk pass them.

"Kate, here he comes," Anna said. "Along with his ever-present, trusty baseball pals. I bet you he says something to you. Funny or not, nice or not, he's going to say something to you, and to no one else." Anna was adamant and pleased with her prediction.

"Stop it." Kate pretended annoyance. "I don't care. Let's start moving."

Anna and 'Clarkie', as Kathleen was known by her friends, were nearly inseparable. Anna stiffened in her reply. "I'm not moving. I waited for you, now you can wait a few minutes longer for me. Besides, I like his friend, Johnnie. And I don't get to see Johnnie unless Danny wants to see you."

"Well," Doris chimed in. "I like the tall one. He is good looking, and he's not shy."

"That's Joe." Anna knew all of the boys' names.

"OK. So it's Joe. That should be easy to remember."

Joan, one of the other girlfriends, agreed with Anna. "You know, Kate, Mickey is right. Danny always seems to look for you in the crowd. He always teased you when we were kids. Remember?"

"I remember. I didn't like it. Well, not all of the time. He always thinks he's funny." It was a half-hearted defense from Kate.

"But he is funny." Joan chuckled.
There was a sudden end to the conversation as the three boys approached. The girls all smiled and nodded to them and the boys did the same. Joe was the first boy to say anything. "Hi, girls. Was it a good day or a bad day at the school house today?"

"A good day," was Doris' bright reply. This was her chance to look at Joe directly and get his attention on her. "No homework. No school until Monday."

Joe liked her friendly, casual comment. He hadn't noticed before how cute and bubbly she was. "What's cooking for the weekend?" he asked.

Before Doris could say another word, Anna looked directly at Johnnie who was her choice of boys. "Oh, just the malt shop tonight, and maybe the team's baseball game tomorrow."

Now Joan added her voice to the banter so she wouldn't go unnoticed. "It's an early home game at 10 am against Eddystone, right."

"Uh Huh." replied Joe. "They're not an official high school team. But all their players are from the school. We should beat 'em. Even with Vernon on their side." He explained what he meant. "Vernon is very good but he can't play everywhere. Best of all, he doesn't pitch. Right, Danny?"

Danny answered Joe, but he was looking at Kate. "Mickey's very good but he is only going to bat 3 or 4 times. We're going to win tomorrow. Johnny P is pitching. He's a sophomore but he's our best pitcher."

There was a slight pause in the conversation. Then Danny spoke to Kate. "Hey, Clarkie. Are you a baseball fan now?"
Anna perked up and looked over and smiled widely at Kate. Kate hadn't said a word and wasn't going to volunteer anything to the discussion because she wanted to prove that Anna was wrong about Danny and her but now she had to answer the question. "Ah, yes, I like baseball, especially our school team. Sometimes it gets confusing. But I like watching you all play."

With his attention solely on Kate, Danny nervously offered to improve Kate's baseball knowledge. "Well, if you are ever confused about the rules or the game just ask me about them. Anytime." He smiled, then turned as Johnnie got the boys attention.

"Let's go fellas. We want to get a little practice in before it gets dark."

Danny, looking again only at Kate, started to move away. "OK, girls. Maybe we'll see you tomorrow."

"Maybe even later tonight." Added Joe.

The boys crossed the street toward the park as all four girls waved goodbye. "OK. Bye."

As soon as the boys were out of hearing range, Ann turned to Kate and laughed. So did the other girls. They all began to tease Kate.

Anna was first. "I told you! Danny is sweet on you."

"He acted like the rest of us weren't here." Doris chimed in. "And he's usually always talking to everyone."

Joan was more direct. "I think you like him too, Kate."

Anna was giddy. "She likes him plenty. She always has, even long ago when he bothered her in class. Only now it means something more. It's love."

"Stop it, Mickey." Kate yelled. "All of you, stop. I'm not going to listen to you. I just might not even go to the school game tomorrow."

No one wanted to upset Kate but Anna couldn't help but laugh out loud. "Yeh, you will. Because I'm going to drag you there. Then you and I can.." she paused, then finished the sentence. "..learn all the 'confusing stuff' about baseball. They all laughed, even Kate.

1935- Mickey vs Danny

The next morning was a bright, warm Saturday morning. Chester High School's baseball team was anxious to play an informal game against Eddystone on Chester's home field. Eddystone didn't have a school-sponsored team but there was enough interest at the school to field a team and several teachers agreed to coach and manage the players. This year's Eddystone team was very successful. One reason for that was the slick fielding and power hitting of their junior class first baseman, Mickey Vernon.

Danny and Mickey, Ordinary Heroes

Mickey and Danny had become friends over the past few years. They were brought together in the circle of talented baseball players in the county and they often competed against one another, and sometimes were teammates. Mickey had size and strength, graceful moves around the bag, and the smooth and quirky swing of a classic left-handed hitter. Danny on the other hand was a feisty, hard-nosed player with grit, great speed, and passion for the game. He did not have a power swing but he hit well enough to earn praise as a leading hitter and infielder in the area. A bonus was that he was a leader and he was well-liked by his teammates. Hell, he was well-liked by many of his rivals.

In 1935, Mickey was in his third year at Eddystone High School even though he lived in Marcus Hook. The school was on East Chester Pike and it was a trolley ride to Eddystone, a ride that passed right through Chester. Why Mickey was enrolled in Eddystone High and not in Chester High was a topic for concern today because today the Chester team was trailing 8-3, and Mickey was the reason.

As promised, the girls arrived at the game, but not until the second inning and they seated themselves on the first base side of the field just behind the Chester dugout. The game advanced at a faster than usual pace and it was going into the bottom half of the last inning. Mickey, the star hitter for Eddystone, had two doubles, a single and a walk and had done most of the damage. None of the Chester pitchers could get Mickey out, including Chester's star sophomore pitcher, Johnny Podgajny.

Now it was Chester's last turn to bat, and they would have to score six more runs in the inning in order to win. The first two Chester batters had already made routine outs. Danny was the next batter and he hoped to keep the inning going with a hit, a walk, an error. Anything. On the third pitch, Danny hit a ball over second base for a single and now he was standing on first base, just a few feet away from Mickey. Danny also knew where Kate was sitting. He noticed her back in the second inning when she and her girlfriends filed into the third row of the grandstand behind first base. He peeked a few times between innings while the

Chester pitcher loosened up his arm before facing the first batter in each inning. He thought Kate looked pretty in her green blouse and white slacks sitting with her girlfriends and talking. Heck, sometimes he noticed that she was even watching the game, at least whenever he batted.

Danny put his mind back on the game situation. The first base coach got Danny's attention as the next Chester batter moved up to home plate. Danny took a short lead off of the first base bag. With two outs and trailing by five runs, he wasn't going to steal or take a big lead off of first base. So he began talking to Mickey who crouched low in a defensive stance just next to first base. Mickey had his glove ready for the ball and closely watched the batter. After all, an infielder who takes his eye off of the hitter could easily get hit in the eye with a ball he never saw coming.

Danny kidded Mickey. "Looks like you guys got lucky today, Mick."

"Not lucky, Danny. We were ready for you guys."

Facing the pitcher and leaning towards second base, Danny said, "You mean you were ready. Your five RBIs crushed us."

Mickey moved slightly farther to his right. "Really. That many? Are you keeping count for me? I don't even do that until the game is over."

"Well, this game is mostly over, Mick. And you know that I always keep track of the score and who's doing what, especially players on the other side."

During all this chatter, the pitcher threw several times to the batter and the batter's count was up to two balls and two strikes. Mickey focused on the batter, changed the subject and asked Danny a question. "Are you going to Legion practice this afternoon?"

"Yep." Danny replied.

At that moment, even before the one-word sentence was fully spoken, the ball was hit. Smack! The ball darted sharply off of the bat and headed directly to Mickey. He straightened up, instinctively raised his glove chest high, and caught the line drive for out number three. Danny who had started to sprint to second base at the crack of the bat pulled up short of the second base bag. The game was over: Eddystone 8, Chester 3. Mickey won and Danny lost. The players from both teams headed to their own benches.

Anna stood up as the game ended. She was probably the only girl that liked baseball and understood some of the rules of the game. She knew the game was over. "Darn. Well, you can't win them all."

Doris showed some interest too even if she spent most of her time looking for Danny's friend, Joe. "It was a good game, not too long. And just like I wish all games could be. No extra innings."

Kate rose from the bench on the grandstand, smoothed her slacks, and yawned. It was fun, but it was too long. "I think they should have a half-time." She added. "They played good. It was just that tall kid who kept hitting the ball."

Anna knew who the tall kid was. "Oh! That's Mickey Vernon. He is really good. He plays on the local Legion team with Danny and Johnny."

"I haven't seen him before." Betty replied.

"That's because he lives in Marcus Hook. He only comes this way for baseball.' Warming up to the subject of boys, Anna smiled. "He's the quiet type. Good-looking though, huh? Tall, dark, and handsome, I'd say. It's a shame that he is only a junior. Too young for me."

The girls started to walk away but Anna stopped. She teased Kate. "Wait, Kate, this is your chance to ask Danny to explain the confusing terms in baseball."

Kate shook her head. "No. I don't know much about baseball, but I do know that this is not the best time to ask him anything."

"Yeh! You're right. Next game, maybe, or maybe later over a soda. He better bring Johnny." Anna was always a step ahead.

The girls walked across the street and now all the fans were gone. Only the players remained and they were milling around their coaches. Danny looked over his shoulder at Kate as she walked away. Johnny noticed him watching Kate. "Go say goodbye to her, Danny. You like her enough."

Danny didn't like that someone noticed his interest in Kate, and he didn't like Johnny mentioning it in front of the other boys. ""I like who? What do you mean? I was just looking for someone."

Johnny didn't let up. "Yeh, I know. Well, you found her. She dressed up just for you. Why don't you go tell her she looks nice in blue? Say something to her."

"Blue?" Danny was confused. "She's wearing green. You're just trying to make me say something stupid to her. She looks pretty OK in green."

"It's blue? OK? Don't ever tell a girl that she looks OK. 'You look OK' is not a good thing to say to a girl. And that blouse she is wearing is not green. You forgot that you're color blind. She's wearing blue. Boy you ought to be glad Kate's not a redhead. You'd always be in trouble."

Danny ignored Johnny and stepped back into the center of the players. He took one last look in Kate's direction, then he turned around and began talking with his teammates.

Danny and Mickey, Ordinary Heroes
1935, Graduation day

Chester High School's graduation ceremony concluded with the proper pomp and circumstance. It was a comfortable summer morning with a gentle breeze and the ceremony ended before the warm sun rose over the shaded tent. Danny with Kate beside him, Anna with Johnny, and all their other friends and classmates were released from the seats that contained them for an hour. With diplomas in hand, they were running around excitedly, greeting family, friends, and sweethearts. Danny and Kate ran over to his Mom, Dad, Unkie, and his four sisters who were all gathered tightly together and smiling happily.

Gushing with excitement, Danny hugged his parents first. "Thanks Mom and Dad for everything. This is great. No more school work. I'm ready for the world. Thanks, Unkie."

Betty, Eunice, Mary, and Peggy were crushing each other in their push to be the first to hug their only brother. The girls were laughing, crying, and speaking at the same time. "Congratulations! Danny. Hooray! Whoopee! Let me see your diploma."

Unkie put his arms around his nephew. "What now, Danny boy? The world is waiting."

"Let it wait a day or two, Tim." Danny's mom said as she kissed her son. "Let my boy celebrate now."

Everyone laughed. It was a happy, memorable moment. It was a happier moment for Danny because he was certain that he would never step inside a classroom again, unless it was something that he wanted to do.

The crowd began to thin out and the last graduates and their families left the event and began walking to their homes. Later that night, the graduates would stay up late with one another to enjoy their new accomplishment, and be excited and even possibly nervous about the new life ahead.

1935, American Legion

The future and its new life would have to wait at least one more day for Danny and Mickey. Their final American Legion game was this morning, one day after graduation. Their careers in Legion ball will end today. This is the final playoff game for the American Legion district in Delaware County. Those players who were eighteen or who completed their senior year of high school had to leave Legion ball and move on to an adult league, or play for one of the highly competitive semi-professional leagues in the Tri-State area such as the Delco League. Beyond those local teams there were the golden rings of baseball: the major league teams and their affiliated farm teams throughout the country.

Danny knew where he would play next year. As a highly regarded infielder, he will work full time at the shipyard and play in the spring and summer on the shipyard's industrial baseball team. That's next year. Right now, his Legion career ends today and he and his teammates were trailing in the final game of the local district American Legion championship game, 3-2. The visiting team was batting in the top half of the seventh (and last) inning. Johnny P. was pitching his last inning regardless of the score at the end of the seventh inning. Johnny didn't want to let the opposition score another run. He wanted to keep the other team from scoring any more runs and enable the Chester team to have a final bat to tie the score 3-3 and send the game into extra innings, or better yet, score the lead runs in the last bat and win the game. Johnny P. was doing just that as he managed to get the first two batters out before he walked the third batter.

As the runner took his slow walk to first base, Danny called time out and walked from his defensive position at second base over to the pitcher's mound. Mickey jogged over from first base. Then Danny said lowly to

Johnny P. "This is it. Johnnie. Give him the stuff. Put this guy away, and we'll go in and get what we need to win it."

"We'll catch anything hit on the ground." added Mickey. "Give it all you got."

Playing third base, Joe signaled two outs to the outfielders, then yelled to the other infielders. "The infield play is at first or second base, fellas. Go for the easiest out."

With the fourth batter in the batter's box, Johnny P. repeatedly threw over to Mickey at first base to keep the runner from getting a big lead towards second base. Now he placed the ball in his hand and from the stretch he pitched the ball to home plate. There was a loud piercing whistle just as the ball was released. Danny timed his annoying signature whistle perfectly.

The batter swung hard at the pitch and topped it so the ball rolled slowly toward first base. Mickey was playing back to hold the runner on base and now he had to charge the rolling ball that was a foot in fair territory along the first base line. Mickey picked up the ball, pivoted around to first base, and blindly tossed the ball left-handed to first base. But no one was there. Then, in an instant, Danny ran from his infield position towards first base and reached out for the ball. He snagged the low throw and slapped the ball and glove on the bag just a split-second before the runner's foot touched first base.

"You're out!" The umpire pumped his right arm emphatically to signal his call. At that same moment there was a loud cheer from the home team's side of the field.

Danny got to his feet, brushed off some fresh dirt and lobbed the ball to the umpire and continued running directly to his team's bench. His team trailed 3-2. They needed one run to tie, two runs to win the game and the championship.

As Mickey came off the field, he patted Danny on the back and said loudly to everyone. "Runs, fellas! We need two. Let's go get 'em."

Now everyone in the dugout was excited, nervous, and talking all at once. The coach was talking to them but only those sitting closest to him could understand what he was saying. It was bedlam but order was needed so the team could communicate with each other. Suddenly, another loud whistle exploded in the dugout. This time it wasn't Danny. It was Mickey, the quietest player on the team. The talking stopped immediately but Mickey didn't say a word. He pointed at the coach who nodded approvingly at Mickey and spoke to the players in an even voice. "OK, fellas. It's sitting here for us. Let's take it back. Here's the batting order. Turk, then top of the order - Murtaugh, Seber, Miller, Vernon."

The first batter, Jimmy Turk, worked the pitcher for a walk. Murtaugh stepped into the batter's box. He already had a single and a double in the game and scored a run back in the first inning. He managed to get an even count to one ball and one strike. The entire bench was cheering him on with baseball chatter. "Danny, let's do it, pal. A walk, a hit, anything. Just get on base."

The third pitch came in fast and away from Danny but he reached his bat out across the plate and met the ball with a level swing. The ball sailed out to right field and landed to the left of the outfielder and darted into the right field corner. Danny used his rabbit-speed and slid safely into second base with a double. Turk reached third base easily and was held there. There were no outs.

Joe Seber was the next batter. He stepped into the batter's box and slapped the first pitch to the second baseman. Danny hesitated between second and third and Turk sprinted for home. Murtaugh ran when the fielder threw home and he arrived safely to third base but Turk was tagged out by the catcher on a fine throw from the second baseman. Seber was safe at first on a fielder's choice. Now there was one out and there were runners on first and third. Miller was a good hitter and he's played well in the series. But he quickly fell behind the pitcher with no balls and two strikes. Now the pitcher had the advantage and he used it. Miller swung at a tough inside pitch. "Strike three!" The umpire shouted. Now there were two outs. Chester trailed by one run with runners on first and third bases.

The crowd was noisy as fans on both sides launched competing cheers and boos that matched the changing emotions that rise and fall from pitch to pitch. The Chester team still needed at least one run to have a chance to win the championship. The one piece of good news for Chester is that Mickey Vernon was now the batter. He was also the leading hitter in the league and the best clutch hitter in tight game situations.

The entire Chester team was leaning on the dugout screen. Miller, Turk, the coach were all offering last minute encouragement. First the coach, "Let's go Mickey. Show them who you are." Then Miller noted under his breath. "A game can't get any tighter than this. Whew!"

Jimmy Turk was more confident. "This is a cinch. We're in boys. Mickey is a rock at times like this."

The noisy crowd became silent as the pitcher began his windup. Danny whistled loudly from third base. Mickey tightened his grip on the bat. The pitch was made. Mickey swung and hit the ball. WHACK!

"Holy crap! He smacked that ball!" Miller trumpeted. "That ball is going to clear the bases. Holy cow!" He let out a stream of additional comments before he left his mouth hanging open while he stared at the ball rising into the outfield.

The Chester coach was jumping up and down and pointing to the outfield sky as the ball carried well beyond the right-fielder. He was as excited as anyone and in an expected manner he announced to the team.

"Yep. Mickey's got a Midas touch with a bat in his hand. Congratulations, boys. It's over. We win."

The three base runners scored easily: Danny first, then Seber followed. Mickey raced quickly around the bases. He could've trotted easily to home plate as the ball hadn't even been relayed back into the infield yet. Finally, the home plate umpire waited until Mickey touched home plate and saw the ball secured in the infield by the second baseman. Then the umpire nodded affirmatively and belted out to the coaches on each team. "My time! Game over. This game is over."

1935, Farewells

With the game over and success fresh in their minds, the Legion players were still standing around the ballfield, talking with their family and fans. Standing in the dugout, Danny and Mickey were talking about the play that ended the top of the last inning and that kept the opposing team from scoring. Almost forgetting it was his homerun that won the game, Mickey shook his head and congratulated Danny. "That was a million-dollar catch that you made, Danny. It was like you were flying." Danny downplayed his catch and the resultant bang-bang out at first base for the last out in the top of the inning as though it was a just his half of a normal infield out made every day. "Well, your throw was amazing. I saw the ball floating in the air and I just dove for the ball, caught it, and landed the ball and my glove on the bag."

Just then, Joe walked over to them. "Yeah you two sure make a good combination. Like Houdini times two." Then he added, "The coach is having some refreshments back at the Lloyd AC clubhouse to celebrate. Are you both coming?"

"I can hang around to celebrate for a little bit." Mickey answered, then looked over at Danny. "But I'll need a ride home." Mickey knew that Danny was never without a solution to anything.

"OK." Danny said as he picked up his glove. "Come to the club house with us. We'll get Turk's friend, Noodles, to give you a ride home later."

The teammates enjoyed the sodas and snacks at the clubhouse and they spoke about this last game and what the end of this Legion season meant for some of them. Johnny was the first to speak. "What a great season. There's nothing like winning a championship."

Joe chimed in. "That's the only way to end your last game of the year and it's special because it's the last American Legion game that we will ever play in together."

Seated at the table and surrounded by his teammates, Danny was uncharacteristically quiet. Now he spoke for the first time. "Yeh! Some of us will move up to the Industrial League next year. Semi-pro for me. I plan to build ships during the day and play ball for Sun Ship after work."

Mickey was only a junior in school so he had another year in Legion ball. "Are any of you guys a little nervous? I'm glad school is out but I'll be back there in September. For you guys, there's no more school. That means serious stuff now, like work."

Johnny grimaced as though he was hit in the gut. "Crap! Up early every day, and work days are always longer than school days." None of the graduating seniors were pleased to hear that.

One happy thought was celebrated with loud cheers when Joe reminded everyone of it. "Yeh!" Joe said. "But we'll get paid. We can put some money in our pockets." They all agreed that having money in their pockets would be a welcome change for them.

Danny made it clear to everyone again that he was ready to put high school behind him. "Like I said, it's the shipyard for me. I got a job there and being a ball-player don't hurt any. I'll play for the company's baseball and basketball teams. More school is definitely not for me."

Mickey had one more year of high school and another year of Legion ball. Nevertheless, Joe turned to Mickey and asked him about some news that he had heard at the barbershop in the neighborhood. "Mickey, I heard yesterday that Villanova offered you a scholarship to play baseball for them after you graduate from Eddystone. Is that right?"

Looking a little embarrassed as he usually was, Mickey replied. "Uh huh. They did. But I'm not sure about it. I don't plan on going to college. I've got my senior year to finish before I decide. Just like you, I'll be glad to finish high school and get a job."

Joe grabbed a handful of shelled peanuts and continued. "How about the pro game? What do you guys think about the big leagues?"

"That's a big nut to crack." Danny offered. "Mickey is the only one getting scouts to come see him. That's why Villanova wants him."

Danny voiced it but everyone in Chester, Marcus Hook, and the rest of Delaware Count agreed. After all, Chief Bender and Jimmy Dykes of the A's and Hack Wilson* of the Chicago Cubs came from Delaware County and all of them were stars in the majors. It sure looked like Mickey was the next best bet to join them there. "Well, that could help all of us." Joe said, grabbing a handful of peanuts.

"Yeh." Danny said. "But we need experience. We need to play in the Industrial League so we get more experience against better players. Then we gotta do well in those leagues before the farm scouts will even look at us."

Joe munching on another mouthful of peanuts was barely audible but nevertheless said. "But when they come to see Mickey, they'll see us too. That's when we have to shine. That's how it helps us." He looked at Danny and said, "We know this is true but we also know that no matter how good someone else is, only your talent will make a scout turn his head and watch you play.

"That's right." Danny nodded. "Until then, we can work hard and plan for it. Right now I'm going home. Mickey, let's go see Turk and get you a ride from the clubhouse to the Hook."

After celebrating at the Lloyd AC clubhouse, the boys gathered their equipment and went to their separate homes. Mickey waited for Jimmy Turk and Noodles and Noodle's car. He had a parting view of his teammates and friends. He called out to all of them. "1935 American Legion champions. That sounds really good."

They could hear him and as they walked every which way to their homes in the various parts of the city and beyond, they held their heads high and put smiles on their faces, and let the sound of their laughter echo across the city streets. This baseball season was behind them, and for most of them it was the last formal league baseball they would play. They were entering the ever-unpredictable world of grownups. Maybe semi-pro baseball was ahead for some of them but for most of them getting a decent paying job was now definitely their number one goal. None of them knew what lay in the future for them, but a peek into a crystal ball would've surprised Danny and Mickey because they would see that they would never again play baseball together on the same team.

***Hack Wilson slugged 94 homeruns and batted in 350 runs in the combined 1929 and 1930 seasons.**

CHAPTER FOUR
GOING SOUTH

1937, Villanova

In the following two years, Danny played baseball for the shipyard team and worked in the shipyard metal workshop with his Dad. Mickey completed his senior year at Eddystone High School where he met Elizabeth Firth, known socially as Libby to her friends and affectionately as Lib to her new boyfriend. Upon graduation in 1936, Mickey accepted a baseball scholarship to Villanova.

Danny also received an offer from Villanova in 1936 but it was an offer to play football, not baseball. He said no. Though he was smaller than most baseball players and overcame that physical size disadvantage, he considered himself too small and too light for the towering linemen that played football in college. Anyway, as he was quick to tell everyone, school was not for him, and certainly not among these growling giants of the gridiron.

The past two years demonstrated that Danny and Mickey shared more than a friendship. They shared a single, driving ambition to play professional baseball. In the 1930's, baseball was the only team sport where you could earn enough money to make a living. Basketball and football were strictly college sports. The only other sports where you could make a living in the 1930s were boxing, wrestling, and horse racing, if you were a horse or a jockey. Mickey was never going to be a jockey, he was too tall. Danny had never ridden a horse and he still thought that only cowboys and Indians rode horses. There was tennis and golf, but those were country club games played in clean clothes. There was no doubt that baseball that was the single choice for them. Mickey was in college, but he was there for the same reason that Danny was at the shipyard, baseball.

Mickey completed his freshman baseball season at Villanova. His biggest success that semester was his batting average and his slugging percentage. A week before having to choose his courses for the second year of college, Mickey made an appointment to meet with his Registration Counselor, Mr. Burman. Mickey decided to leave Villanova and the day had come when he had to tell his counselor. This would be the first time he told anyone at the school. His Mom, Dad, and, of course, Lib, were the only people who knew. He had not even told Coach Jacobs, Villanova's baseball coach, about his decision.

Mickey knocked lightly on the open door and entered the school counselor's office. Mr. Burman was a middle-age man who liked his job, loved baseball, and was particularly fond of Mickey. He had been a Registration Counselor at the school for seven years. "Good morning, Mickey" was the cheery greeting from the counselor. He pointed to a single chair and said. "Please sit down."

After they were seated, Mr. Burman moved a few papers from the center of his desk and placed them into a filing tray. "You didn't tell me on the phone why you were coming to see me, Mickey." He held that thought for a moment, and began speaking again. "That's OK, I presume you are ready to choose your semester courses. So I have a copy of the course selections for the semester here. Did you decide what courses you will take next year?"

Mickey wanted to get this meeting done as quickly as possible. It took him a lot of time to make this decision, and he didn't want to drag it out any longer. He wanted to be quick about it and be done with it.

"I'm not taking any courses, Mr. Burman. I've decided to leave school."

The counselor was visibly stunned by this news and by the calm manner in which Mickey relayed the news to him. "You're withdrawing from school?"

Mickey looked across the desk and said in a controlled voice. "Yes, sir. That's correct. No courses. The baseball season is over here at Villanova. I'm leaving school."

Settling back into his tall chair and allowing a few seconds to let this bombshell announcement settle in his brain, the counselor asked him. "Why are you withdrawing?"

"College isn't for me, sir. I've been transferred into three different curriculums in one year: Engineering, Accounting, and now Business. None of them fit me. School doesn't fit me." He paused but Mr. Burman didn't speak. He wanted Mickey to continue talking so he could gather his own thoughts and provide a perfect response that would pull Mickey back into Villanova.

Mickey continued. "I like Villanova. I do. But books and I aren't a good match. I love baseball more, just by itself."

Despite searching for the right words, the counselor didn't find a perfect response. He said the only thing that came quickly to his mind. "Are you sure about this? Does Coach Jacobs know this?'

"No, sir. He doesn't know it yet. You're the first person at Villanova that I've told." Mr. Burman leaned forward a little and regained his normal cadence of breathing: air in, air out, etc. He made a sincere suggestion to Mickey. "Don't you think you should talk to the Coach before you withdraw from school?"

"I guess I should, but this way is better for me. You see, Coach would ask me to stay and I might not be able to say no to him. But I know leaving school is right for me. If I stayed, it would be the wrong thing for me."

Mr. Burman took another full breath of air and continued. "Well, I wish that you would think some more about your decision. Getting a college degree will help you greatly in the future. Baseball is giving you that opportunity."

"Yes, I know that, sir. I appreciate it, too. But college isn't for me. Actually, playing so much baseball for the team against so many good college teams convinced me how much I want to play baseball all the time."

Speaking more like a father than a counselor, Mr. Burman's next statement sounded more like a command than the well-meaning advice that he wanted to convey to Mickey. "Son, you can't play baseball all the time. You have to have a job, a career." Mickey understood that, and he had prepared his best answer for that argument. "That's just it, sir. I want baseball to be my job, to be my career."

Obviously, this meeting had become more than a student/counselor discussion on course selection and such things academic. Mr. Burman understood Mickey's dream but he realized the consequences of giving away a college education. "Mickey, that's a long shot, even for a player with your talent. Think about it some more. I'll speak with Coach Jacobs now. Do you want to come with me?"

"No. I'll see him later, after you speak with him." Mickey's voice was now lower and his words were barely audible. "He's a really good man and he is the best baseball coach I ever had."

Mr. Burman rose from his chair and walked around to the front of his desk. Mickey got up slowly. He stood about five inches taller than the counselor, but he didn't feel his full height just now. He didn't like disappointing people. He didn't like making anyone feel bad because of something he did. But he also knew that he was doing the right thing for himself and for his future. It was a gamble but he was confident in his talents.

Mr. Burman offered his hand towards Mickey. "All right, Mickey. I hope we will talk again. Until then, come see me with any other questions, especially if you change your mind. Villanova really wants young men like you on campus. I'll talk to Coach Jacobs. Goodbye for now."

"Goodbye, Mr. Burman."

Mickey turned away from the desk and opened the office door. He stepped out through the waiting lounge, then exited down the hallway. It was his last day as a student at Villanova. It was also the definitive beginning of his dedication to pursue baseball as a career. In less than a year, he would be accompanied by a fellow Legion teammate on a journey that would change both of their lives.

1937 A volunteer fireman

Many fathers and sons from Chester and the surrounding communities worked side by side at the manufacturing plants along the river. Danny's father had worked in the shipyard for several decades and he was helpful in getting Danny hired there when he graduated from high school two years earlier. The ship yard owners also knew young Danny was a talented ball player and they wanted him to play for the company teams in the very competitive Delco Industrial League. It wasn't long before the shipyard became a central part of Danny's grownup life. The shipyard wasn't what he wanted to do for his whole life, but it was a fortunate possession in the midst of tough times everywhere in America.

During these few years after high school, many of Danny's waking hours away from work were spent with his high school sweetheart, Kate Clark. She became the person of primary importance to him. Whenever his family or his friends wanted to find him, the first place they would look for him was at Kate's house. If he wasn't there, there were only two other places where he could be found. During baseball season, he would be on a baseball field. Anytime there was a fire in the neighborhood, he would be there. Danny was a volunteer fireman.

He joined the Franklin Fire Company while in high school and he was an enthusiastic member ever since. He became interested in fire-fighting while watching members of his family respond to fire emergencies. His Uncle Tim was a life-long member and later became the Fire Chief at Franklin Fire Company.

Fire-fighting was in Danny's blood and he loved the adventure and the excitement of responding to an emergency of any kind; he even enjoyed false alarms. But the two major benefits of being a fireman were the camaraderie that he experienced with his fellow firemen, young and older, and the satisfaction of aiding someone who was in danger from a fire or from some other frightful event. The firehouse became a second home for him and he certainly couldn't say that for Kate's house. Sure he was there a lot too and though he knew that Kate's Mom and Dad liked him, he was certain that they were pleased when he said good night to them and to Kate and went home. Yep. The firehouse was a perfect home away from home. Maybe better than home? It was like a private club house, often times it included hot meals, and there was always plenty of laughter and many hands of cut-throat pinochle.

Although he was a junior member in the beginning years and remained a volunteer, he wanted to do things correctly and be the best fireman. He never missed a fire call when he was at home or in the area and he prided himself on being the first to arrive at the firehouse. It wasn't so difficult for him to be first. After all, he was young, ran fast and he lived only a few blocks from the Franklin Fire Company building. Whenever the alarm sounded he ran out the back door and jumped over two neighbors' fences to get to the firehouse even quicker.

One Sunday afternoon the fire alarm went off and Danny ran out the back door. He jumped the two fences and raced a few blocks to the fire station. Once in the fire station, he threw on his fireman's coat and hat and managed to get on the back of the fire truck just as it pulled out of the fire house. He was pleased with himself since he was once again among the first to respond. With the fire siren wailing and the fire truck racing around several corners, Danny was thrilled and anxious to be at the center of the activity. The race to a fire was the most memorable part of being a fireman. The longer the ride, the more fulfilling was the experience. This time the ride was short, and within a few minutes the firetruck stopped. Everyone standing on the truck's side and rear running boards stepped onto the street and headed immediately towards the smoking building. Danny ran from behind the truck and stopped suddenly. He was surprised to see that he was standing in front of a neighbor's house on his own street, and he couldn't hold back an embarrassing smile when he realized that the fire was on his street. When he heard the alarm, he ran out through the back door, jumped the fences and raced all the way to the firehouse so that he could be among the first to arrive at the fire when all he had to do was walk out of his front door to be the very first fireman to arrive. Fortunately for his neighbor, it was a small kitchen fire that issued no flames and mostly smoke and was contained very quickly with little damage to the house. Humorously, it was a fire that he could've put out with a fire hose while standing on his front step, but he arrived too late.

Of course, there were more serious fire calls. Danny would never forget an alarm that took his fire company to the West End of the city. It was a residential home and the fire and smoke was extensive. As a volunteer, Danny assisted the more experienced fire-fighters and this evening he was pulling the hose along the sidewalk to the fire scene when he heard a voice coming from a curtain of black smoke at the rear of the house.

"Over here. Someone give me some help. Over here."
Danny heard the voice clearer as he moved into the smoke and then he saw a fireman carrying a woman out of the back of the house. ""Here. Take her and find a safe place for her. She needs medical attention."
Danny stretched out his arms and the fireman placed the woman onto them. She wasn't a big woman and her eyes were closed and she seemed

unconscious. That combination made her feel even heavier. Danny was not big but he was strong. He found the strength that he needed to carry her away from the smoke and laid her gently on the grass under an oak tree. He waited for a few minutes that seemed so much longer but no one else joined him. Then he left her briefly to summon first aid attention. He quickly returned accompanied by a Franklin colleague who was carrying a medical bag. Danny stood by the woman while the fireman checked the woman's pulse and breathing. Danny was now oblivious to the sights and sounds of the other fire-fighting activities behind him. Although there were no visible injuries or burns to consider, the silent checks for the woman's vital statistics made Danny nervous. He was soon speechless and dazed after the attending fireman spoke to him in a solemn tone.

"She's gone."

'Gone'. It was the single word that echoed in his ears. 'Gone.' He knew that meant she was dead. The woman that he carried away from death's grip was 'here' a minute or so before but now she was 'Gone'. She was no longer here in the land of the living. This was Danny's first introduction to the suddenness and finality of death in human form. He was numbed. Unfortunately, within only a few years the numbness would fade into acceptance when he became a constant witness to the frightening power and randomness that death wields upon the living in the midst of war. More so, he understood that fire-fighting was a serious endeavor, linked to life and death, and that even flameless fires could be fatal. The race to be first to the firehouse became less important. He was unaware that these years with the fire company would prepare him somewhat for a larger challenge ahead.

1937 Ships or Baseball?

Like young people in love, Danny and Kate spent as much time with one another as they could possibly find between each of them working their separate jobs and Danny's year-round sport activities. The evenings were usually full of short walks where they were alone and where they could be serious or mostly just laugh about almost anything. Tonight, though, would be a little different.

Danny had been working at the shipyard for the past two years and it hadn't been easy. The shipyard could be a dangerous place to work in fair weather or foul weather, inside the shops or outside on the dry docks. The steel plates and the welded ship sections were massive and required movement using large fixed and mobile cranes. The various lifting equipment was vital to transferring all of the ship components from the many work stations to a dry dock area where the ship sections were welded together into a massive vessel, that when finished, would travel across the great oceans of earth. The equipment in the shipyard required experienced operators, and above all, safety was of prime importance. Even so, accidents occurred and sometimes they happened more often than other times. When they happened, those were the worst days to be in the yard.

Danny worked alternating shifts in the shipyard because he was required to be available to play on the company's semi-professional sports teams. It was officially an unofficial part of his job. This week the team had four games scheduled. So Danny was working the first shift, 7:00 am to 3:00 pm. It was a bad day to work at the yard.

Bad news always spreads quickly, and earlier this morning bad news ran swiftly through the city that there was a fatal accident at the shipyard. It was the third fatal accident this year, and these fatalities were preceded by a string of bad accidents in the previous year.

Kate heard the news. Shortly after dinner she was waiting by her living room window for Danny to come to her. Depending on the shift that he worked, Kate knew when to expect him to walk up the street because they only lived a few blocks away from each other. She watched him approach now and met him at front door. Taking his hand, she was glad to be able to have him here safe and sound.

"Joe told me about the accident at the yard today. I was so scared and worried."

"I was fine, Kate."

She was so frightened when she first heard there was an accident, even more so when she learned it happened in the same building where Danny was working this week. "Was it near you? Did you know the person who was killed?"

Danny answered solemnly, "I was nearby. The steel plate wasn't hoisted very high. I heard someone shout and I saw the plate slip from the cables carrying it to the welding area." He lowered his voice and spoke slowly. "Then I saw it drop and heard all the noises that followed. It was terrible." Kate wrapped her arms around him. "I'm so sorry, Danny."

He let words rush out from his soul. "I knew the crew. But I didn't know the fella real well. I knew him just enough to say hi, and small talk sometimes. He was young, only a few years older than me. I don't think I'll ever forget it."

Fearful that Danny might not want to hear what she was about to say but more fearful that she might be sorry if she didn't speak up now, Kate added softly. "Danny, you've been in the yard for two years now. That makes five accidents near you. Two people were killed. Maybe you should work somewhere else."

Danny knew the dangers that existed in the shipyard but it wasn't easy to find work that paid thirty-five dollars a week. "I know. I know." Danny said. "My Mom says the same thing. She is so worried that she's even telling me that I should go and try professional baseball after all. Unkie is always pushing her to let me go to a farm-league tryout. I think that he's finally convinced her that I'm ready and that baseball is a lot safer for me."

Kate and Danny had often talked with one another about the next level of baseball. She wanted Danny to have his chance in the game but she knew that he would have to leave his home, and her. She was fearful that he might not come back to her. Nevertheless, she heard herself say. "Unkie is right. You are ready. Do it."

Danny was conflicted. "I don't know, Kate. I can't just quit. I can't go and leave my Dad there. He's worked in the yard for more than twenty years. He shows up every day and night. I can't just quit on him. And I can't leave you here. Plus I need the job and the money if we're going to get married someday."

Kate stood up and walked a few steps further away from him. "I can wait for that as long as you're safe." She turned back to him, and addressed his concern for his Dad. "Your Dad does what he has to do. I'm sure he wants you to have more choices. Talk to him about it."

Danny stood facing Kate, "We already talked. He told me to go for the tryout. He told me to just go down there. He said I can come home if it doesn't work out, that the shipyard job can wait."

Kate was surprised that Danny and his father had talked about following a baseball career. "When did he say this? Why didn't you tell me?"

"It was only yesterday. He told me when we were walking home from work that Unkie spoke to him about letting me leave the yard for a shot at baseball."

""What did your Dad say about that?"

"He told me to go after my dream. That I should give it all I got and that I can come home when I'm ready. He said this is why his Dad left his home in Ireland and came to America. Because here you can be more than ordinary."

Her eyes were beaming. Kate was happy that Danny had finally gotten his Dad's spoken permission to try baseball for a living. Maybe everyone was getting nervous about the shipyard. "Gosh. That's wonderful." She said. "He said all that."
"He did." Was Danny's proud reply.
"Well, then do it."
"It's not that easy, Kate. These are tough times. I feel like I'd be selfish, leaving everybody behind just to do something for myself. I can't do it. I'm lucky to have a job. My family, and us too, we can use the money that I'd be throwing away."

Kate was near to tears. "Danny, I love you. I want us to be together. But your mom and dad and Unkie are right. You told me most people don't like your uncle. He's cranky, rude at times, and he is hard to please. Maybe he drinks too much. But his redeeming quality is that he loves you above anything else. Listen to him, listen to all of them. Listen to your Dad."

"I know, Kate. I want to, but.."

Kate was struggling with her emotions, holding back her tears. "You tell me all the time that Unkie always repeated something to you when you and he were having baseball catches." Taking a breath, she asked him, "Do you remember what he said?"

Then without waiting for a reply, she said. "He told you then and he's telling you now ... "if you want the ball, sometimes you have to go get it. You have to move your feet, you can't wait for it to come to you." Kate took another breath. "It's true now. If you want baseball in your life, go get it."

Danny reached out and pulled Kate into his arms and he kissed her hair. She whispered into his chest. "I will wait here for you to succeed. I know you'll come back to me."

It was a moment that transforms young love into lasting love. Danny lifted her face to his, he softly wiped the tears from her eyes, and kissed her again.

"Kate, you know I will. I love you too much to stay away."

1937 Big League Tryouts

A few winter months passed and on a chilly spring morning, Danny arrived at a ball field in the city's East End with a few of his friends (Turk, Noodles, Johnny). They began to stretch and loosen up while they waited for rides that would take them across-town to begin trying out in front of a group of big league baseball scouts. This tryout was arranged annually by the two local major league clubs that played in near-by Philadelphia: the Philadelphia Phillies of the National League, and the Philadelphia Athletics of the American League.

Here at this gathering spot, no one was hitting baseballs. They were intent on stretching and tossing baseballs back and forth. They brought their bats but they were swinging at the air only. No one was chasing fly balls or fielding hard grounders now. There just wasn't enough time to do any serious baseball drills before heading cross-town to the tryouts. They were excited and anxious.

Noodles, a hard-hitting catcher with a playful and quirky personality, was swinging a bat to loosen his arms and shoulders, and Jimmy Turk, a speedster and former high school quarterback, was sitting on the field stretching his legs and arms. In the infield, Danny and his close friend, Joe, were tossing a baseball back and forth. They were all waiting for their chance to play in the big leagues.

Danny and Mickey, Ordinary Heroes

Noodles was cold and since he never kept anything to himself he said to no one in particular. "Brrr. Hey, guys, can it get any colder in April? "

Danny laughed. "Noodles you ain't cold. You're just shaking because you're nervous."

"Ok. I'm nervous, too." Noodles readily agreed. "But it's still cold." Jimmy Turk and Noodles who were friends since grade school understood one another and neither one held words back from each other. Jimmy let Noodles have it with both barrels. "Noodles, shut your trap. If you had a sandwich in your hands, you wouldn't feel cold. The only time you're not cold is when you're eating, or when its 90 degrees outside, and you just finished eating."

Hearing but ignoring Turk's comment, Joe caught a ball thrown by Danny, then took it out of his glove and tossed it back to Danny when he noticed all of the fellas on the field. "Danny, how many guys do you think will be at tryouts this morning?"

"I don't know, Joe. More than we want to see there. That's for sure."

"How many do you think they'll choose?"

"I suppose as many as they like. Unkie tells me that sometimes they want different things in a player, and sometimes they don't see what they want. So, they don't pick anybody. But he says give 'em everything that you got. Don't hold nothing back."

Turk interrupted them. "Where's Mickey. Isn't he coming with us?"

Noodles answered for Danny. "Yeah. He's coming. Heck, he's probably why the scouts are here today. Mickey V., the hitting machine."

"Yep." Danny answered as he looked around for any sign of Mickey. "He's got to be at the top of their list. So since he's bringing the scouts here today, we gotta shine today."

Danny didn't see Mickey, and not seeing him, he was staring to get concerned. "It's getting late. We're gonna have to leave soon. I hope he gets here soon. This is one ride he doesn't want to miss."

Jimmy saw him first. "Here he comes." He called out to the others. "Man, is he sweating. He must've run all the way from the Hook. Him and his long legs."

Mickey ran across the field just as they were all told to climb into one or the other of the two pickup trucks that were ready to take them to the tryout in the West End of the city. Mickey hopped onto the truck and turned to Danny and to the others in the truck. "Whew! I just made it." Mickey recognized all of the faces in this truckload of tryouts. Then he asked aloud. "Hey, does anyone know if Hank Miller got here?"

Danny looks around quickly. "I didn't see him."

Hank Miller was a colored kid who lived near Chester and Mickey had played against him in a few semi-pro baseball games. Mickey was impressed with Hank's talent. "I saw him yesterday and he didn't know about this tryout. I told him that he ought to join us today. He is a top notch fielder and hitter, and he's a really good pitcher, too."

Danny yelled over to Legion coaches who were seated in the front of one of the other truck and asked the front seat passenger. "Mr. Carter, is Hank Miller in the other truck?"

"No, Danny. He's not here, and he ain't coming." Mr. Carter then turned to the driver. "Let's go."

Mickey was puzzled and he called over to the coach. "What do you mean? He ain't coming."

"Look, Mickey. Colored players have their own league and their own tryouts for colored players only. You ought to know that by now. He ain't coming with us today, or any day, ever."

Mickey was not pleased with the coach's reply. "Can you just wait a few more minutes? Just in case he does come."

"No." Mr. Carter's responded. "We got to go now. Hank and all the colored boys will play in their own league, in front of their own fans, against very good players with big league talent. He'll play plenty of baseball."

Mickey was still incredulous. "In their own league? It doesn't make much sense to me. It's just baseball."

Mr. Carter wanted to put an end to the discussion so he gave the last reason that is usually offered when something doesn't seem correct and can't be easily defended. "It's no big deal, Mickey. That's just how it is. Now sit back. Let's go. We don't want to be late. Today is everybody's big chance."

Danny and Mickey sat back in the truck, exchanged glances and turned to look back across the empty field as the two pickup trucks pulled away from the curb and headed toward the city's West End. Some of their own excitement was lessened as they realized that 'everybody' didn't include Hank Miller. How could it? It sure didn't seem like Hank was going to get his big chance today."
They arrived quickly at the tryout location. There were nearly a hundred ballplayers standing all along the edges of the ball field. Standing on the infield with the baseball scouts were several local newspaper reporters. Family members, friends and local fans were also sitting and standing around the perimeter of the field. When everyone was positioned, a short

man in a dark suit motioned to the players to move to the center of the ball field. All these young men had waited for this moment and none were more nervous than Danny and Mickey. After all, baseball was the king of sports in America, it was the Great American Pastime. Tryout camps like this one were held all over America. In 1937, they were at the beginning of the road where a professional baseball career began.

These tryout camps always ended a little sooner than every player wanted them to end because there was always something left that a player wanted to show the scouts, maybe another time at bat, or a chance to throw several more pitches, or run like a rabbit around the bases one last time. At the end of this long day, Danny and Mickey had the best tryout performance of the Chester-area boys. Both of them were eventually offered contracts with separate minor league teams. Mickey's hitting impressed all of the scouts and he was signed to an American League farm team on the Eastern Shore area of Maryland and received a signing bonus. Danny's hitting was average and his smaller size put him at a disadvantage to baseball scouts looking for the power hitters that they eagerly sought in the new golden era of the homerun hitters like Ruth, Gehrig, Wilson, and Foxx. Fortunately, Danny had exceptional infield skills and he was swift on the base paths. His above-average hitting percentage combined with these skills earned him an offer from a National League farm team also on the Eastern Shore, but he was not offered a bonus. Young Johnny Podgajny also impressed the scouts with his pitching but he was still in high school. He would be signed the following year by the Philadelphia Phillies.

Their amateur baseball games were all finished. Danny and Mickey started their professional careers in the same farm league on the Eastern Shore in Maryland and competed against each other. They were happy to be accepted into the world of professional baseball. Their newest playing fields were not much bigger or better than their sandlots fields at home but they knew the bigger prize was ahead of them.

Danny and Mickey, Ordinary Heroes

1937 Rookie League

The first season in the low minor leagues passed quickly for both young players. The excitement of being chosen as future players in the major leagues produced mixed feelings. One was the relief that came from having a team acknowledge their ability and the second was the anxiety of realizing that the game would become more competitive than ever. This was just the beginning and everyone around them belonged here. A more immediate and noticeable change for them was their drop in income. They were now making less than they did at their jobs in the shipyard and refinery. For example, Danny's wages fell from an average of $140 each month in the shipyard to just $60 a month for baseball. It was clear right away that playing baseball for a living wasn't going to make them rich.

It wasn't surprising that Mickey advanced swiftly through the Washington Senators' farm system. He was a classic left-handed batter who hit line drives with power and regularly batted above the high-performance batting average mark of .300 (three hits in every ten at bats). This was one of several statistics that baseball executives and Managers used to separate can't-miss players from their teammates who had to bring other skills with them to supplement their lower hitting averages. Mickey was identified early as being among these cut-above-the-rest ball players, a potential star.

Danny progressed at a slower pace. His below-average size and his lack of power were initially the negative physical features that stood out to most Managers, coaches and scouts. The exceptions were those few scouts who had a keen eye for the fielding skills and the speed that Danny possessed and packaged with his acceptable batting average, between .250 and .280. There was something else a keener eye saw in Danny. He was a feisty ball player who had a passion for the game and displayed leadership qualities. He accented this persona with an exceptionally contagious and dry, funny sense of humor. This was always a welcome antidote to the repetitive, sometimes, drudging life of a professional ball player.

Naturally, some games were more memorable than others either because an unforgettable happening occurred in the game, or because the games pitted the two friends as adversaries. Danny and Mickey played very few games against each other but one such game was played a few months into the first long season.

Danny's Class D Cambridge team hosted a hometown game in the middle of July. His team of rookie players was trailing early in the game with two outs in the fourth inning. Danny was the batter and as he walked to home plate, his Manager shouted instructions to him.

"All right, kid. Just wait for a good pitch then put the bat on the ball. That'll get the runner to third. Don't forget to run like hell to first. Got it?"

"Yeh, coach. I got it." was Danny's reply.

After taking two balls and fouling off one pitch and missing another, Danny set himself in the batter's box and waited for a good pitch that he could hit. The Manager leaned over the dugout railing and called out. "That's it, kid. Make sure it's a good one."

As Danny prepared for the pitcher's delivery, the catcher squatting behind him needled him with a few words of distraction. "OK, pal. This one is headed right at you."
At that moment, the pitcher completed his stretch and threw the ball towards Danny. The ball came over the plate but Danny knew it was low and beneath his knees. He clutched his bat tightly. Then pulled it back. **Whoompf!** The ball hit the catcher mitt.

"Strike three! The umpire yelled. "You're out!"

Danny turned in amazement and looked at the umpire. "What? It was low." The umpire disagreed with Danny. "Strike three, son."

With the decision final, Danny tossed his bat into the air in frustration and looked disdainfully at the umpire. His Irish face was angry and his hands hung tightly at his side in balled-up fists. At the same time while Danny stewed, the umpire looked up at the bat and saw the bat rise to its highest point in the air. "Son" he said. "You owe me ten dollars when that bat hits the ground."

"Ten dollars!" exclaimed Danny?

"Yep, Ten dollars." The umpire bellowed. That's so you don't do it again."

Danny with frantic urgency looked up and located the bat on its downward path to the ground. He quickly lunged for the bat and was just able to grab the top of the bat before it hit the ground. For his mighty effort, he landed in the dirt, on his back, with the bat on his chest.

The umpire wore a wry smile on his face. "Nice work, son. That's the best play I've seen all day. You saved yourself ten bucks. But you're still out. And don't throw the bat again."

Danny got off the ground, dusted himself off, and as he walked away from home plate, he muttered under his breath to no one in particular. "Holy crap. That was close. Ten bucks is a lot of money, especially on sixty dollars a month. No wonder the ump is always right."

1937 - Fan Interference

On another occasion, Mickey's team again visited Danny's Cambridge club in an Eastern Shore League game. The game advanced into the fifth inning and Danny as usual was playing second base when he booted a hard-hit infield grounder. It was his second error in the game, a rare occurrence for him. A fan in the stands behind first base didn't like it and screamed out towards Danny on the field. "Hey, shorty. You're a bum. If you wanna get in a big league game, you should have to buy a ticket." There was a silent pause, and the fan added to the insult. "And throw your glove away. It ain't helping ya. Try a bucket instead." Then the fan laughed loud and long.

The first baseman for Danny's team looked into the stands, then said to Danny. "That guy's a shit-head, Danny. Don't pay him no mind." Danny heard the fan alright, and he didn't like it. "Well, he's been riding me for four innings now. It's getting stale."

The inning ended with no runs scored but as the Cambridge team came off the field, the same fan continued to yell at Danny. Danny had enough of it so he looked up into the stands and motioned for the loudmouth to come down onto the field. The fan just sat there eating a hotdog and ignored Danny as Danny went into the dugout. Danny wanted to slam his glove down on the bench but before he could, his Manager walked over and gave Danny piece of sage advice as old as the game itself. "Don't let that guy get under your skin. It's part of the game. Keep calm."

That was sound advice and he nodded his head affirmatively to the Manager. Out on the field and standing at first base, Mickey was able to get Danny's attention and signaled to his friend that he should relax. Danny nodded to Mickey and sat on the bench, placing his glove right beside him.

The game moved on to the bottom of the last inning with Cambridge still trailing 3-2 when Danny's Manager who was positioned in the coach's box next to the third base bag sent a runner from second base to home to try to score the tying run, but the runner was thrown out. It was the final out of the game and Cambridge lost the ball game. Just as the umpire signaled that the game was over, a now familiar voice rang out from the stands. "Hey, bird-brain! There was no chance to score there. You deserve to lose. Why don't ya get on a bus and go help some other team lose. And take that blind second baseman with you. You bum!"

Danny's Manager looked up and recognized that it was the same guy that badgered Danny. He turned and yelled back to the noisy fan. "OK, loudmouth. Why don't you come down here and send me back?" The Manager stood there for a few seconds looking menacingly at the fan. He was sure that if this guy didn't come down for Danny who was shorter and lighter than himself, he's not likely to come down at all. It seemed like a safe move. But, he was wrong.

The loudmouth fan rose from his seat and he kept rising. He was big, like houses and trucks are big. "I'll send you, alright." The fan said. Then he jumped down from the stands and stepped onto the field. The Manager looked at this bulky, muscle-bound, farm-boy, thought quickly, and yelled to Danny. "Danny, I got him down here for you. Now you handle him."

Danny was in the dugout and he hadn't seen the size of the fella. He came out of the dugout and onto the field, and in one lightning second the loudmouth fan clobbered him. It was Danny's last ever on-field conversation with a fan. He never got a word in and his team lost.

CHAPTER FIVE
CROSSROADS

1940 Day Shift

For nearly a century, professional baseball players had little if any voice in their baseball careers after they signed their first contract. The teams controlled all future baseball-related matters. What level of baseball they played, when and if they were promoted to the big leagues, what city they were traded to, even what position they played on the baseball diamond were all determined solely by the owner of the team. Most importantly, the team owners negotiated salary directly with the players. This negotiation was usually lopsided since it often resulted in the owner dictating what the player would accept for each season, less or more, and it was often less. The owners were businessmen and the ballplayers were employees.

Because the salary was minimal and only paid during the baseball season, it was common practice for players to return home after the season and find other work during the late fall and early winter months. So Danny and Mickey went back to their previous jobs. Danny was back in the shipyard and Mickey returned to walking the pipelines at the local refinery. They both worked at these jobs until spring training began each February.

In 1937 and 1938, Mickey's progress in the minors continued at a fast pace. In 1939 at 21 years old he was promoted to the majors. He joined the Washington Senators and appeared in his first game in the majors as a pinch runner in Griffith Stadium in Washington, DC. Only a day or so later, he started his first game for the Senators in the 'Taj Mahal' of all baseball ballparks, Yankee Stadium. It was even more memorable for Mickey because his first game in 'the house that Ruth built' took place only four days after Lou Gehrig delivered his emotional "luckiest man alive" speech.

The following year, 1940, another Chester High graduate, Johnny Podgajny, was called up to the Phillies. They needed pitching and Johnny was expected to see a lot of work. Among the hometown trio, only Danny was still waiting for his call to the majors. He played well in the minors for the past three years using his grit, speed, and infield skills. He appeared at second-base, shortstop and even third base for several minor league teams and played at increasing levels of competition. Unfortunately he lacked that most desirable skill that baseball Managers hungered for in this 'golden age of baseball'. He didn't hit homeruns. He lacked over-the-fence power. Danny didn't consider this a weakness, it just wasn't a strength. Everyone in baseball who was familiar with Danny's baseball skills knew it. His Uncle Tim knew it. Only Danny's Mom thought that it wasn't important. After all, everyone can't be a Babe Ruth.

The 1940 season was over. It was mid-week and Danny was back working the day shift at the shipyard. Unkie as usual took some time from his city job and stopped by his sister's house to find out if tonight's dinner would be to his liking. He wasn't particular in his taste for food so he was most likely to stay for dinner whenever he came to the house near the dinner hour. Nellie's home was his home away from home.

Nellie and Unkie were standing in the kitchen. Nellie was preparing the meal and Unkie was watching her work and was determined to stay out of her way. "Nellie, is our boy coming straight home from the shipyard?"

Moving a pan onto the stove, Nellie talked over her shoulder without turning away from the pan. "Yes, he is. Then, like every night, I suppose he'll go over to Kate's house after dinner."

Smiling behind her back, and noting to himself that her tone portrayed some annoyance with Danny's routine, Unkie changed the subject and made the same announcement to her for the millionth time as though he just thought of it for the first time. "Nellie, you know that our boy is going to move up this year. I know it. He's held back because he don't hit homeruns. But he can help so many teams in the majors play better. A lot of teams need Danny's speed, fielding and clutch hitting in the big leagues."

She usually answered him differently depending on her mood and the amount of available energy she had. Tonight, she was tired and she didn't have much left for engaging in a lengthy and spirited discussion. So she simply asked. "If that's so, why isn't he there yet?"

"Tis his size, like always." Unkie said. "It's always been his size. Yet, he always produces better overall numbers than the big, slow ones."

Just before Nellie could respond to her brother and repeat the same question that she just asked him, Danny's youngest sister, Peg, entered the kitchen with a bounce in her step. As always Peg's greeting was bright and cheerful and accompanied by a question and a request. "Hi, Mom, is Danny home yet? Can my new girlfriends meet him?" Unkie waited for Nellie to respond to Peg.

"No, Peg, he's not home.' Nellie answered. You know that he doesn't come home from the shipyard until four o' clock. And he might be a little later today because I asked him to bring Dad home with him." She looked over at Unkie, then back to Peg. "Your Dad hasn't been feeling well lately. So Danny will wait for him. Anyway, you know Danny doesn't like a fuss over himself."

"It's not a fuss, mom. He said I could bring my friends, this once."

Unkie began laughing and said. "Well, Margaret, my sweetie, will your girlfriends settle for us? I'm Danny's famous Unkie and this is Danny's darling mom?"

Peg crossed her arms and looked sweetly at Unkie. "Unkie, you're only famous to us. And Mom is just.. Mom. Now if you can bring us Mickey Vernon, then you're talking."

Interrupting their playful conversation, Nellie put an end to it. "Off with you now Peg. It also happens to be that Mickey is also at work right now down at the refinery. So, tell your friends to settle for your Unkie, or no one today." Clearly, if Nellie wasn't in the mood to dally with Unkie, she certainly wasn't going to listen to her youngest daughter's whining.

Frustrated, but sensing a child's sensitivity of danger signals from her parent, she turned to leave the kitchen. "OK, I'll go now. But we will all be back at four."

As she closed the door behind her, she heard her mom's final words that won the battle. "Make certain that you come back alone. I won't be feeding dinner to you and to your girlfriends."
Changing subjects but riding along the same train of thought, Unkie continued to make light conversation. "Nellie, that Vernon boy is going to be a star, you know. He even looks like a blossoming matinee idol."

Nellie moved plates from the kitchen counter to the table. "I'm glad for Mickey, and I wish the same for Danny, for all of them boys. I don't want them at the shipyards or in the refineries. It's dangerous." Nellie stopped setting the table and looked solemnly at her brother who had always been her dearest friend in her life. "Unkie, I surely don't want them in the army. I just want them safe. If I had my way, they'd always be home just like my four girls." She walked over to the sink, placed her arms on the edge of the counter, and stared out of the window. She recalled a foggy image in the past. "Remember when the Great War took all of our young men away. It was for only a year and it wasn't good. Some never came back."

"I remember." He replied dolefully. "God knows I remember. I pray that no ill wind blows this second German war towards us. I hope we just send ships and oil overseas. Nothing more". He paused, then brought them both back into the present. "What's for dinner, Nellie? I'm as hungry as I've ever been."

1941 "I'm Gonna Miss Him"

Mickey completed his first full year in the majors and celebrated by asking his high school sweetheart Lib to marry him. So on March 14, 1941 just before the 1941 season, James Michael Vernon and Elizabeth Firth of Leiperville were married in St. Luke's Episcopal Church in Eddystone. They decided that they would live with Lib's parents. They were both comfortable with the arrangement since Mickey would be travelling for eight months of the year.

This same year, Danny was a leading player for the Houston Buffalos, a St. Louis Cardinal farm-club affiliate. It was rumored that St. Louis' General Manager Branch Rickey wanted to move Danny into the Cardinals major league infield for the new season. But during spring training, Danny's year took a sadder turn than he would ever had imagined.

Danny Sr.'s earlier illness did not pass and grew more serious as 1940 ended. He died suddenly in mid-March, 1941. Danny left spring training to join his family in making preparations for his dad's funeral and to take his new position as the surviving male of the family and assume responsibility for the entire family. He was not the oldest child but he was the only son. He arrived home with most of the funeral arrangements already completed. The burial service would be conducted in the Chester Rural Cemetery.

The Chester Rural cemetery was so-named because it was located on the very northwestern edge of the city, a rural and less densely area away from the busy market center of town where most commercial businesses, retail shops, and factories were located. Like most cities, Chester's population growth and its newer housing would eventually circle the center of the town. The cemetery was outside this circle.

The procession to the cemetery was preceded by a funeral mass attended by family and friends at St. Robert's Catholic Church. The solemn mass celebrated his father's life and his resurrection into God's hands. On this cool spring morning, a group consisting mainly of family gathered inside the cemetery around a freshly dug opening in the ground and next to the opening lay the resultant mound of fresh dirt. They watched as the parish priest, holding a single prayer book with a black leather cover, followed the pall-bearers who carried the casket and walked slowly and carefully up to the grave site. Once the casket was securely placed on slings stretched across the open grave, all movement and sound ceased. Only the sound of mourning, muffled sobs and tears being held back were heard. The priest recited a litany of prayers with accompaniment from the attendees. A stilled, solemn silence signaled the end of prayers until the silence was softly broken by the priest's final dedication of the corporal body into the earth below and Danny Sr.'s spirit was sent skyward to heaven above. "Dear God," he intoned. "We commend Daniel, loving husband, father, brother, and our friend to your care. We are comforted in knowing that he will receive a heavenly body and that his spirit now has eternal life in heaven. Amen." In unison and in earnest, everyone replied. "Amen."

At that moment, Unkie stepped to the right of the priest and announced to everyone that they were all invited to share a noon meal with the Murtaugh family at the family's house. He ended his brief remarks with his head uplifted. "Nellie and the children thank you for joining them today to bid goodbye to Daniel."

The mourners began to depart, some going to their cars, most walking varied distances to their homes. Danny and Kate decided to take the long walk to the Murtaugh house. Danny wanted some rare time alone with Kate. Just as Danny and Kate began to leave the gravesite, Unkie walked up and embraced Danny, lingering for a moment. Then he asked his nephew. "Danny, we'll see you at home for lunch? OK?"

"Yes. Tell Mom and the girls that Kate and I are going to walk home, for the fresh air."

Unkie left them. Danny and Kate walked a little further along the edge of the cemetery grass before exiting the main gate and crossing the street to the sidewalk on the opposite side. Walking hand-in-hand, Kate spoke first. "Your dad was a fine man. He loved you and your sisters dearly."

Danny was barely audible in his reply. "I know he did. It just wasn't something that you'd hear him say too often. That was his way."

Kate wanted to sooth him by sharing her fond remembrance of his father. "He was a quiet man. Your Dad never wasted words when they weren't needed. He was proud of you and he loved you. He loved all of you."

This made Danny smile. "He really liked you, Kate."

She put her hand on his shoulder. "I think that was because he knew how much I loved his son. That's why he liked me."

"Maybe so. But he also saw what I saw. How special you are." Taking a deep breath, and trying to keep his words from breaking apart, he managed to say. "I'm going to miss him."

"He worked hard." Kate added. "He knew his responsibilities."

Danny's voice began to gain strength and he said almost cheerfully. "Did you know that he didn't care for baseball? He liked soccer. A game he and his father played. They called it football. He wanted me to play soccer, and so I did play it in school. But he understood how I felt about baseball." He took a breath. "When I was leaving for Maryland, he told me to hold nothing back, don't quit, don't make it easy for them to send me home. He said, always show up, especially when the odds are the toughest. His told me that his life, his family, the shipyard, weekly paychecks: these are good things. But if a fella wanted something specific, you had to get off your ass and go after it. He said it only once but once was enough. It was one of the very few times that I ever heard him curse. Maybe that's why I've never forgotten it."

"Danny, I'm sure that a single curse or even a thousand curses won't keep your Dad out of heaven."

Danny raised his head and looked at the clear sky above. "Heaven? Yeah, he'd like that." Then he laughed. "I just wonder if he'd know anyone there."

Kate was pleased that this walk and conversation was helping Danny to recover a little from the heavy sadness he felt. The salve of humor could often be applied to soothe a wound or dampen anger so that the path ahead was less difficult for the next day's tasks. This was always so with Danny and his family, as it was with many Irish families. A careful, measured dose of humor, even scarcely enough to lighten dark days, can cure so many ills.

1941 Houston Calling

Danny returned to Houston for his second year in the very competitive Texas League. He continued to play well for the Houston Buffalos and he was batting .316 in mid-season. Amazingly, he had already stolen home six times before June 30 and his hitting, defense, speed, and even his whistle, made him a player for big league scouts to notice. He was hopeful Branch Rickey would soon move him up to join the pennant-contending Cardinals. But he still hadn't gotten the call that he had worked so long and hard to receive.

On a weekday morning at the end of June, he was in his hotel room in Houston when his phone rang. Stretching for the phone, he reached across the narrow bed and nearly knocked the lamp off of the night table. "Hello. Yeh, this is Danny. Fine, coach. How are you? Nothing much. Just sitting around. Waiting to go the ballpark."
Eddie Dyer was the Buffalos Manager and he had been in baseball for his entire life as a player, a coach, and a Manager. This baseball lifer was very fond of his feisty second baseman. He and Danny got along fine. But this

morning Danny could hear a serious, business-like tone in Eddie's voice, sort of like a man who was going to tell you that your loan didn't go through or that you were a dollar short on your mortgage payment. "Did Mr. Ankenman or Dutch call you this morning?"

Mr. Ankenman owned the Houston team. He was a hearty baseball fan, and wanted, really wanted, his teams to win. He was pleased however when a player was promoted to the major leagues as a promoted player meant extra dollars to the farm league owners. However, he preferred to send the best players to the big leagues after his own club's season had ended. Making money was fine but he wouldn't mind holding a good player down on the farm long enough to win his own league.

"No. No one called. Why?" Danny sat up on the edge of his bed. It wasn't easy to tell if Eddie was glad to hear that no calls were received but he proceeded to give Danny instructions on what to do when this 'call' reached him.

"Oh, OK, good. Well, look, when they do call, play dumb, like my call to you never happened. Like you and I haven't spoken to one another today. OK?"
"Yeah. Sure." Danny was more interested now. "Haven't spoken about what? What's up?"

Now Eddie's voice filled with excitement as he remembered how he felt when he first received similar news a long time ago. "I have some great news for you. You are going to the Big Show, the big leagues. The Phillies just bought your contract from the Cardinals. You are being sent up to the big time. The Phillies are in Cincinnati today and tomorrow. So pack your bags."

Eddie stopped speaking for a few seconds to allow the news to settle in Danny's head. "Mr. Ankenman called me an hour ago for your phone number so I figured I'd wait a bit and call you after he gave you the great news." Eddie took another much-needed breath of air and proceeded.

"I'm sorry that I got to you before he did. But he'll call today." He waited for some words from Danny, then added. "Congratulations, kid."

Danny remained silent. After the longest minute, and recovering from being physically shaken, he finally responded to his Manager in a nervous voice. "You're not kidding me, are you, coach? The big leagues, the Phillies. Holy cow! That's my hometown."

"Nope. I'm not kidding you. It's legit. I wouldn't kid anyone, and especially not you, not about the big leagues. You earned it. I'm getting off the phone now, so keep the line open for Mr. Ankenman. You can celebrate tomorrow. Right now, you gotta get to Cincy and put on a big league uniform. Call Dutch for information and travel tickets. I'll talk to you tomorrow. So long, major leaguer."

"Wow! Thanks, coach." Danny was between laughter and tears.

Danny was still holding the phone to his ear and he didn't want to let go of it. He grinned wildly. He put the phone on its cradle, then he stood up and let out a loud whistle. He took a big breath and began to laugh. Then he picked up the phone and dialed Kate's phone number. It seemed to him that the phone rang for an excessive amount of time until he heard the voice he was hoping to hear. "Hi, Sweetie. Are you sitting down?" He paused. "Guess what? You're talking to a major leaguer." There was happy screaming immediately on the other side of the phone with a few seemingly incoherent words mixed in with the explosion of joy. "Yep. I'm going to the big leagues. To the hometown Phillies."

"Oh, Danny, that is wonderful. It's just what you always dreamed about."

"It's my dream for both of us."

"Does this mean that I'll see you soon?"

"Not this week but soon. The Phillies are in Ohio now. So I'll go there today. But we'll be together a lot more now that I'm with the Phillies. Philadelphia is a lot closer than Texas."

Feeling dazed and giddy at the thought that she would see him soon, Kate exclaimed. "I can't wait to see you. Can I tell anyone?"

"Not yet. I didn't get the official call from the team owner. The Skipper told me." He explained. "I have to leave the line open. Then after I get his call, I'll call my Mom and tell her to tell the girls and Unkie. Did you know it's also Mom's birthday today." He laughed a little as he thought to himself that he already planned to call his Mom in a few hours to wish her 'Happy Birthday'.

"Anyway, I'll call you back. After that, you can tell the whole world. I'll call you back soon. I love you."

"I love you, too." She started to cry. "Now, I'm crying like a baby."

Danny wanted to celebrate longer with Kate but he wanted that phone call from Mr. Ankenman even more. He managed a last sentence. "I'm pretty close to crying too. Bye, Kate."
They hung up their Bell telephones at the same time placing the receivers down on the cradle.

Danny soon received his call from Mr. Ankenman and it was quickly followed by a 'dream-come-true-call' from the Phillies. Catching his breath and pinching himself to be certain that he was fully awake and not dreaming, he called his Mom, and spoke to his sisters, and of course, to Unkie. The last call exhausted him with joy. But he had one last conversation to share. He picked up the phone and dialed long distance again. Danny just wanted to hear her voice at this moment.

Sounding as if she was restraining herself from both laughing and crying, Kate answered the phone. ""Hello, Danny?"

With his eyes closed, Danny spoke warmly into the phone, envisioning Kate as though she was right in front of him.
"Kate, it's official. I got my calls from Mr. Ankenman and the Phillies. It feels great!"

"That's wonderful."

"But you know I forgot to ask you something?"

"What?"

Now, having waited for this moment to come, Danny asked in his sincerest and most serious manner. "Kate, will you marry me?" Then he held his breath and closed his eyes.

Too excited and nervous to wait for Kate's reply, Danny began talking hurriedly. "Kate, I'll get a raise now. I can buy you a ring and I can support the two of us." He paused. "We agreed that we would marry when the time was right. Well, here it is, right in front of us. I didn't want to do this when we were 1600 miles apart, but I can't wait another day." He asked again. "Will you marry me?"

Almost shouting into the phone, Kate interrupted him. "Danny, stop talking. Let me answer you."

He stopped talking. There was silence on either side of the phone line until Kate said in a soft, clear whisper. "Yes, of course I will marry you. I've said yes to you a thousand times already in my dreams. Even across a million miles, the answer would be the same. Yes! Yes! Yes! I'll marry you."

Kate waited for what seemed to be world's longest second as Danny was unable to form any words. Then Kate asked a most reasonable question. "When can we get married?"

"After the season ends." Was Danny's quick reply. "You make the plans."

"Can I tell anyone?"

"You can tell everyone. I already told my Mom and the girls that we're getting married."

"You did? But you hadn't ask me yet?"

"I know. I took a chance. And now I know I'm the luckiest guy in the world."

Their conversation continued with soft murmurings, and laughter, as they spoke about their plans for their future together. They were both so excited and talked so long that that they nearly forgot Danny had to be in Cincinnati that same evening.

They said their goodbyes reluctantly but with the certain optimism of young lovers who knew their lives were changing forever.

1941, Shibe Park

The last time Danny was in Shibe Park, the Philadelphia Phillies' home ballfield, he paid to get into the game and didn't get any closer to the field than the wooden bleachers over-looking leftfield. He and his buddies had to take a small journey to get to the park, a journey that included a bus ride from 6th and Welsh Streets in Chester to the trolley station on Chester Pike in Sharon Hill, then a trolley ride to Upper Darby where they transferred to the elevated train (El) into Philadelphia's 30th Street Station and finally a passenger train ride to the ballpark at 21st and Lehigh Ave in North Philadelphia. Whew! It was nearly a cross-country trek in 1941.

This time it was different. He was sitting in the Phillies' locker room getting dressed to play in his first big league game for his hometown team. He couldn't wait until this day arrived and now he couldn't stop being nervous. He was living his dream but now he was on the other side of his dream. Now he was on the side where he had to perform just the way that he always dreamed that he would perform: getting hits, scoring runs for his team, and making plays that would get players on the other team out. Fortunately, he really knew that he didn't have to do it all by himself. His teammates would help. A bonus for Danny was that this occasion would also be a small reunion with his high school and American Legion buddy, Johnny Podgajny. Although Danny was older, this was Johnny P.'s second year on the Phillies' pitching staff so he was sure that his fellow Chester High School graduate would keep him calm tonight.

A few minutes later, Johnny entered the locker room and saw Danny sitting alone on the bench putting on his new team uniform. He walked over to Danny's locker and he picked up Danny's small, weathered, baseball glove.

"Danny, you can't use this glove. It's got a hole in it. I saw it the other day in practice."

Danny reached out and took his battle-scarred glove from Johnny. "Johnny. It's just a small lucky hole. That's all it is. It's part of my game. It's what got me here."

'Small. My ass." Johnny groaned. "A golf ball could fall through that hole."

"Maybe? But not a baseball". Danny smartly replied. "I'd never let a baseball get away."

Johnny was adamant. "You're in the Bigs now. And that glove won't keep you here." Then he lifted his equipment bag from his shoulder and placed the bag on the bench next to Danny. Reaching into the bag, Johnny pulled out a baseball glove. "Here ya go, buddy. I got you a new fielding glove. It's my welcome gift to you. Go teach it to catch."

He extended the shiny new infielder's mitt towards Danny and added. "Besides, all your family and friends are here tonight and you wanna look like a big leaguer. This way you might even catch a few baseballs if you don't pass out from excitement first."

Taken by surprise and overcome by his friend's kindness, Danny accepted the new glove and put it on his left hand, pounding his right fist into the center pocket of the glove. He was barely able to talk. "Wow. That's swell, Johnny. Thanks. I'm sure that it will suit me and the Phillies." Trying to regain his composure, Danny humorously adds the only positive thought that came into his mind. "Now if I miss anything, I have an excuse. It's the glove. And it's your fault."

Johnny's responded with his own Chester neighborhood savvy. "No you don't. No excuses. Not if I'm pitching."

1941 "We Need Runs."

Danny did not start the game and as the game advanced into the bottom of the seventh inning, the Phillies trailed 4-1 and sent their first batter of the inning to home plate. Hans Lobart, the Phillies Manager, stood on one of the dugout steps. He shouted over to Danny sitting at the opposite end of the bench. "Murtaugh, you're pinch running for the first man we get on base. Be smart. Use your speed. That's what got you here. We need runs."

The Phillies batter soon drilled a line drive hit into right field. Time was called and Danny immediately replaced his teammate as a pinch runner at first base. Standing on the first base bag, he could hear his family and friends cheering his name. His private thoughts were screaming inside his head. 'Danny's in the Big Leagues. I'm here!'

The first base coach congratulated him and instructed him at the same time. "OK, kid. Welcome to the big leagues. Now, look for the signs."

Danny's mind was racing and he focused on the pitcher's motion and delivery. But he was also thinking to himself, 'OK, Danny, just shake the nerves. This is a piece of cake. You watched this catcher and pitcher for four innings. You can run on them. It's a perfect beginning for you. Speed is your best tool. Everything is in your favor.'

The pitcher knew that Danny was inserted into the lineup to steal second base so he watched Danny closely. He threw over to first base a few times to keep him close to the first base bag. Because of these throws to first base, Danny had to stay close to the bag and that meant he would have a late start and a small lead. All this activity by the pitcher made Danny's chance to steal second base more difficult. The pitcher looked over at Danny again and he tossed the ball one more time to first base. Now the hometown fans started booing the pitcher. The next pitch was thrown swiftly to home plate. Danny, who was leaning towards second, faked to run, then headed back to first. The pitcher threw to home plate. It was ball one at the plate.

A teammate's voice from the dugout offered encouragement to Danny. "OK, Danny. Ball one." Now, getting accustomed to the crowd noise and having settled his nerves a bit, he began thinking and prepared himself for action. 'It's simple. Left foot first, right foot next, move, keep the head down, slide feet first into the bag.' He tensed. He was ready.

The pitcher threw two more times over to first base and Danny dove back safely into the bag both times. He rose from the dirt, brushed himself off, and took a few cautious steps off the bag and leaned toward second base again. The next pitch was rocketed to home plate. Danny moved toward second base as the pitch headed to the batter. He was already on his way to stealing his first base in the big leagues and he heard someone from the dugout yell. "Go! Go! Go!"

All Danny's energy and concentration was targeted on reaching second base before the catcher could catch the ball and deliver it to second base before Danny arrived there. Then the fickle hand of fate intervened and although Danny's left foot correctly stepped over his right leg, his right foot unexpectedly tripped over his left foot. Down he went in a tumbled heap. Fortunately, he had gotten only a few feet off first base, and not so far away from the bag that he couldn't get back to first before the catcher's throw, but he was too jumbled up in feet and legs, and too stunned, to get back quickly. The batter swung and missed the ball and the catcher's rifle-like throw went to first base and not second base. It was right on target. Danny was lying in the infield dirt trying desperately to crawl back to first base when the first baseman caught the ball and tagged him out.

"Out!" He heard this one word loud and clear above all the crowd noises. The umpire's decision was painfully easy.

Lying on the ground, he heard the Cincinnati first baseman say. "Welcome to the big leagues, kid. Too bad you got your pretty, new uniform dirty for nothing."

So, Danny was in the big leagues. He opened his career in his hometown and he was living a dream come true. Sure, he was lying in the infield dirt, embarrassed; but his spirit was in the clouds. Not even this inglorious start could diminish his joy. He was happy that this happened in the fourth inning of a meaningless game with no outs rather than in the last inning of a World Series game trailing by one run with two outs. 'Thank you God.'

1941 Wedding Bells

Danny's first major league season did get better. He hit and fielded well and he led the National League with 18 stolen bases even though he played in only 85 games. Most importantly, he signed a contract with the Phillies for the following 1942 season.

As planned, six weeks after the season and a few days after Thanksgiving, he and Kate were married in St. Robert's Roman Catholic

Church in Chester. This large, dark gray stone church still stands handsomely on the corner of Twentieth and Providence Avenue. The church building itself sits back from the roadway and rests on an elevated piece of ground that rises several feet above street level. It is located in the most prosperous part of the city and provided a beautiful setting for Danny and Kate's traditional Irish-Catholic wedding ceremony. Kate was a beautiful bride and Danny looked youthful and handsome. Danny was quiet throughout the formal service and almost speechless except for his very audible and absolutely necessary repetitive responses of 'I do.' The couple exchanged marriage vows, received the holy sacraments of the Eucharist and Holy Matrimony, and at the conclusion of the wedding Mass they received departing guests as everyone exited the church.

Danny and Kate stood at the beginning of the reception line just inside the front door of the church. Danny's mother, Nellie, and his Uncle Tim were next, followed by Lib's parents, Clarence and Catherine. Before the first guest reached the receiving line, Danny turned to his mom and said in a soft voice. "Mom, I wish Dad was here." Nellie put her arms around her son and said, "I do too, Danny." Then she put her head on his shoulder and added warmly, "I know that he's seeing all of it."

The introductions and good wishes from guests in line continued for ten minutes or so before Mickey and Lib appeared in front of the wedding day couple. Mickey grasped Danny's hand and kissed Kate at the same time. Danny looked relieved to see them here. He hadn't seen either of them inside or outside the church before the Mass began. He thought that they may have lost their way there.
"Thank you, Mickey. Thank you Lib. I hope you're coming back to the house to celebrate with us." Danny hugged Lib. He smiled at both of them. "You kids are still honeymooners yourself."

Looking now at Kate, Mickey smiled and said. "It's a great day, Kate. Now we have the best company in the marriage club. We'll see you back at the house." Lib, beaming at them, offered a final word. "We are so happy for you."

The line of guests dwindled down to zero. Danny and Kate kissed, hugged, exchanged handshakes and pleasantries with all of the guests. The priest and the altar boys received traditional gratuities from the groom's Best Man. It was time for the wedding couple to take a brief but noisy horn-blasting, tin-can rattling, ride from the church to Nellie's house.

As the new bride and groom prepared to enter the car, Unkie rushed towards them. He kissed Kate, and hugged Danny.
"Daniel, my boy. You have a lovely bride. Kate, you have a lovesick, happy Irishman who will always treat you like a queen. A poor queen possibly, but a loved queen. Congratulations to you both. Now, Danny, I'm off to have a happy whiskey and to toast your Dad."

With this said, Unkie stepped back from the car. He felt just a tad-bit melancholy but happy at the same moment. He, Tim Mc Carey, knew that his best work was done. He was proud to see Danny had become the young man his Unkie hoped he would be. After today, Danny would share that path with someone else more important in his new life. He liked Danny's choice. He whispered privately to Kate. "I'll still be here, God willing. But there's not a better person to be with him when I'm gone."

The reception back at the Kate's parents' house was fun for all and filled with happy conversation and laughter. The house party lasted into the night and guests slowly drifted away. There was a small cluster of neighborhood boys that formed in the rear yard. These were Danny's young neighborhood fans who Unkie invited in for cake and ice cream. This impromptu party signaled the end of the day's celebration. Though Danny and Kate had disappeared, unnoticed, hours ago.

The newlyweds spent a honeymoon weekend in the nearby Pocono Mountains in Pennsylvania. Somehow, Danny survived a weekend without baseball and without playing any practical jokes. Life was just as he had always hoped it would be. His pretty Kate was beside him. They were on their own and he had a job at home and a career in baseball. How did he get so lucky?

1941 "It Ain't Good."

Several weeks later, Danny and Kathleen were relaxing in their newlywed apartment in Chester. Except for their hours at work, they rarely left this honeymoon 'suite'. Danny had his off-season job at the local shipyard as a stockman moving pipe, valves, fittings, and other components from the storehouse to the many assembly floors, and Kate worked in a near-by business office. On this Sunday morning, they had just returned from attending late Mass. Kathleen was preparing a late breakfast for them, more like a honeymooners' lunch. Danny was seated at a their little table that barely fitted into a slightly bigger kitchen

Tying an apron around her waist, the new bride cooed at Danny. "Do you want scrapple or bacon with your eggs, hon?"
"Scrapple is good for me." He answered.

Danny reached over to the far side of the kitchen table and turned on the small radio. He dialed in some soft big band music. In front of him, lying on the table were his favorite parts of the Sunday paper – the sports page and the Sunday comics.

"Kate, it looks like we might have a cold winter this year. I think we'll be glad to be in Florida in a few months. It'll be pitchers and catchers in two months. Then, we go. You're gonna need a bathing suit and some shorts."

Kate cracked the eggs and dropped the raw egg whites and yolks into the frying pan, then she pushed the scrapple gently around in the other pan. "I'm so excited. I've never been that far away from home before."

"You won't be away from home, sweetie. You'll be with me in our home. Our home will be wherever we are. Even if I'm at the ballpark without you, I'll be thinking of you. Then before you can lock the door, I'll be back. I'm just 15 minutes away from you."

Balancing her new kitchen skills, Kate watched the eggs cook carefully and let the scrapple brown, "Yes. I know home is wherever we are as long as we're together. I just meant that I'll be away from my family and everyone else for the first time."

Danny got up from the table and walked over to Kate and wrapped his arms around her. "I know what you mean, sweetie. I love you and it's gonna be OK. We're going to be just fine. You'll see. Nothing's gonna be in our way now. Just you, me, baseball, and maybe a little one. Whenever that comes."

They embraced for a few moments, holding each other tightly. They were happy to be alone in their own home. Everything had turned out the way they hoped it would. No, Kate didn't want to end the embrace, not even to turn over the eggs and the scrapple.

Just then, a voice abruptly interrupted the music on the radio. The announcer spoke in a clear, steady and grave manner. "Attention. Ladies and Gentlemen. We interrupt this broadcast with a special news bulletin of serious importance. The White House has just confirmed that the United States Naval Force at Pearl Harbor in Hawaii was attacked today by a large Japanese air and sea armada. Many US military personnel have been injured and many US vessels and airplanes were damaged in the attack. The unprovoked attack took place at 7:53 am Hawaii time; 12:55 pm Eastern Standard Time. More details will be forthcoming on this station. The White House is preparing a formal message to be broadcast later this evening. So allow me to repeat……"

Danny and Kate were frozen in their embrace. They were both holding their breath and stared at the radio. They exhaled once the news report was finished. Then Danny turned off the radio. He didn't wait to hear the second recitation of the same frightening news.

Kate was first to speak. "An attack? Japanese? Pearl Harbor? Where is that? What does all that mean?" Kate asked him.

Danny was still trying to put the announcer's words more clearly in his mind and organize the words into an orderly fashion but he answered Kate on instinct. "I don't know what it all means, exactly. But it ain't good. I guess it means that all our plans might change. I'm not sure about Florida now. I'm only sure about us."

Within hours, the United States declared war on Japan; within a few days, Germany acting as an ally of Japan, declared war on the United States. At that moment, no one was sure of anything, especially not Danny and Kate. Their perfect honeymoon world had come to a sudden halt in less than ten days. Like so many other young people around the world, their long-term plans were now short-term plans. How fast things could change. Danny thought to himself. 'How unlucky can a fella get?'

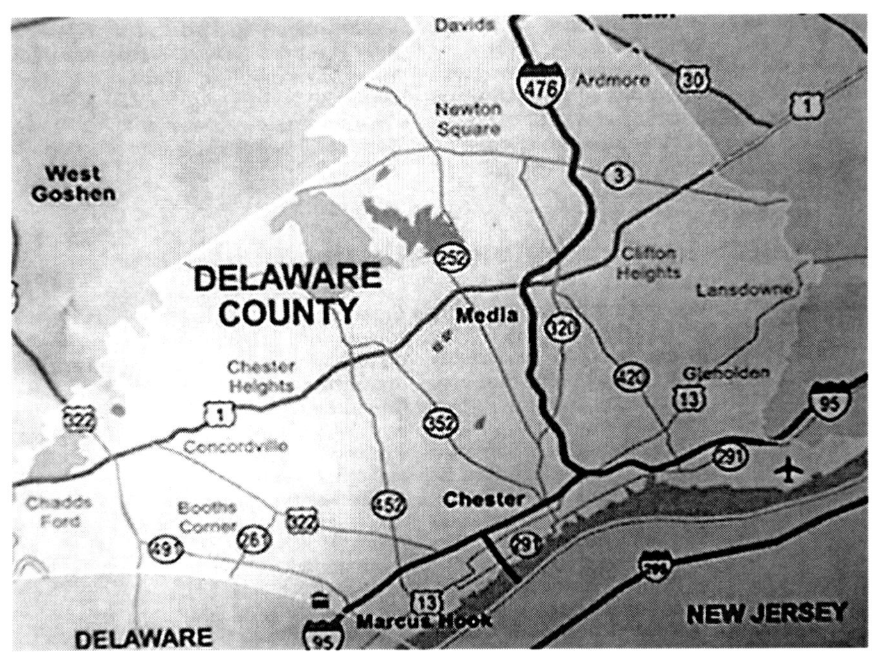

Chester, PA (est.1682), the only city in Delaware County. It is located southeast of Philadelphia along the Delaware River.

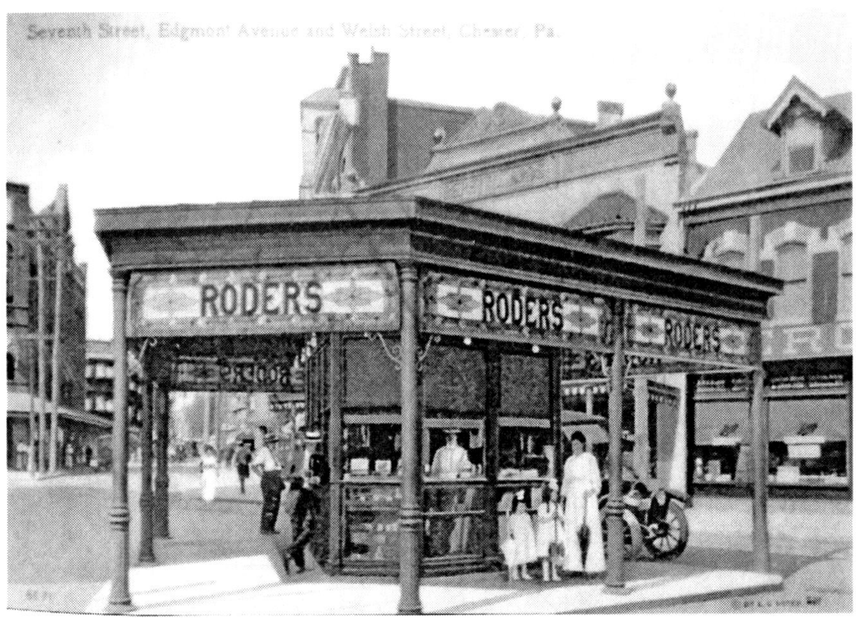

Roder's News Stand, downtown Chester, PA. Still there and still selling newspapers in 2016

Mickey Vernon
Washington Senators

Danny Murtaugh
Philadelphia 1941

Danny and Kate graduated from Chester HS in 1935

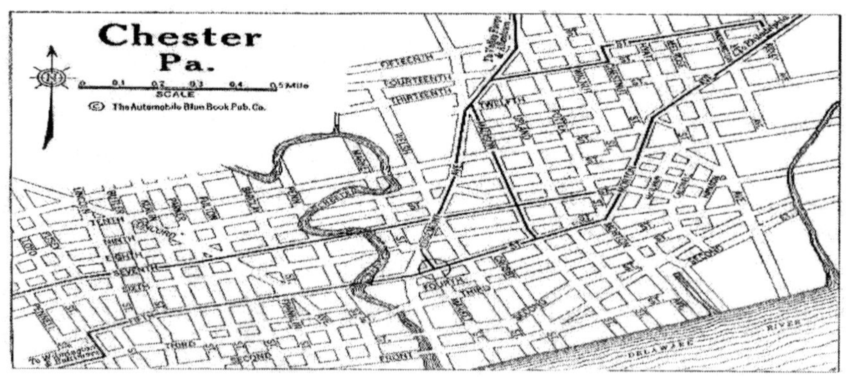

Map shows center of Chester. Danny was born on Barclay Street, left of creek that runs into the Delaware River.

Sun Shipbuilding in WWII.
worked at Sun Refinery

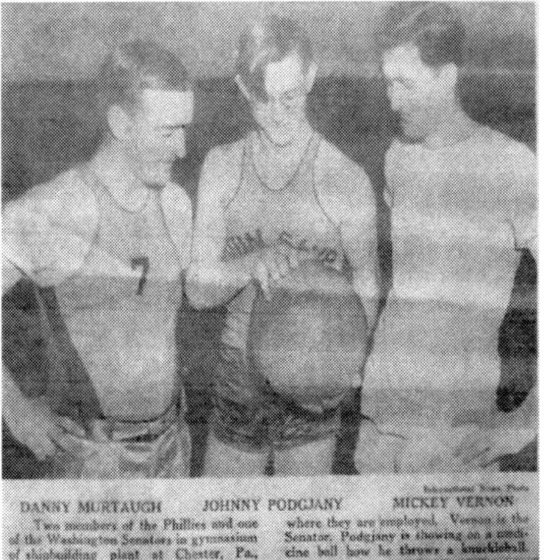

Danny, Johnny Podgjany Mickey
& Mickey 1941 off-season

Forbes Field, Pittsburgh, PA.
Home of the Pittsburgh Pirates, 1909-1970

Danny and Kate's wedding, November 28, 1941. St. Robert's Catholic Church. L to R, Groomsman, Uncle Tim, Eunice, Danny and Kate, Kate's father, Groomsman.

Babe Ruth hit right-field wall in 1924. He was 'out cold', but revived, and stayed in the game.

Franklin Fire Company, 1910 Danny, his father, and Unkie were volunteer firemen here.

CHAPTER SIX
WAR

1942, Roosevelt's Green Light

The 1941 Christmas holiday season was wrapped in more urgency and thoughtfulness than usual as the preparation for war dominated the national conscience. No one knew what changes a world war would visit upon our country and its people and it was a very tense and solemn period all over the world. For more than two years, the Allied and Axis countries in Europe had already battled each other mercilessly. Now in a matter of days, America was at war against two major military powers, Japan and Germany. Suddenly, the Atlantic and Pacific Oceans didn't seem wide enough.

Within a month of the bombing at Pearl Harbor and amid the frantic actions to mobilize the country for war, there were varied opinions on whether to proceed with the 1942 season of professional baseball. The National and American League owners looked to the White House for a decision whether to continue playing baseball in the midst of war. Previously, in 1917 when America entered the First World War, the major leagues suspended play for one season. This time after much discussion and deliberation, President Roosevelt issued a formal and public letter on January 15, 1942 to Judge Landis, MLB Baseball Commissioner, pronouncing his "wish to have the professional baseball leagues continue to play for the good morale and entertainment of the general public but especially for the men in uniform." This letter was informally referred to as "Roosevelt's Green Light Letter."

So like most players in the major leagues, Danny and Mickey continued to play baseball and they added another full season to their career statistics. Danny played his second season for the Phillies and Mickey played his fourth season for the Washington Senators. During the off-season, they worked at the same places where they worked before the war. Only now the work was more important than ever as Danny built war ships for the Navy, and Mickey provided oil products for all of the armed forces on land, sea, and air.

During this 1942 season, Danny played 144 games for his hometown Phillies leading them in the field but struggling at the plate. He finished the season with a batting average at .241. Overall, he played good baseball and was making a place for himself in the big leagues. At home, he was even more successful. He and Kate introduced a baby boy to the Murtaugh clan. Timmy, named after Danny's Uncle Tim, was born at 8:30 am on May 6, 1942. Fittingly enough, Kate was obligingly sympathetic to Danny's career because she managed to deliver baby Timmy between two scheduled games against the Brooklyn Dodgers. The Phillies had a two game set, a May 5th night game in Philadelphia followed by a May 6th day game in Brooklyn, when Kate, assisted by divine providence, delivered Timmy after the first game. This timeliness made it possible for Danny to rush to Chester Hospital to be with Kate and his new son immediately after the night game in Philadelphia. He spent a few hours with them and then he hurried to catch a train back to Brooklyn, NY. He arrived at Ebbets Field and played in the day game. It was the most exciting twenty-four hours in his life and he was back to wondering again just how lucky can one guy be.

The excitement of Timmy's birth didn't fade but as the season neared an end, there was something bothering Danny. He knew that he had a decision to make. The news from the battlefront was not good. He began thinking about the war and his role in it. His friends enlisted or were drafted into military service. He understood the importance and the value that baseball, movies, and music all lent to the country's morale, and the leisurely distraction and peacefulness they each brought to the country. But in the end, he didn't think he should be playing baseball while so many others were fighting in the war. He and Mickey spoke to each other often about their predicament, and they were in agreement – they would enlist. What was more difficult than the decision to enlist was when and how to tell their wives. Danny would be leaving Kate and Timmy for an uncertain amount of time, maybe even forever.

1943, "I'll Come Home."

Following the 1942 season, Danny and Kate's apartment was busier and happier than any previous off season. Certainly the addition of Timmy into their lives made it so. Danny also worked more hours at the shipyard this year than he did last year. In fact, everyone at the yard worked longer hours to replace ships lost at sea and to build newer vessels to support the Allied forces' increasing attacks against Japan and Germany in 1943.

Kate's mother spent a few days each week minding Timmy while Kate contributed to the war effort by working in an office downtown. Naturally, any hours that Danny was not at work were filled feeding and playing with his baby boy.
The whole country was so busy in 1943 that it seemed to have arrived onto the calendar much quicker than expected. The war had continued for more than a year and there was a no sign that an end was near. In fact, the opposite seemed more likely, the war was lengthening and it was settling into a fearful normalcy.

In deference to the need to conserve fuel and commodities during the war, major league baseball executives made a significant change to its spring training regimen in 1943. All of the teams were encouraged to cancel the traditional gathering of players and teams down in the warmer air and brighter skies of Florida and instead conduct their training camps closer to the club's home city. Subsequently, the Philadelphia teams established a practice site in Hershey, PA, seventy miles west of Philadelphia.

While America's participation in the war entered its second full year, baseball continued to entertain the people at home and the troops overseas. It was common to see photos and newsreel footage of a group of soldiers tightly gathered around a stateside radio listening to a ballgame in a barracks; or sailors and GIs hunkered around a battery-operated radio kit listening to the same game from somewhere halfway around the world from home, in either direction, east or west. There was a shared assuredness that everything at home was safe and unchanged, everyone was waiting for all of the men and women to come back home after this war was over. Baseball was comforting.

An annual event that marked the half-way point of the professional baseball league season was the July 4th national holiday that honored and remembered America's fight for independence and celebrated the freedom that is inherited with citizenship in the United States of America.

In 1943, the Phillies played a long stretch of home games just before and after the July 4th holiday. During this stretch of games, Danny was home with his family for a few days. The last home game of this series ended in the afternoon and Danny was scheduled to leave with his team to go to one of the other seven cities in the National League.* Dinner had ended a half-hour earlier and now Timmy was sitting up in his playpen, his chubby legs spread wide to give him the proper balance to sit on the playpen's padded surface. His dad had just finished rolling around the carpeted floor with his son and carefully placed a pile of wooden blocks in front of Timmy. It was time for Timmy to entertain himself while mom and dad shared some time with each other.

Kate finished washing the dishes and placed the dishcloth on the counter. She walked into the living room and sat on the couch next to Danny. "Danny, you hardly touched your dinner. Didn't you like it? I made your favorite."

"It was great." He smiled. "Just like always."

"Was there something wrong with the meat loaf?"

"No, not at all, hon. I wasn't very hungry."

She persisted. "Do you feel OK? Did anything happen at the game today that you want to talk about?"

"Really, Kate. I feel fine. Nothing happened at the ballpark. I guess I just don't like to leave you and Timmy."

She accepted that as the cause for his quiet mood because leaving to travel with the team wasn't anything he ever wanted to do. But she was sure there was something else he wasn't telling her, something that seemed to have taken a presence in the room with them. "Something's bothering you, Danny. I know it. Tell me. What is it?"

Danny knew Kate could read him like he was an open book. He also knew that he had put off this conversation with Kate for too long. He decided to speak with her during this home stand but they were all having such a happy time, he didn't want to break the spell. This time he had to give her an honest answer. "OK, hon, you know how I feel about me continuing to play ball while everybody, all the guys, are fighting in the war."

This is what Kate feared she would hear and what she knew had been left unsaid and unresolved. She had prepared a response to his personal dilemma if he did voice it.

"Danny, you're not the only one home. Lots of men are working, building ships, airplanes and tanks, and playing ball. You're doing both. You are right where the country and the President wants you to be. You're boosting soldiers' morale, and giving everyone something positive to focus on, and sometimes take their minds off the war, even for a little bit. You're making people happy. And you're needed to help build warships for the war.

"I know but I'm not happy. I feel like I need to do more, to be on the same team with everyone else. Not to be safe in a baseball stadium."

"You are on the same team. You're doing what the country wants you to do: what only a few men can do – hit and field and run in the big leagues. It's an important job for our country now. Yes, it's safe. And yes, I'm happy that you are safe. Your battlefield is here, on this side of the world. I know I'm selfish. I want you to be safe. Timmy and I want you to be safe. Timmy and I need you home." She was so close to crying but she was determined hold her tears back.

He listened and he could feel Kate pleading from the depths of her heart and hoping he would agree with her. "Of course, I want to be safe. I want all of us to be safe, Kate. But this is war. I feel like I'm sitting this war out. I'm not really doing all that I can do."

Now tired, worried, and frightened by what she may hear Danny say next, she said softly. "Danny, I don't want you to be anywhere but here. You're finally where you want to be. You're playing like you always knew you could. It's your dream that you worked so hard to reach." She started to cry, then continued. "You worked so hard."

"I know. It's what I want too. It's what I always wanted to do. Except that baseball doesn't matter so much now. It will only feel right when everyone is back here. When everyone is back home."

Hesitating, and fearful, she whispered quietly, almost inaudibly. "But everybody's not coming home."

Now Danny turned and looked deeply into her eyes. He rested his eyes in hers for a few long seconds, trying with his will power to make Kate feel his sincerity. "I'll come home, sweetie. I promise you."

With tears in her eyes, she reached for him, and they embraced. Before the war, they measured their love for one another by the amount of time spent together or by the number of times they called each other on the phone, sent flowers, exchanged trinkets, and shared all the little things that meant so much. Now they measured their love by how their hearts grew, making room for an increased love for one another, yet their hearts were never burdened by this abundance of love, by its plenteousness.

Kate barely whispered. It was more like a prayer. "I love you. So much." There could be only one response and Danny replied. "I love you."

***Prior to 1964, there were only eight teams in each of the two leagues. Since then teams have been added in several phases of expansion. Today there are thirty teams representing twenty-two cities in the US, and Canada. In 1990, inter-league games were formally scheduled during the regular season. These games match American and National League teams against one another and count towards a club's official win/loss record. Thus, a team's wins and losses against a team in the opposite league can determine their final standing in their own league.**

1943 Buckley Airfield

Danny appeared in one-hundred and thirteen games for the Phillies in 1943 and batted .273 before he was inducted into the army in Philadelphia in August 1943. Once he was sworn in, he requested a transfer to the Army's newest branch of service, the Army Air Corps. It is likely that Danny's decision was influenced by his sister Peg's husband, Captain Dale Bennie Wilson. Captain Wilson was a pilot in the Army Air Corps. Danny liked what he heard from Bennie when he was told that after the war there was a strong possibility of having a job flying commercial planes. Danny reasoned it was something to fall back on after he finished playing baseball. This wasn't the first time he thought about what he might do to earn a living when baseball ended for him. He didn't want to continue working at the shipyard. He wanted to start a new career.

Danny was soon transferred to Buckley Airfield in Colorado. After some military training and a complete physical evaluation, it was discovered that he was color blind. He was greatly disappointed even though he shouldn't have been too surprised. His pal, Johnnie, always told him that he was color blind. Danny now remembered that Johnnie was correct those many years ago – Kate's blouse was blue, not green. They joked with each other about his 'color blindness' when they were kids but now it was definitely an obstacle to flying airplanes because he must identify different color instrument lights and markings on enemy aircraft. Danny's blue sky was green. So he was disqualified as a pilot, He was disappointed but he remained in the Air Corps and continued playing for his army base's travelling baseball team.

During the war years, the Navy, Army, and Air Force formed baseball teams that were very competitive with one another. Teams consisted of enlisted men and draftees who were experienced players and most teams sought out professional and semi-professional athletes. If you were able to hit, field, or pitch a baseball with skill, you were assigned to a military base where baseball had a serious focus on winning. This friendly competition often softened the hard edge that military life imposed on recruits. Danny's Buckley Airfield team was such a team, travelling across the west and southwest representing the base pride and entertaining sailors and troops before their audiences sailed away to sea or marched off to combat. Often, these service teams were invited, more correctly commanded, to participate in bond-raising events throughout the country. Danny participated in some of these games.

During a pre-game warmup in Colorado, Danny and other infielders were fielding ground balls tossed to them by the first baseman, then they stretched their arms loose by throwing the ball back to the first base bag. The first baseman prodded him. "Are you going to play in the War Bond Drive game at the Polo Grounds in New York next week?"

Danny bent over and fielded a ground ball, then he threw it smoothly to first base. "I guess so."

After catching the ball from Danny, the first baseman quickly removed it from his glove and bounced it speedily along the ground to another waiting fielder while he continued to talk to Danny. "Boy, that's really something," his teammate added. "I heard it's a big deal. The President might even be there."

Danny continued to stretch his arms and shoulders in between fielding grounders and he replied. "I guess so." But his face was emotionless.

"Wow! Movie stars? Actresses? Maybe the Babe…?" the first baseman added.

Not showing much interest in the subject and not sharing his teammates' enthusiasm, Danny flatly responded. "Yeh, I guess they might all be there."

The shortstop who was standing twenty feet to Danny's right and was waiting for his groundball, looked slightly puzzled. "Geez, Irish, aren't you even a little excited? How about if you stay here. And I'll go. Actresses are a good enough reason for me. Someone else can have dinner with Babe Ruth."

In fact, actresses and Babe Ruth were the last things on Danny's mind but he understood his teammates' excitement and envy. He realized too that he didn't want to appear to be ungrateful for his good fortune.

"No. No. Fellas. Sure, I'm excited alright. But I'm mostly excited because I'll be near my hometown, and I hope I can get a 24 hour pass to go to see my wife and son."

This was something that his fellow airmen could appreciate. They knew now that Danny wasn't being nonchalant or snobbish about his skill level and social fame. They knew that like them, he was just more excited with the opportunity to go home, even for only 24 hours.

Warmups ended and the sandlot game began. The first batter took ball one, and then he hit the second pitch, a line drive rocket, towards Danny.

Instinctively, Danny reached to his left and snared the ball. The sharp popping sound of the hardball slamming into his leather glove felt great and natural.

"That's out number one!" Danny called out to his fellow infielders. Then he looked over at the first baseman, smiled widely and said. "This thrill never gets old."

The game continued. In a game, Danny was in the most comfortable part of his world but he knew that he was about to make another difficult decision. He felt guilty playing baseball while others fought. How was he going to tell Kate?

1944 Infantry Boots

Baseball continued to dominate Danny's contribution to the war. He played well, ate well, and was a good soldier. However, the news from Europe and the Pacific was full of reports listing losses of men and women. He felt that he was less of a soldier than he could be, giving less than he was capable of doing. He accepted that his commanding officers considered his role as a ballplayer as an essential entertainer to be important and to have a higher value than if he fired a rifle in combat. There were not too many soldiers who could entertain others with a baseball on a grassy outfield and a dusty infield. Baseball they decided was his 'call to arms.'

Less than two months after the War Bond game in New York City, Kate received a letter from Danny. It was a routine weekday and Kate had just returned home from her job downtown. Her girlfriend, Doris, who worked alongside her came home with Kate to share a light dinner. As a matter of routine, Kate's mom would bring Timmy home to Kate shortly before nightfall. Removing the letter from her mail box always excited her. She carried it into her apartment and picked up a metal letter opener she always left available on the end table in the living room.

As Kate deftly opened the letter and began reading it to herself, Doris was less patient. "Well, what's Danny say?" She politely asked. "Can you read some of the letter to me? I haven't received a letter from Joe for two weeks now."

Kate was half-listening as she quietly continued to read the letter to herself, then she paused and spoke out loud. "Danny says he was in Kansas and played against a team of college all-stars. It was fun. He misses me." She paused again and her voice lowered. "He says that he still wants to stop playing baseball and do more in the war."

"Tell him no." Doris almost yelled. "Tell him to stay there. I wish Joe was playing baseball."

Kate's heart and mind agreed completely with Doris but she held back her truest feelings. "I can't tell him to do less than he feels he should do, Doris. He and I have gone over this so many times. He can be stubborn." Kate took a breath, and quietly added. "He wants to transfer to the infantry. That means shipping out... overseas."

1945 Shipping Out!

A week later, Danny was on sitting on his bunk and he was finishing another letter to Kate. He wrote that he requested to be reassigned to the 97th Infantry Division. In the letter, he told Kate he would be training for several more months before shipping out. He didn't tell her the 97th Infantry Division had been undergoing warm weather combat training in Louisiana for the past several months. They were training to prepare for a June 1945 invasion of Japan. The Allies in Europe believed that D-Day invasion at Normandy had the German army in full retreat across the western front in Europe*. This meant that a larger force of American forces could now be fully concentrated on Japan. Danny didn't mention Japan in his letter to Kate. Even if he wrote it in his letter, it would have been censored and removed, or stricken from his letter. The rumor of an invasion of Japan was getting stronger as the slow, brutal, island battles in the Pacific continued to claim so many lives. The Japanese leaders had made it clear to Washington they would not surrender at any costs. Regardless, rumors or not, no person in uniform was authorized to share any military data, plans, or opinions with anyone. The message to all was summed up in one of the earliest and popular slogans of the war. "Loose lips sink ships."

On this day, no one, certainly not the commanding officers of the 97th Infantry Division, could foresee that within six months after the D-Day invasion, a German counterattack in December 1944 would stop the Allied advance through Belgium and force a change in combat orders for the 97th. Tokyo will have to wait. The 97th was needed first on the western front in Europe. Danny wasn't going to land in Japan after all, at least, not yet.

Danny was lounging on his bunk and finishing the letter to Kate when his bunkmate came running into the near-empty barracks. The soldier nearly fell through the screened wooden door. "Irish, did you hear the news?"

Danny raised his head and was hopeful that the war was over. "No. What news?"
"We're shipping out."
Danny put his pen down and asked. "Shipping out? When? Where?"
"Well, buddy." His bunkmate replied. "I heard we ship out as early as tomorrow." Then he added. "We're going to Tokyo. Where else?"

In another moment a few more members of Danny's platoon entered the barracks. One of them overheard the word, Tokyo, and he corrected the first soldier's comment on their platoon's destination. "Tokyo? Hell no. I heard its Berlin. We're going to kick Hitler right in the ass."

There was a cacophony of shouting and cheers as more soldiers streamed into the barracks. Many of them were repeating varied battle cries. "To hell with Tojo.", "Let's get Hitler.", and a few spirited, forward-looking soldiers cried out. "French girls! Viva la France."

Danny didn't know where they were going but neither place sounded safe. Under his breath, he prayed. "Well, Lord, I got my wish. Now give me your strength." He left his letter unchanged. He signed it, folded it, sealed it, then he walked out of the barracks to post the letter.

***On June 6, 1944, the combined Allied Forces launched the largest air and sea invasion in history on the Normandy beaches in France. Operation Overlord was its code name and it was a huge success. The German army was surprised and was pushed back deep into western France and Belgium. With the steady production of bomber and fighter planes provided by a mobilized American industry, massive bombing support enabled Allied soldiers to continue their successful forward ground movement into Germany. Germany was retreating. Berlin was the main target.**

1945, Ulithi, somewhere in the South Pacific

The war in Europe was swiftly turning against Germany as American and British forces combined ground and air attacks in its westward march to Berlin while Russian troops moved steadily from Russia into Eastern Europe and on to Berlin.

In the Pacific, fierce, bloody battles were repeated daily as US marines, sailors, GIs, and airmen defeated the Japanese and captured, one-by-one, a string of strategic islands that led from Pearl Harbor to Japan's mainland and ultimately, to Emperor Hirohito's palace in Tokyo, the capital city of Japan.

Mickey was stationed on one of those strategic South Pacific islands, Ulithi, the most important island in that string of captured islands. The US military command decided that Ulithi, an atoll that is situated in Micronesia and that lies among the Caroline Islands in the South Pacific, would serve as the most strategic island in the US Navy's plan for invading Japan. Ulithi was located three-hundred and fifty miles southwest of Guam and thirteen hundred miles south of Tokyo. The US Navy and Marines first occupied the island atoll in 1944 and were feverishly transforming it's lagoon into the largest naval station in the world, capable of holding and servicing seven hundred vessels. This naval station was selected to become the command post and staging area for the forthcoming invasion of Okinawa, and for the later invasions of Japan's mainland cities. The US Navy Construction Battalions, CBs, commonly referred to as 'Seabees', spent months clearing away the jungle foliage here and increasing the number and the size of airfields recently captured from the Japanese. These airfields were now American bases and they were being prepared for use by US bombers, fighter planes, and the massive number of invasion troops that would gather here for the attacks on Japan.

Mickey had been on Ulithi for several months, arriving just after the Marines secured it. Secure, however, was not the same as 'safe and quiet'. Everyone on Ulithi was subject to sporadic aerial attacks by Japanese fighters and, occasionally, light bombers. These deadly attacks were meant to endanger and kill Americans and to delay and prevent the work on the airfields. Regardless of the attacks, American bulldozers, dump trucks, and other heavy equipment operated eighteen hours a day. The only reason that the equipment did not run for twenty-four hours a day was that the use of lights at night made the airfields and living spaces easy targets for Japanese night raids.

There were other construction projects that were a priority on the island Commander's list. The island's new ball field was one of them. The Seabees (CBs) were more than happy to build a ballfield that would provide some distraction from the daily grind of war. Baseball at home and across the seas was a short-range healthy antidote to the strains of war. One seasoned member of the Seabee battalion who was assigned to supervise the building of the ballfield had been a groundskeeper for a farm team in Nebraska. He called over to a younger member of his construction crew. "Hey! Mac, don't forget that we gotta keep an area open to make a ballfield near the barracks. The colonel wants the men to have something to help keep their minds clear and their bodies fit."

Yelling loudly so he could be heard over the construction noise, Mac answered. "OK. I'll do that. I know the colonel likes his baseball. I heard that he played in college and just missed the big leagues." The supervising Seabee laughed. "Uh huh. It seems like all high ranking officers always just missed the big leagues. Is that why they are all in the Army and Navy?"

Curious, the younger Seabee innocently asked one last question. "What position does he play?"

In his flat monotone Nebraskan manner, the Seabee leader ended the discussion with an eternal hierarchal truth. "Any position he wants to play, son. He's a colonel."

1945 Mickey on first

Though the lagoon was large with several atolls surrounding it, nothing on the island was very far from anything else. Less than two hundred yards away from the soon-to-be ballfield, the Colonel was in his office seated on a wooden folding chair behind a makeshift desk as he received a verbal report from a Lieutenant updating him on the current status of the many and varied construction activities in progress. Summing up the report, the junior officer was pleased to inform the Colonel that overall there was good progress on the landing strip, the officer quarters, the barracks, and the warehouses. The junior officer continued. "We are also accumulating any surplus wooden planks and crates to be used for the bleacher section at the baseball field. The ball field should also be ready at the end of this week."

The commanding officer was relatively young for his rank, under forty years of age, and though he knew that this was a war zone, he was hopeful baseball would remove some of the anxiety of war, even if it was for only a few hours at a time. "Good, Lieutenant. It's important the added airfield is ready for aircraft use as quickly as possible but at least level and outline the ballfield so we can play games. Everyone can stand and watch the first couple of games." "Yes sir. I understand, sir." He saluted the Colonel, then he turned to leave.

The Colonel suddenly had something else he wanted to say to the Lieutenant so he motioned him to stay. He knew many of the local ballplayers were working double shifts on the airfield in order to meet the deadline to have the air strip functional as soon as possible. But he was also excited about welcoming the Navy's star baseball players into Ulithi next week to play several games against his local team. He certainly didn't want his own players to be too tired or too sore to play their best. He wanted to convey to his junior officer the importance of getting the field completed and the players rested. He spoke as though it was an after-thought but his words fell crisply on the young officer's mind. The younger man had spent many days and nights in the Colonel's command. He knew when the Colonel's intended meaning was more important than his words and light tone. The colonel's request/command was simple. "Lieutenant, make sure that our ballplayers get some rest before the all-stars get here. I want them ready when these island-hopping Navy all-stars arrive next week. It would be memorable to upend our service cousins. It's something I'd long remember and it will be fun, a nice friendly distraction from dodging bullets and choking on dry, wind-blown sand. Of course, it'll be more fun if we win."

"Are you going to play, sir?" The Lieutenant asked.

"I plan on playing some. I played varsity in college, mostly infield. I'm not sure which position I'll play here."

Smiling and glad to have the chance to polish the Colonel's ego, the Lieutenant beamed. "Why, sir, I'd think that you could play anywhere you'd want to play."

"That's what I think, Lieutenant. After all, rank does have its privileges. But with Vernon here, I can rule out first base, even if I am the Colonel.

1945 Under fire

It was game day. Soldiers, sailors, Seabees, and marines crowded onto the wooden bleachers. All of them were sitting in the full morning sun admiring the Colonel's new ball field. Dressed in light summer-issued clothes they all appeared to be back home on a weekend pass in Anytown, America. Except that it was impossible to not know that you were not home watching a baseball game in somebody's hometown because everyone here was carrying a government-issued steel helmet and any sound of overhead airplane engines caused everyone to lift their heads and search the skies for aircraft, identifying them in a split second as "ours" or "theirs".

Meeting their deadline as always, the Navy engineers and the Seabees used their bulldozers to do yeoman work that made the Colonel proud of the new ballfield. There was some growth that mimicked grass in the outfield areas, though it was really a mix of grass, weeds, and low shrubs. The infield was entirely a mixture of small stones, dirt, and sand blown up from the nearby beaches – the word 'sandlot' would be stretching the compliment a bit. Impressively, the once uneven, lumpy, palm tree-lined site's most noticeable new features were its flattened, level surface, perfectly measured to duplicate the exact dimensions of a professional baseball diamond. The distances from the pitcher's mound to home plate, and the distances around the bases were copied straight from the major league baseball manual. Only the distances from home plate to the outfield's wooden fence were shorter than the actual distance in a big league ballpark. The home plate to outfield fence distances were scaled down to three-quarters of a major league outfield fence's actual distance. After all, they were on an island, and land was limited. It was also unlikely anyone was going to smash a 340-400 foot homerun with the wind always blowing in towards home plate.

The day for the exhibition game arrived. Mickey's local team practiced on the field the day before so the visiting Navy all-star team took the field first for warmups. This barnstorming team of elite players from several bases in the states had been flying around the captured Pacific islands to entertain the men and to compete against any local team that the base could put on the field. There was only one requirement for the players on Mickey's team. They had to be assigned to Ulithi. Mickey and a few other "recruited players" were 'specially assigned' to this local island team. One other noteworthy addition to the field's appearance was creatively added by the Seabees. Out in the deepest part of centerfield just beyond the outfield fence stood a tall billboard-like structure that stretched towards the cloudless sky. A large flat wooden panel was nailed onto it, and painted on the panel in extremely large battleship gray letters was a greeting that brought a smile and some refreshing laughter to all. It was a homage to the common spirit that filled the hearts and minds of the island's newest inhabitants. The sign simply read, **'WELCOME TO YANKEE STADIUM'.**

So the stage was set and here in the middle of the Pacific, a game of baseball, America's Greatest Pastime, was ready to begin. The umpire walked out to home plate and told the visiting all-stars to leave the field; then he signaled Mickey and his teammates to take the field to complete their final pre-game warmups.

Soon, the lead-off hitter left the visitor's makeshift dugout and stepped across the loose mix of dirt and sand and into the batter's box. Finally, the crowd of sunbaked and energetic fans focused on the pitcher. The sole judge and arbiter on the field stepped silently behind the batter and the catcher and flipped down his protective face mask. He shouted that most action-packed command. 'Play Ball'.

1945 Delay of Game

The Navy all-stars were as good as their advanced billing. They led 6-4 as the game moved into the bottom of the sixth inning. Ulithi never led in the game. Now, the home team had two men on base and Mickey was coming to the plate. Mickey already had a few hits that led to a few runs and he wanted to continue to do more to help his team score at least two runs in this last inning of regulation. Two runs would tie the game and the game would at least go into extra innings, three runs would win it outright since the home team always has the last bat. The first few pitches to Mickey were carefully thrown off the plate. Mickey fouled one of the pitches and the count was now two balls and one strike. Just as the 2-1 pitch was released towards Mickey, the sound of a low-flying plane was heard, followed by the rat-a-tat-tat echoing sounds of machine-gun fire. On trained reflex, Mickey kept his eye on the ball and swung and hit the pitched ball hard but he never finished watching its journey towards the tall Yankee scoreboard in centerfield. Completing his follow-through, he heard more machine-gun fire, then the piercing scream of the air raid siren. He dropped his bat. "Holy crap! Japs!" He looked over to the on-deck batting circle and saw the Colonel also drop his bat and yell at the top of his lungs. "Take cover! Everyone! Move!"

In the chaos, the sudden exodus of fans from the stands and ball players from the field was swift but surprisingly calm. Nevertheless once clear of the open field, men and women scattered in every direction towards the safety of the air raid trenches that lined the camp pathways or under any visible cover to protect themselves from the fast, repetitive and powerful rain of 'hot lead' bullets zipping all around them. People were hurdling themselves into narrow air raid pits, frantically holding onto the steel helmets that covered their heads.

Mickey raced to a trench and as he ran, he grabbed a slower teammate, dragging the fellow into the trench with him. The sandy ball field and surrounding area was being peppered with steel bullets and the resultant pieces of dirt and stones rose up like shrapnel from the impact of the

Japanese Zero's gunfire. Then, as quickly as the attack began, it ended. The siren was still wailing as everyone rose from the ground and the practice of checking for injuries and for damages began.

Mickey lifted his head from the pit and found himself squeezed into a trench with several soldiers including the teammate that he dragged in with him. It was the right-fielder. He patted Mickey on the shoulder. "Thanks Mickey. I run like a catcher. I wasn't going to out-run that Japanese Zero's bullets without your help."

Mickey got on his feet and dusted himself off. He removed his helmet and said to the slow right-fielder. "This is one of the toughest away games I've ever played. I'm never going to complain about tough fans again. Even my hometown A's and Phillies fans aren't this bad."

After recording the injuries and damages from the attack, the game was officially declared ended. According to standard baseball rules, the score of an unfinished game reverts to the last fully completed inning. Since the last full inning completed before the attack was the fifth inning with the all-stars leading, 6-4, the Navy all-stars were declared the winners. What no one saw in the midst of the attack was that Mickey's ball rose quickly off his bat and flew high over the centerfield scoreboard. It cleared the Yankee Stadium sign. It was a homerun that would've given the local team a 7-6 walk-off win. But the game ended without discussion. It was one homerun that Mickey would never get credit for hitting. He didn't know he hit it out of the park. He didn't care. He was just thankful for the Seabees' man-made trenches and the American-made steel helmets.

CHAPTER SEVEN
WAR WEARY

1945 Letters home

While Danny was away, Kate's weekdays were routine. Like so many other young women she worked to support the war effort and of course she supported herself and Timmy. She usually arrived home from work at 4 PM, checked for mail from Danny, prepared something for dinner, and waited for her mom to bring Timmy to her for the evening. Then she started the routine all over again in the morning. She was in the middle of such a normal day on a Tuesday afternoon as she arrived home from work, and walked up the stairs to the second floor, and opened her apartment door. She placed her purse and house keys on the end table and sat in Danny's favorite chair. In her hand she held that day's special prize, a US Army APO postmarked letter she had just removed from her mailbox. She smiled when she saw her name on the front of the envelope, Mrs. Daniel Murtaugh. It was at least two weeks since she received her last letter from Danny, but it always seemed like a week of months.

She opened the letter carefully, making certain the envelope was not marred in any way. These envelopes were much more to her than a holder for the letter inside. They were other-than-worldly sachets that both protected and carried Danny's words to her across land and sea. They formed a golden chain that connected her and Danny; the one concrete possession that proved to her that he was out there and that he would be coming home soon. He had touched this same letter and now she was touching him.

Kate reclined into the softness of Danny's chair. She read the letter out-loud so she could hear and almost feel the words, Danny's words. She liked to speak his words out loud. Once heard, they easily filled her mind, and then travelled inside her to find a permanent place in her heart. She moved her lips and began to read…

> *Dearest Kate, I miss you and I think of you more each day. I want to be with you, to hold you and never leave you. I'm happy to hear that you are busy working at the office, and volunteering at the USO canteen. You know I never washed a dish in my life, an advantage of having three sisters. But this is one time that I wouldn't mind doing dishes, all the dishes in the canteen, in the world, all day long, if it meant that I could be with you at the end of the night. We're being told that there may be a delay in our families receiving our next letters for a while as we are expecting new orders and might move to a new base location. I just want to let you know so you won't worry if you don't get a letter from me right away or if they arrive much later than before. You can still use my current APO address, so write as much as you always do. I will write the same and hope that my letters move quickly to you. The infantry routine is getting easier and I am training on something new every day. Time goes by fast. I'm glad that I transferred to the infantry. I mean I liked the army air corps guys and I wanted to be a flyer and everything, but this is where I need to be now, unless I could be with you. Last night, like almost every night, I dreamed we were together. These dreams never get old. ....*

Kate stopped reading and dabbed her eyes with a tissue. She was smiling and crying at the same time. She said out loud to herself. "How can I cry and laugh at the same time?" She missed her Danny so much. She pressed the envelope and the letter to her damp cheek. She was fearful of where he might go next.

1945 Le Havre

Eight months passed since the Allied invasion took place on the beaches at Normandy in France. After heavy fighting to capture a beachhead at Normandy, the Allies made continued progress along the western front and advanced steadily towards Germany. But in December, 1944, the German forces launched a large-scale offensive counter-attack through the Ardennes Forest in Belgium. This unexpected attack from the Germans became a series of fierce battles fought for two months in extremely cold weather. The Battle of the Bulge, as it became known, was bloodiest during the 1944 Christmas season in eastern Belgium and western France. The German army slowed down the Allied advance and inflicted many casualties. American officers with units under German attack were instructed to stand their ground and were firmly commanded 'to hold at all costs.' With much valor and sacrifice, the Allies regained the initiative and drove the enemy forces back into Germany but the Americans suffered great losses and their troops were exhausted. It was clear fresh troops from America would be needed to reinforce the Allied forces and continue to push the German army back into Germany.

Danny and his fellow GIs in the 97th infantry Division were among the troops that were thrust into instant combat. Trained for jungle and beach combat in hot weather, they were hurriedly issued clothing suitable for the cold weather conditions that they would endure in the dark, frosty, woods of France, Belgium, and Germany. In fact, the 97th would even march into Czechoslovakia.

1945 Cigarette Camps

Danny's ship sailed into Le Havre which is a major seaport in the northern end of France. He was accompanied by the entire 97th Infantry Division. Once they landed, the division spent a few days getting organized at Camp Lucky Strike, one of the many 'Cigarette Camps' that were a series of Allied entry and exit points in Western Europe that occupied enormous space around the cities of Le Havre and Rouen. The camps served as dual way-stations for thousands of troops: wounded and wearied troops of recent battles who made their way from the battlefields in France and Germany, and fresh troops like Danny and his buddies who marched to the same battlefields to replace them. Within a day or so, the newest troops would be fighting the German army on German soil.

The reason for the slight but necessary delay at Camp Lucky was logistic. The full complement of the 97th Division's individual parts, separately shipped to Le Havre, needed to be gathered together again and reunited as one army division before launching itself into battle. The 97th operations personnel raced to catch up to its infantry and artillery units while supplies and equipment to support all of them was patiently collected and confirmed to be ready to attack the Germans.

When all the pieces were fitted, the 97th moved out of Le Havre and began their long march into the woods. The terrain didn't change as that area of France and Germany was abundant with trees, wild forest growth, narrow rivers and supple valleys. The primary targets of the US Army were on the other side of the forests - the industrial cities west of Berlin, like Dusseldorf, and then Berlin itself. The 97th Infantry Division's goal was to be a part of the Allied force that would defeat the enemy troops and capture these industrial cities that were the last bastions of German military production for the German Third Reich.

Prior to this campaign, the woods and open countryside in the Ruhr Valley had been largely untouched. That was no longer true. The war came late here but it showered havoc and devastation onto the valley in this final drive to Berlin. Danny was never going to forget the difficult march across eastern France, south into Belgium and then east into Germany and beyond. The division faced resistance every step along the way, at times it was brutally fierce as some of the opposing German troops were being led by SS commanders who vowed that their units would fight to the death. There would be no surrender. Every mile of the German homeland was being vigorously defended by a final mix of desperate, hardened, Nazi SS troops who commandeered newly conscripted troops, both old and very young, all novices to war and to the death that accompany it. These were the last remnants of the soon-to-be-defeated German army of the Third Reich. This was the last major ground offensive of the war in Europe. Major tank battles, full infantry attacks and small deadly skirmishes were fought in villages, towns, and cities between February and May. The history books will refer to this months-long stretch of battles as the Battle of the Ruhr Valley.

1945 The Ruhr Valley

Danny could think of a thousand other places where he'd rather be. Though he didn't regret his decision to join the 97th infantry, he couldn't stop thinking that he could still be in Colorado ending his day at Buckley Airfield, maybe playing some pinochle or poker.

Here in the heavily forested German countryside, it was cold in the daylight even when the sun lifted itself high and fell brightly on the trees and meadows beneath it. When night fell, the darkness placed a lid on the forest and everything under it froze. In Danny's own favorite part of the world, it was also cold, but not this cold. Not bitter cold, not 20 degrees F and accompanied with a chilly wind. Everything around him had been frozen for the past two weeks. It seemed that the world had been covered in ice or snow since his platoon left the 97th division HQ in France that was now more than one-hundred miles behind them. He wanted to be part of the fighting army and now he was in the war every day and night. The towns, hills and valleys and forests all ran together in his mind. He wished every day that this war was over and that he was home. So did everyone else.

Sleep was a luxury and it didn't come often as Danny and his platoon moved steadily deeper into Germany. When he did sleep it was a deep sleep because he was exhausted from the combination of the marching and the constant bitter cold. Once asleep, his mind would sometimes wander in dream sequences where he was home again with Kate and far away from the perils of war.

A typical dream sequence would contain little to no dialogue, just movement, affection and gestures between him and Kate. They are home and alone in the dark. In the background he hears the soft haunting strains of 'Stardust'. Danny's and Kate's eyes are filled with longing for each other. There is no war. There is only the two of them sharing time together as it was always planned to be before the war. There is a peaceful quiet that envelops them. In this dream, there is no war. There is no separation. Just the two of them alone.

But as always, a call to arms, or sentry duty, or just the smell of hot coffee would bring him back to the reality of war, and of course, the bitter cold. He was in that faraway place when he was awaken roughly by his Sergeant. "Murtaugh, wake up. You have guard duty in ten minutes."

The sound of the Sergeant's voice interrupted Danny and Kate's reverie. It was always a rude awakening that separated Danny from the warmth of Kate's arms. He would open his eyes, rub them vigorously, and try to clear his mind. It usually took a minute to face the cold truth. He wasn't home, but worse than that, Kate's wasn't with him.

Danny stumbled with his words and said confusedly to the Sergeant. "Huh? Oh. OK, Sarge. Guard duty. Ten minutes. Yep. OK." Then still not thinking clearly, he innocently replied. "OK. Then wake me in ten minutes." Sergeants don't take orders or requests from enlisted men and the Sergeant barked a response. "Hey, soldier, you're not home with your nanny or you're Mommy. I want you awake now! Use the ten minutes to shake the cobwebs and have some coffee before you take your position. Now!"

Danny started flexing his arms, then did the same with his legs. His eyes were fully open now. "Yes, sir. I am ready, sir."

Inside the fox hole shared by Danny and several other GIs, a boy-soldier, maybe seventeen years of age, tried to make conversation to keep his mind off of the cold surroundings.
"Damn." He said drawing a word from his newly acquired army-language dictionary. "How the hell did we get here after all them months training in the heat of Louisiana and landing on sandy beaches? This ain't no Pacific island I ever heard of. Jesus, if it gets any colder, the bullets will freeze in mid-air."

Another young soldier added. "Well, that might be a good thing if all the guns froze and the bullets just stopped before they hit anybody."

Reaching for a cup of coffee, Danny was still flexing his arms and legs and he added. "I don't know, kid. I would be worried that one of you young guys might just run right into one of those frozen bullets." The Sarge decided to throw his two cents into the topic and he said to Danny. "Hey, Murtaugh, that's funny. But you're from Pennsylvania and you'll probably dumb enough to like this cold weather."
"No, Sarge, I don't like freezing weather. In Philly, we go inside when it's this cold." Danny picked up his rifle and rose to his full height to take his position on guard duty.

Just then, **Thwack! Thwack! Thwack!** Three shots rang out. Each shot hit immediately behind the soldiers with all of the bullets just missing the Sergeant's head. The bullets made heavy cracking sounds when they pierced the bark of a single tree: first one crack, then a second, and then a third, all three bullets moved so fast that the bullets seemed like they hit the tree at the same time and the three sounds were echoes of a single bullet. In an instant, all hell broke loose! The Sergeant instinctively took command and shouted to everyone. "Hit the ground! Stay down. Down! Down! Seek cover."

All of the men dropped quickly to the ground. It appeared that one soldier was struck by shrapnel from the bullets hitting the tree. All eyes now searched the tall trees, and the underbrush and the fallen tree branches around them. Now there was just cold silence. In the pitch-black darkness, no one could see or hear anything. Whispering to the soldiers lying face down in the grass and dirt, the Sergeant took control. "No one move! It's likely a sniper. We have to find out where the shots came from." He thought for a moment, then said. "Lee, Clarke, Murtaugh. You three crawl over to that clump of large trees" He motioned to a line of trees roughly 100 feet away to the left. "Take these binoculars and one of you climb the tree and get some surveillance all around us. Be careful. No noise. Look high and low."

All three men began to move slowly, crawling on their stomachs towards the designated trees. It took a few minutes to reach the base of the trees. Now someone had to climb the tree. Danny wasn't fond of tree climbing. The only climbing that he ever did was back in basic training. Nevertheless, he was the senior soldier in the small group, so he volunteered. "I'll go up. You both keep watch for any movement by anyone other than our guys."

Private Lee, a young soldier from Arkansas, put his arm on Danny's rifle to stop Danny's movement up the tree. "No. old man, I'll go up. I'm younger and I've been climbing trees since I was five. I used to hunt from a tree. Give me the binoculars. You'll take forever to get up the tree." Danny knew that Lee was right so he handed him the binoculars and said lightly to the younger soldier. "A regular Indian scout, huh? Well, we didn't have many trees where I grew up. OK, kid, you go up. Just don't drop the glasses on my head. Be careful, and be quiet."

The young soldier climbed slowly but effortlessly up into the tree. The kid was right Danny thought to himself. The younger soldier was a lot quicker and looked as comfortable as a monkey in that tree. Everything was still quiet as Lee reached the top half of the tree. It seemed like thirty minutes had passed but it was only a few minutes since the first shots rang out. Lee continued to climb a little higher, then he settled on a branch that jutted out from the main tree trunk. He lifted the binoculars and looked out through the tree foliage. He saw that not a single man in the platoon was moving. Danny and Clarke laid flat on the ground and scanned the woods from the base to the tops of the trees, ready to fire at the first sign of movement, or noise. Assuming responsibility for the patrol, Danny instructed Clarke. "You look to the left, up and down. I'll look to the right, up and down. If you see anything not in our uniform, shoot it." Just then, Lee moved slightly in the tree, he whispered down to Danny. "Psst. There is nothing to our rear, and nothing to our left. Let me turn…..just.."

Thwack! Thwack!
Two shots rang out loud, followed by rapid, flat, dull thuds, hitting something simultaneously. Lee froze for a moment in the tree. He stopped speaking, not making any sound. Then the tree limb shook and Lee fell hard to the ground, dropping maybe 30 feet out of the tree. He was lying only a few feet from Danny. Clarke couldn't believe his eyes. He stared at the youngster lying on the ground and without taking his eyes off of the fallen soldier, said to Danny. "Jesus! He's been shot. The sniper shot Lee."

Hugging the ground, they looked to their right, then to their left, they scanned the trees and ground cover quickly, but they saw nothing. Danny waited a minute or so and crawled over to Lee. He checked Lee's wound and pulse, and crawled back. "He's dead. He's gone already."

What now? Danny thought. Lee wasn't the first GI[*] that he'd seen killed but he was the youngest and he never got used to losing a fellow soldier. He always felt a cold chill and shivered for a moment every time a fellow soldier was hit. He and Clarke stayed low to the ground and waited for what seemed like an endless time. After making a personal vow that they would come back for Lee after they found the sniper, they crawled back to the Sergeant, There wasn't too much to report. The Sergeant saw it all happen from just a short distance away.

Looking upward to the black sky, the Sergeant calmly said, "Men, we can't afford to wait here much longer. The moon is getting higher and soon we will be like sitting ducks in a shooting gallery. This could also be a planned holding strategy so that more German soldiers can advance on us and surround us." Thinking for a few moments, he pointed at three soldiers. "Connor, Clarke, Watson. The three of you move forward slowly and see if you can get to the other side of this path, then find the bastard and out-flank him. He will likely want to move to another position. Stay low and quiet. We will keep an eye out for any other movement. If you draw fire, we may be able to find him from his rifle spark."

Danny who had been thinking of Private Lee interrupted the Sergeant. "Sergeant, send me in place of Clarke. He's already done his part tonight. I'm the senior soldier here and I might be luckier than some of these young guys." Trying to down-play his concern, Danny added some morbid humor, "If I'm wrong, it won't be the first time, but it will likely be the last time."

The sergeant understood Danny's request. "OK. Murtaugh, you take charge. Clarke, you stay here with all of us. We'll provide cover. Good luck soldiers. Get the kraut bastard. Then let's get out of here and get back on the road to Berlin."

The platoon waited in place and Danny's patrol moved stealthily towards the right side of the path, and into the woods, staying very low to the ground. Advancing slowly but steadily, they halted and laid low to listen and watch for movement. Connor took this opportunity to whisper to Danny. "Do you really feel that lucky tonight? How much luck do you think you need to beat the devil?

Danny wrinkled his forehead and answered matter-of-factly. "Luck? I have as much luck as the next guy. But I mix my luck with a few prayers. I'll take my chances with luck and a prayer. You see I know the other guy ain't Irish. I just hope he's not praying to the same God I'm praying to.

The three-man patrol continued to move a little farther from the platoon and they neither saw nor heard anything for nearly a half hour. The moon had risen higher and this provided increased light to aid them in their search for the sniper. It also meant that the sniper now had more light to see. As they inched themselves slowly through the dark forest, they soon found an empty German canteen at the base of a tree where they noticed the ground was freshly trampled. They figured that he was either still in this tree or he had recently climbed down from the tree. Danny motioned for them to spread out and carefully search a wide area around the tree. They found nothing, and heard nothing.

"It looks like he's gone." Danny said. "Maybe he's a loner after all."

Connor wasn't so sure. "I'm still nervous."

They were all nervous. Danny offered them his opinion. "I guess he's done enough to slow us down. I gotta think he knows the moon helps us too."

Watson who had been silent and alert this whole time finally spoke for them all. "Maybe so. I just hope he never figures out how scared we are."

Danny signaled them to stop. "That's enough searching. Let's go back and report to the Sergeant. Stay quiet. Keep low. Let's go!"

They turned to head back when they heard a crunching sound. There was a slight movement in the brush just ahead of them and suddenly it was quiet again. A patch of clouds crossed in front of the moon and the increased darkness made the silence more ominous.

Watson looked to Danny. "What was that? Did you see anything?"

Connor whispered at the same time. "Shhh! I heard it too. But I can't see a thing."

Danny cautioned them both. "Don't move, speak, or breathe."

Connor motioned animatedly to a patch of bushy growth next to nearby trees. Against the partial moonlit sky, they could see the outlined shape of a soldier walking towards them. It wasn't a GI*. Watson raised his rifle to fire. Danny touched Watson's arm and motioned for him not to fire. He whispered to both of them. "Let's try to capture him. We'll take him to the Sergeant. Maybe Headquarters can learn something from him."

Watson was frightened. "I don't know." He countered. "It seems safer and easier just to shoot him."

"Not if his buddies are anywhere near us." Danny replied.

Danny directed the two younger soldiers to stand a few steps in front of him, one on each side of the path. He made a chopping sign to signal to Watson and Connor they were to attack the German, knock him to the ground, and short of killing him, silent him quickly. Danny readied his rifle to shoot the German if he resisted too much, and to be ready to fire on any other German soldiers who might appear. Danny made a chopping sign as the enemy soldier passed between the two Americans. Then he commanded. "Now!"

The sniper was startled by the English word coming from just a few feet directly ahead of him and raised his rifle but at that same moment he was quickly disarmed and taken to the ground by Watson and Connor. After a brief struggle, the German lay bruised on the ground with Danny's rifle pointed at his head. "Well, Fritz, you're coming with us. One sound or one wrong move and you are dead. Understand?"

The three Americans marched their captive back to the Sergeant who learned from the prisoner that the German unit in front of them was retreating further into the woods and planned to bivouac outside Dusseldorf. The Sergeant sent the German soldier back to division headquarters for more questioning.

The long night finally ended for Danny and his young buddies. They settled in place on the damp ground and were glad to be able to rest for a short while. But before they fell to sleep, they said a prayer for Private Lee and vowed to remember him for his courage and sacrifice in the Ruhr Valley. Danny never climbed another tree.

*** During World War II, "G.I. Joe" became the general nickname for all American soldiers, no matter what branch of the Army or Army Air Forces they were serving in, including US Marines and Navy personnel. The original term G.I. was used as an abbreviation for "Government Issue" or "General Issue" and was stamped on military trash cans and buckets to identify equipment made for U.S. Army inventories and supply houses. The term "G.I." came into widespread use to identify a US soldier with the start of the military drafting of young men in 1940. The use of "G.I." expanded quickly from 1942 through 1945 and grew to be an acronym for US soldiers in action comic books and toy action figures.**

May 1945 V-E Day

The 97th Infantry continued its' long, embattled, trek east through Germany and southeast into Czechoslovakia. There was continued resistance in the cities and towns around Dusseldorf and all the way into the western Czech countryside. Some conflicts were full fierce battles while others were smaller but no less deadly skirmishes. As rumored earlier, the German soldiers who remained did not retreat without showing virulent resistance.

There were other difficult and unpleasant discoveries that lay ahead for some members of the 97th infantry. During a deeper advance into Czechoslovakia, units of the 97th captured a German prisoner concentration camp and liberated the emaciated survivors. These concentration camps were unforgettable places that haunted many of the GIs who liberated the camps and who saw the horrors that the predominately civilian Jewish prisoners endured. The American soldiers who liberated the camp never forgot what they witnessed but many seldom spoke about these concentration camps when they got home. The pure evil of Hitler and his Third Reich was on full display in the remnants and records of the living and the dead that were found in these camps, and in the abandoned and decimated towns and villages where whole communities of men, women, and children were murdered. The few remaining survivors were forced to watch their homes burn before they were transported into similar camps and also murdered.

The steady advance of the 97th Infantry was interrupted with the shocking and sad news that President Roosevelt was dead. The president died on April 12 while resting at his retreat in Warm Springs, GA. Although he was recently elected to his fourth term as America's President, he had been seriously and secretly ill even before the election. It was a sorrowful loss for the American people and for the Allies but the war continued. Vice-President Harry Truman from Independence, MO was quietly sworn in as the thirty-third President of the United States. He would soon make momentous decisions to end this war, and to go to war again when the post-war peace was broken in the Far East.

Though the news of Roosevelt's death was heartbreaking, the Allied advance to Berlin was unstoppable. American, British, and French troops pushed into the German capitol from the west, while at the same time, Russian troops pushed from the east. Within three weeks, the long-awaited good news that everyone had waited so long to hear was broadcasted. The date was May 8, 1945. It was a less than ordinary, blandly-named, middle of the week day; not a more significant, joyously sounding day like a Sunday, or even a playful, relaxing sounding day like Saturday. It was a Tuesday. It seemed ironically fitting that the ugly war and all its horrors would end on a non-descript, routine Tuesday.

Danny heard the soul-lifting news from his Sergeant who was standing on the hood of an army jeep just outside a make-shift mess tent in the woods somewhere in Czechoslovakia. Addressing Danny and all of the members of his platoon, the Sergeant shouted loudly amid muddy tents, and the charred cooking pots and dented steel helmets scattered across the campsite. “Men.” He said. “I am happy as hell to tell you that this damn war is ended!” An immediate and thunderous roar of joyous shouting, whooping, and hurrahs erupted. There were numerous hugs and even kisses exchanged among the war weary soldiers. Danny provided his own, personal signature whistle. Some soldiers froze in place and stared up at the sky, thankful that it was true but unable to believe it at first. Others shed tears of happiness and felt bountiful relief that they survived this war.

The Sergeant continued his announcement to his troops.
“I was told today to tell you US Army generals met in Berlin today with German officers who under instructions from Germany’s highest commander, Admiral Donitz, signed an unconditional German surrender. The war is over. It’s over! This goddam war is over!”

There was more shouting, whistling, cheering. Even louder than before. Danny stopped whistling and he knelt in place, made the sign of the cross, and quietly prayed. “Thank you, God. I’m going home. We’re all going home.”

The unconditional surrender was signed by the German Army High Command. Adolph Hitler was dead. He committed suicide in an underground bunker in Berlin on April 30, 1945. The war in Europe officially ended on May 8, 1945 and the eighth day in May is still celebrated as V-E Day, Victory in Europe.

As a footnote of history, the US troops of Company B, 387th Infantry Regiment, 97th Infantry were reported to have fired the final shots in the European theatre on May 7th**

But the war wasn’t over for everyone. America was fighting two wars. The war in Europe had ended but the war with Japan continued. Mickey was still on Ulithi in the South Pacific and Danny and the 97th Infantry Division would stop fighting in Europe and come home but only long enough to exchange winter clothing for lighter clothing suitable for fighting the Japanese in the steamy jungles on the Pacific islands and on mainland Japan. Within two weeks of arriving in the US, they would sail to the Pacific Ocean to join the massive US Armed Forces for the invasion of Japan.

***American troops, including the 97th Division, liberated several of these concentration camps while fighting in Germany and in the Czech Republic. Theresienstadt, Flossenburg, Dachau, and Bergen-Belsen are a few of the infamous names of such camps. A year earlier in the spring of 1944 all of the people in the town of Kosice in Slovakia were taken from their homes and forced to watch as their homes and synagogue burned to the ground. All 15,700 people were murdered: some nearby in the forest where they were first forced to dig large pits that were used for their burial. Others died later in the Auchwitz-Birkenau camp in Poland.**

****On May 9th, the day after the German surrender, six hundred Russian soldiers were killed in battle at Silesia (eastern Germany). The war was officially ended the day before but in 1945 information often travelled too slow and arrived too late at the battlefront.**

May 1945 Ulithi Naval Base

The news from Europe was received in the United States with enormous joy and grateful relief but there was still an abundance of tears and sorrow that continued to rise daily from the farms, towns, and cities throughout America. Death was halted in Europe but many Americans were still dying in the South Pacific. The local movie theaters provided updated newsreels showing actual battle footage from the action in the South Pacific. Actual film footage showed US Naval bombardments and US Marine landings at Iwo Jima and Okinawa and brought home to Americans the images of sailors, soldiers, and marines suffering death and injury. Mothers and fathers, sisters and brothers, wives and children watched and wondered if their GI was on that island, in that battle, and possibly in that film.

The Navy and Marines would fight for sixty-two days before they overran and secured Okinawa, a key island that would be used as an airfield for the future invasion of Japan. This single island victory involved more than 500,000 US troops and resulted in the tragic loss of 14,000 American soldiers killed and 36,000 wounded. It was a steep price of American lives. It was of no comfort to know that the Japanese losses were much greater. Nearly 140,000 native islanders were killed.

While the battles for Okinawa and other islands were being fought, the buildup of forces on the small island atoll of Ulithi where Mickey was stationed had transformed this once peaceful lagoon into the largest naval station in the world. Ulithi was becoming the launching pad for the massive US invasion of Japan.

Once an island was secured, idle hours increased between military duties and general activities. That's why Mickey and a fellow sailor were leisurely sitting under a palm tree outside their island barracks awaiting mess call. The sailor had been on this island for over six months and like everyone else in the Pacific, he was frustrated with the pace of the seemingly endless war.

"Hell, Mickey. It's taking weeks to chase those Japs off of Okinawa. That's a lot of our good men, lost and wounded. It will take us forever to do the same to Tokyo. This war will never end."

"It will end, alright." Mickey replied. "But it can't end too soon."

The sailor nodded his head in agreement. "You know, Mickey, I didn't think we had so many airplanes, and ships of all kinds."

"I don't suppose we did at the start of the war", Mickey answered. "Many are brand new and they keep coming from back home, a lot are from my home town." Mickey couldn't help wishing he was back there now. "We need them all.' He added. "Some don't last too long."

A second sailor started to walk into the barracks but when he saw Mickey sitting outside the barracks, he walked over and sat next to him. He said excitedly to Mickey. "Vernon, did you know that the Cardinals are in first place? Yeh, my Cardinals, Vernon. Whaddya think of that?"

Mickey was used to hearing this razzing from just about everybody on the island. They knew who he was and all of them had their own favorite baseball teams. None of them were Washington Senator fans. Mickey supposed the Senator fans were all shipped to Europe.

"It's still early, Hank. Heck, the Senators could be in first place now, too. But I wouldn't get too excited about it yet."

Hank laughed. "The Senators in first? I wouldn't get too excited, either. They would need a legion of angels to get there." Then Jerry piled on and kidded Mickey. "Hey, Mickey, maybe if they get that close, they'll come and get you and put you back on the field."

"No chance." Mickey shook his head side to side. "I got a job right now. I don't think Uncle Sam will give me time off, even for a World Series. Anyway, I think we might be in Tokyo by then."

With that said, they all looked at one another, nodded, and raced to the mess hall. Gourmet or not, no one missed a meal.

1945 Invasion Plans

Mickey and his fellow sailors as well as the rest of the world were not aware that America's military leaders were preparing for a much longer war because Japanese Emperor Hirohito and his military commanders had already refused to surrender. The Japanese military was massing fifteen divisions of men and firepower on their coastlines and the US military had already scheduled target dates for a costly and bloody invasion of Japan. The invasion of Japan was scheduled for two separate attacks: Operation Olympic on November 1, 1945 at Kyushu, Japan's southern home-islands, and a second invasion in April 1946 at Kurjikuri, the gateway to Tokyo. Privately, the US military estimated that 450,000 Americans would be involved in the first invasion (Operation Olympic). The US government had already ordered 500,000 Purple Heart medals* in anticipation of the number of casualties from the two planned invasions. Thankfully, as events unfolded, they were not needed.

*** These medals remained in government possession long after the war. As recently as 2010, sixty-five years later, one-hundred thousand of these WWII medals still sat in a US government warehouse.**

Johnny Podgjany (L) and Danny ((R) are cheered by hometown friends at Phillies game in Shibe Park, September 1941

Mickey practicing his perfect batting stroke

Danny's heavy lumber

Danny, US Army, 1944

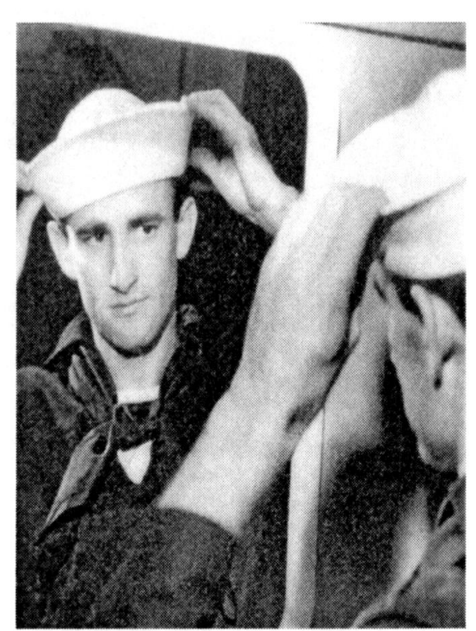

Mickey, US Navy, 1944

Danny, Buckley Airfield 1944

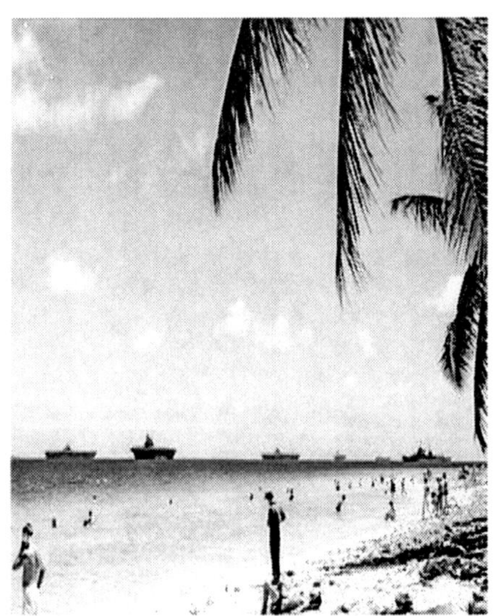

Ulithi, Caroline Islands
South Pacific, 1945

During WWII, ballfields like this were built to entertain troops. Mickey's homerun was hit on a similar field 1945.

US troops battled German soldiers every mile from Normandy to Berlin. Danny and the 97th Infantry fought in France, Germany, Czechoslovakia.

PFC. James W. Reese
Medal of Honor, 1943
Mt. Vassillio, Sicily
August 5, 1943

J. William Reese, 1920-1943
Chester Rural Cemetery
Rest in Peace

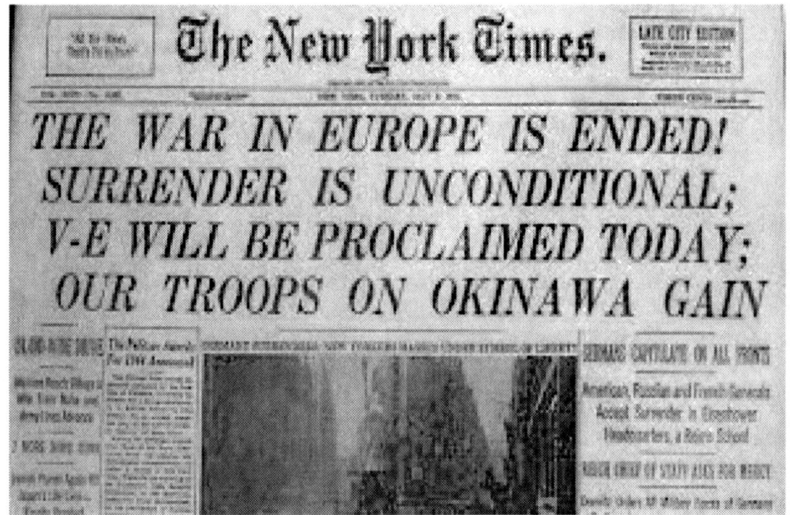

The New York Times.

THE WAR IN EUROPE IS ENDED!
SURRENDER IS UNCONDITIONAL;
V-E WILL BE PROCLAIMED TODAY;
OUR TROOPS ON OKINAWA GAIN

GERMANS CAPITULATE ON ALL FRONTS

American, Russian and French Generals Accept Surrender in Eisenhower Headquarters, a Reims School

The beginning of the end of WWII,
V-E Day, May 8, 1945

CHAPTER EIGHT
1945 COMING HOME

1945 Chester Train Station

The end of warfare in Europe meant that Americans GIs - men and women - would return home. Realistically, not every GI was going to be sent home at the same time. There was still a great need for troops to be sent to defeat the enemy in the Pacific and the 97th Infantry Division was specifically trained for island invasion and jungle warfare. So Danny and the 97th were whisked back through Le Havre, destination Tokyo. This time they were mustered for exit through one of the 'City Camps' in contrast to 'Cigarette Camps' at entry. The 'City Camps' were named for American cities. So a GI might enter the European war zone through Chesterfield (a cigarette camp) and leave the war zone through Cincinnati (a city camp). Their reward for a three month's tour in the Ruhr Valley was two full weeks at home before sailing to Japan.

Danny's path home brought him through Philadelphia to Chester's downtown train station. The station was located at Sixth Street and was the city's main train station. The remaining southern destinations for this local passenger train from Philadelphia were at Highland Ave. in the west end of the city, then Marcus Hook, and then much farther down the line, Wilmington, DE.

On this day, a small crowd had gathered a half hour early at the station and they stood close to the area where passengers normally disembarked. The few outbound passengers who were waiting to board the southbound train once it stopped politely stepped back away from the train tracks that welcomed the arriving train. The station trainmaster stood on the platform next to the ticket window and made a formal announcement. "Now stand back, please. The train will pull into the station in just a minute or so. Back away from the edge of the platform.

You must allow the incoming passengers to depart the train before anyone boards the train."

"I see him. I see him."

The small crowd could see the train's billowing smoke lifting from its smokestack a half-mile or so up the track and now it was heading directly for them. Unkie was tall enough to see above most people's heads since the crowd consisted mainly of women and children. The majority of men and many young women were either away from home in the armed services, or at work supporting the war. Unkie herded the family close around himself and voiced instructions. "Nellie, Kate, girls. Here, get in front of me. We want Danny to see you girls first. We don't want him to miss your bright beaming smiles."

Kate held tightly onto Timmy, and stood anxiously in front of the crowd, and faced toward the train's arrival. "What a grand day this is." She whispered to Timmy. "Daddy's coming home to see us."

Holding his cap so the rush of wind from the approaching train wouldn't blow it away, the trainmaster asked Unkie an obvious question. "Well, Mr. Mc Carey, is this the train that you expect your nephew to arrive on?"

"It is." Unkie smiled. "It's been two years since we've seen him. He's coming back from winning the war in Europe."

"That's a fine thing then that he's home." The trainmaster politely tipped his hat to Unkie.

Unkie noticed the gesture and he was proud for Danny. "Yes. He's home but only for a short while. He is home for two weeks then his unit will travel to California and ship out to the Pacific. There's one more war to win."

The conversation was interrupted as the train dragged itself noisily into the station, then it slowly, laboriously, stopped to position itself alongside the middle of the long platform. Regardless of their ages, and despite an original intention to stay lady-like as their mom had requested of them, Danny's sisters all began shrieking loudly.

"I see him. I see him." Peggy yelled, not being lady-like at all. "He's standing by the door. See him. See him. He's waving at us."

The train's car door opened, and the first figure to step down was Danny, smiling, eyes twinkling, resplendent in his Sunday army best. He nearly missed the bottom step as he appeared to leap from the train. His face was beaming brightly from ear to ear, and the first words he spoke expressed his happiness and gratitude for this moment. "Wow! Oh my God!" The words sounded more like a prayer of thanks, and less like a greeting.

He looked instinctively for his Mom, found her, and smiled, then he saw Kate and Timmy standing next to his Mom. Kate stood breathless and felt anchored to the platform as she watched him come to her. He dropped his bags onto the platform and stepped through the happy cluster of family and friends. Kate placed Timmy into Danny's arms. Danny was surprised how much Timmy had grown in the past year. He was no longer an infant, but now a little boy. Danny hugged and kissed his son, and squeezed him tightly. He embraced Kate and held her close. He kissed his mom's smiling face amid her tears, and shared quick kisses with his sisters and his aunts, all the while he managed to keep one arm around Kate and his other arm held Timmy firmly against his shoulder.

This circle of family and friends was full of joyful noise and quiet tears and he acknowledged all of them. At the trainmaster's request, Danny and the small crowd slowly moved like one single figure away from the train. This enabled the Trainmaster to manage the discharging of other arriving passengers and the loading of new passengers before the train moved down to its next station stop, Highland Avenue. Once loaded, the train departed leaving amid an echo of laughter after having delivered enough treasure to the Murtaugh family for one day.

June 1945 Alone together

Several hours later that same day, Danny and Kate sat side by side in their bedroom at Nellie's house. This was their first time to be alone together in nearly two years. Downstairs, the house was filled with family and a constant stream of friends and well-wishers who continued to stop in to welcome Danny home and to see him in the flesh. He was overwhelmed by it all.

Kate was overwhelmed too. Sitting on the bed next to him, she could only laugh like a giddy girl on her first date. "I just can't stop looking at you. I don't want to let you out of my sight, not even for a second. I'm so happy." She almost sang the words to him.

This was perfect. This was everything Danny had envisioned in his dreams. Kate was perfect and he was here with her. "Hon, you are all I thought about. Here I am, and you're right in front of me. It's so good to be home with you, and with Timmy."

They embraced, kissed softly, lingered, and then slowly pulled themselves apart. With a last sigh, they reluctantly headed back downstairs to join the celebration. They were thinking the same thing, but they both left it unsaid. How long will everyone stay, how long before we can really be alone?

June 1945 some will never come home

A few days later, the morning was nearly over when Danny came down from his upstairs bedroom and greeted Uncle Tim who was seated on in a large, comfortable chair in the front living room.

Rubbing the sleep out of his eyes, Danny greeted Unkie in a daze. "Hi! Unkie. Geez! I must've been really tired. I didn't hear anybody leave or come into the house this morning." Rising half-way out of the chair, Unkie gathered the loose sections of the morning edition of the Chester Times, the city and county's only daily newspaper, and handed it to Danny. "Well that's a good thing, Danny." Unkie assured him. "You have a lot of sleep to catch up on these days."

Taking the local paper out of Unkie's hand, Danny thanked him and then added. "You're right. The extra sleep sure does feel good, but I don't want to waste a moment here, or miss anything while I'm home. "He paused, and asked. "Where is everybody?"

Unkie put his right hand up to his chin, thought for a moment as if Danny's question was difficult to answer. "Well, let's see. Kate is out getting groceries from the nearby American Store. Everybody else is at work."

Taking a seat on the sofa, Unkie and Danny continued to talk about family and friends. With the war's ebb and flow and its forced separations, Unkie was glad to have this opportunity to talk with his nephew. "Because all you young guys are away, your sisters and their girlfriends are working in the offices and metal workshops. There are a lot of women at the shipyard too. You wouldn't believe your eyes. And your mom is as busy as ever doing laundry for some and cleaning for others. The scary truth is that the women are doing a fine job without men. I just hope they don't like working so much so that they won't come back into the house."

Opening the paper, Danny struck a hopeful note. "Well, we might all be coming home for good, soon."

"Yay, all of you", was Unkie's reply. "And tomorrow wouldn't be soon enough."

Danny glanced over the war headlines and looked for some local news. Then he turned to the Times sports page. In his opinion this local paper had the best sports page in the Tri-State area. He told people many times that it was better than the Philly sports pages. He had really missed his local paper. As he read a few headlines in the sports section, he commented on some familiar person or fact, then express some surprise. "Wow! The Cardinals and Senators are at the top of the NL and AL standings."

Closing the paper, but not putting it down, Danny spoke for the first time about the future. "Unkie, once this war is ended, a lot of players will be heading back to spring training." It was clear that the future had suddenly became a new concern for Danny and other returning soldiers. During the last four years, no one thought too much about the future, at least not a future without war. Now that one war had ended, and hopeful the war with Japan was nearing a conclusion, it was likely that peace and prosperity will be the next challenge for America.

Already things were beginning to look promising. Men who left jobs to go to war were promised that their old jobs would be given back to them when they got home. This was certainly good news for many but there was a different concern for Danny and professional players. Going back to play baseball wasn't the same as rejoining your train crew, or shipyard gang. Hitting a fastball, stealing a base, diving on the ground to catch a ball were job skills that could lessen over time, or there could suddenly be a new young kid who just might be much better than you are. The opportunity to get your old position back only meant that you get the right to try out again. Baseball required performance. Two years in the service didn't erase Danny's skills but those years took some youthful zip from his arms and legs. Even his eyesight wasn't as sharp as before the war.

Unkie sensed his nephew's self-concern and answered enthusiastically. "Danny, you'll be ready when the time comes. You're be kicking dirt and chewing tobacco. It'll be like you never left the field."

Danny liked what he heard from Unkie and didn't expect to hear anything less from him but he knew what lay ahead. "Well I won't be just like I was when I left. I did a lot of hiking, belly crawling, and sweating in the army. I just want an honest tryout at my old position."

Unkie wanted to calm Danny's fears so he repeated a conversation that he heard on the radio. "I'm hearing that the league will mandate that all ballplayers who left to join the military will get a first opportunity to get their jobs back, just like industry workers who left factory jobs."

Not really sounding convinced, Danny stood up to leave the room. "I hope so, Unkie. But every ball club wants good hitters, nifty fielders, and crafty pitchers. It doesn't hurt any if you can steal a base, or slam a round-tripper. Let's see what happens when they fill in the lineup cards after the war is over."

Danny hadn't mentioned to anyone where he and the 97th were going after this short visit home. They could all easily guess but no one wanted to spoil these happy days while he was home with all of them. But Unkie had already decided that when no one else was around, he would ask Danny directly. This was his first opportunity to ask his nephew the million dollar question. "Tell me, Danny, if you can. Are you going to the Pacific?"

Tight-lipped at first, then taking a deep breath, he looked at Unkie and said. "I don't know exactly. I only know that we board a troop train two days from now and head west. That's all I know."

Before Unkie could press him for more details, the front door opened. Kate walked into the room carrying a bag of groceries. She smiled at Unkie and walked over to Danny and kissed him. "Good morning sleepy-head." Then she addressed Uncle Tim. "Hi! Unkie." She placed the groceries on the table and smiled again at Danny. "I saw Libby and she said that she received another letter from Mickey. It was dated two weeks ago and he asked her if you were coming home now that V-E Day arrived. He hoped that you would come home and stay stateside."

"I'd sure like that." He smiled. "I guess everyone will focus on Japan now and hopefully shorten that war so Mickey and all the others can come home soon, too."

Kate returned and sat next to Danny. "Libby told me Mickey said in his letter that he's as safe as he can expect to be in the middle of a war. She's going to come by tomorrow to see you."

"OK, Kate. That's great! Lib knows that I want Mickey back here as much as she does. We all do."

The young couple looked comfortable sitting on the sofa, like they could sit there all day. Suddenly, the room felt crowded so Unkie stood up. "Well, I'll leave you two alone before everyone else gets home. Danny, I'll keep rooting for the Phillies or the A's to win the pennant. It might seem impossible for either team but we Irish know that miracles only happen when the impossible is needed." Unkie laughed at his own wry humor and walked out the front door.

The door had barely closed when Kate and Danny embraced. After a long kiss, Kate pushed Danny away, smiled and whispered. "Let me put away the groceries and then we can relax." Danny released her hand, laughed and said "No. Let's relax now." He promised her. "After we relax, I'll help you put the groceries away." They both laughed.

Later, Kate went into the kitchen to put the groceries away by herself, and Danny sat in the parlor and began to read the newspaper's general news section that included war events, and a twice-weekly list of the names of local men and women recently wounded, killed, or missing. This public list was released by the government only after the families of those men's and women's names on the list were formally advised by the respective branch of service.

Reading this casualty list Danny remembered that before he entered the army, James W. Reese, a local Chester boy and a 1938 graduate of Chester High School was killed in Sicily and was posthumously awarded the nation's highest military award, the Congressional Medal of Honor*. During this short visit home, Danny sadly discovered that since he was last home in 1943, there were many additional young men and women from Chester and the surrounding communities in Delaware County who were killed, wounded, or were missing.

He didn't know them all but he knew they were all loved and missed by someone, and they were never coming home again. He stood, placed the newspaper on the chair, and walked into the kitchen. He put his arms around Kate while she was emptying the bag of groceries. He kissed her neck and squeezed her tightly. He didn't ever want to let go.

***PFC James W. Reese died on August 5, 1943 on Mt. Vassillio in Sicily. He was twenty-three years old and a private in the 26TH Infantry, 1ST Division.* see commendation on official MOH award certificate.**

August 1945, V-J Day

Within a few weeks, Danny was reunited with the 97th Infantry in California and shipped out to Tokyo. The war in the Pacific continued on its hectic, bloody pace as the entire might of the American Armed Forces focused on pushing the Japanese farther back and closer to their own island homeland just as they had pushed the Germans back into Berlin. Danny and Mickey were among the hundreds of thousands of men and women who were now in the Pacific preparing for the invasion of Japan. The combat for the islands leading to Japan remained brutal and even though the Japanese continued to lose one island after another, they would not surrender. The hopeless and suicidal defense of their homeland was costing Japan and America many additional human lives. The final turning point of the war occurred on August 6 and 8 when a new weapon was unleashed on Japan that ended the war overnight.

The newsreels shown later in theatres across the United States of America and the world brought onto the screen the enormous explosions that blasted all matter within the two targeted cities. Movie audiences were universally held spellbound by the weapon's total and instantaneous destructive power. The birth of the atomic age and its attendant weaponry would soon end the world's largest and deadliest conflict in history.

The first of these 'atomic bombs' was dropped on the Japanese city of Hiroshima on August 6 after America issued warnings to Japan's leaders that immense destruction would befall their major industrial cities unless they agreed immediately to an unconditional surrender. There was no response from Japan before or after the first bomb was dropped on Hiroshima. With Japan still refusing to surrender, a second atomic bomb was dropped two days later on Nagasaki. These two cities were destroyed with only two bombs. The devastation was instantly catastrophic. Many lives were lost and those who survived the bomb blast suffered greatly from the resultant radiation, then died. It was expected that this Armageddon would soon force Japan to accept an unconditional surrender.

But as late as August 14 Japan still had not agreed to an unconditional surrender. Now well past the point of no return, President Harry Truman authorized that another atomic bomb be dropped on a third Japanese city. This was communicated to Japan's Emperor Hirohito who promptly agreed to sign the unconditional surrender and did so on August 15, 1945, a day that would be thereafter referred in America as V-J Day, Victory in Japan.

History records that America's decision to drop the atomic bombs on Japan was based on the growing forecast that catastrophic American casualties would be incurred during a land invasion of Japan. A formal peace treaty was signed by Japan on the battleship, USS Missouri in Tokyo Bay on September 2, 1945. The war with Japan was over. Danny,

Mickey, and millions of other men and women were going to come home. Just as it was arranged in Europe, the servicemen and women were to be sent home based on the number of points accumulated by their specific military service and their time served.

Of course, some men and women would never come home. Others who were wounded or who were prisoners of war took longer to get all the way home to their families. In the final summation, the US government reported nearly 420,000 Americans died in Europe and in the South Pacific. An additional 670,000 were wounded, and 130,000 were captured and held in German and Japanese prison camps. More than sixteen million Americans served during World War II.*

---

*An estimated 80 million people were killed across Europe, Africa, and the Far East during the Second World War. Military personnel accounted for 25 million of this unfathomable number; civilians accounted for the remaining 55 million. The USSR (27 million) and China (20 million) suffered the largest loss of life. In many countries, the number of wounded far exceeded its number of fatalities.

December 1945, Mickey comes home

The war was over. After four months, America was struggling to get back to a normal pre-war routine. The festive mood from V-E Day in May and from V-J Day in August remained but there was an increasing realization that the pre-war normal would never return. Most of the world and America had changed. There were many young men missing from the towns and cities, and many more men and women who returned home would have to overcome the physical and emotional damages caused by the war.

Mickey sailed back into the states and arrived in California on Christmas Day, 1945. As soon as his ship docked, he took his government-issued cross-country train ticket for Philadelphia and traded it in for its cash value, then added the difference in cash so that he could purchase an airplane ticket to fly home. If he couldn't be home on Christmas day, he would try to be home the very next day.

The cab delivered him to the Los Angeles airport's main building and he approached the ticket counter in his Navy uniform and inquired about the cost of a one-way ticket to Philadelphia. The ticket agent smiled at him and wished him a Merry Christmas and said. "That is twenty–three dollars for you, sailor. The plane will leave from Gate 3 in an hour. You should be home just after midnight in Philadelphia." Finally beginning to relax now that he had his ticket and was ready to board the plane, Mickey flashed a wide grin. "Thank you, sir. Merry Christmas to you."

Mickey was still a sailor in the Navy but he knew that in only a few weeks he would become a civilian again. He walked to the gate carrying his ticket tightly in his hand.
It was literally his ticket home.

After sleeping through the long flight, he landed at Philadelphia airport in the early morning hours of the next day, December 26. He took a Yellow Cab from the airport to his in-laws' home in Leiperville, approximately twelve miles south of the airport. The cab glided silently for the final 100 yards and stopped in front of the house. Mickey tipped the driver, stepped lively out of the cab and walked to the front door. Before he could knock on the door, the door opened and Lib stood in front of him. He didn't move. He dropped his bag and then Lib leaped into his arms and Mickey wrapped his long arms around her. He was home and he was safe. He hid his tears in Lib's long dark hair. No one noticed his tears because everyone was crying, even the family dog.

January, 1946 Danny comes home

On the other side of the world, Danny wasn't so lucky. He spent his Christmas in Tokyo. He was a member of the US Army Occupation Forces where he was assigned to assist in rehabilitating the sports facilities at Stateside Park, one of the many venues that was built for the 1940 Tokyo Summer Olympics that were never held.

Like every military person overseas, Danny was focused on coming home. The Armed Forces created a Victory Points Program at the end of the wars to determine the order in which armed forces personnel would be released from active duty. A total of 85 points was required before a soldier or sailor could be sent home. The points were accumulated by receiving a specific number of points awarded for certain milestones or events during a person's military service. The events ranged from the total number of months in the service, an overseas assignment, battle participation, medals earned, and so forth. A form was provided to all military personnel that must be completed and submitted for tabulation and verified by Army personnel. Danny was anxious to complete his Victory Points Form and go home. He entered the Meiji Hotel in Tokyo that served as US Army Tokyo Headquarters and approached a soldier sitting at a desk located just inside the hotel lobby.

"How do I qualify for a Victory Pass home, Corporal?" he asked.

The corporal looked up at Danny and held up a multi-page form that he offered to him. "Here fill this out this. Then take it over to the desk back there in the right corner. The First Sergeant will tell you how many victory points you have."

"How many do I need to go home?" Danny asked.

The corporal heard this question at least a hundred times a day. His answer was always the same. "Ask the Sergeant. You need 85 to get in line. You might have enough to go home now or you might need to earn more."

Danny accepted the paper and walked to a desk against the far wall. A wooden nameplate rested on the front of the desk with 'First Sergeant' engraved on it. No name was written on the nameplate and there was no sergeant sitting behind the desk. A paper sign with 'Out to lunch' handwritten on it was taped to the front of the desk.

Seeing this, Danny rolled up his Victory Points form, sighed and turned around to walk out a nearby door. Just as he began to exit the doorway, Bam! He bumped into another soldier who was entering the room at the same time.

"Excuse me, buddy." Danny mumbled to the soldier as they both recovered from the small collision.

"That's OK soldier. Smaller people, narrow doorways here. There's barely enough room for both of us."

At that moment, both men glanced at each other and stood perfectly still. They immediately recognized one another, and they both grinned. The second soldier spoke first. "Danny Murtaugh! Well I'll be a monkey's uncle. When did you get here?"

"Holy cow! Arky Kraft!" Danny was surprised to see a friend from his hometown standing in the doorway. "I've been here since September. Geez! It's great to see you. You are the first neighborhood face that I've seen outside of Chester during this whole war. Here we are on the other side of the world, and a guy from the south end of Chester and a guy from the east end of Chester meet in Tokyo."

Both Arky and Danny stepped away from the doorway and stood in the lobby. Arky extended his hand and continued excitedly. "What unit are you assigned to? What brings you to Tokyo? Other than a free cruise from Uncle Sam."

"I'm with the 97th but I'm hoping to go home soon. I just got this Victory Points form and I need to see the First Sergeant when he comes back from lunch. Are you here to check on your points, too?"

Arky looked over his shoulder at the vacated desk in the corner. "No. I work here. Victory Points huh. Do you know the First Sergeant? There's a long waiting list to see him. But it always helps if you know the right guy." This wasn't surprising to Danny as he knew there was always a long waiting list to see anybody about anything positive in the Army. But this wasn't going to help Danny.

"No. I don't know him."
"Sure you do, Danny." Insisted Arky.

"No, I don't think I do."

Arky grabbed his own arm, turned his shoulder sideways, and pointed to his stripes. "Sure you do, Danny. I'm the First Sergeant." With his mouth open so wide that a bird could've flown into it, Danny stared at his friend. "You are?"

Sergeant Arky Kraft removed his cap and smiled. "Yep. I am."

Danny finally managed to close his mouth before he caught a Japanese wren in it. Arky finished laughing and said. "Look, fill in that VP form with your army induction date, your number of days overseas: where, when, what action you've seen and so on. If you have any more questions about it, just bring it over and we'll finish it together. Right now, I got a few things to get done. Give me a half-hour."

"That's great, Arky. I'll bring it to you when I'm done." Danny walked over to a card table, sat on a metal chair, and began completing his VP form, his ticket home.

Working together, Danny and Arky completed Danny's Victory Points Form. Within a month Danny was officially credited with enough Victory Points to be sent stateside. He arrived home in February 1946 only a few weeks before the start of spring training. The good news was the war was over and some things were beginning to return to normal. Another good thing was that the Phillies baseball camp wasn't going to be in Hershey,

PA any longer. Baseball was back to normal. Spring training was going back to warm and sunny Florida. So was Danny.

CHAPTER NINE
STARTING OVER

1946, Starting Over

Danny returned home to Chester just before Phillies began spring training. He barely had time to kiss Kate, hug Timmy, and pack his bag. It seemed as though the war happened a long time ago. But the war affected everyone and required adjustments. The war experience was something that would never be forgotten by Danny, Mickey and all the other men and women who lived through it.

The morale of the country's citizens and soldiers benefited greatly from the decision to have professional baseball continue at full speed through the war years. The level of skilled talent may have been reduced but the game's appeal to Americans was never any greater at home and overseas, whether on ships, in foxholes, and in Quonset huts, and in make-shift barracks in Europe and in the Pacific. The 1945 World Series paired the perennial basement-dwelling Chicago Cubs against the Detroit Tigers. The Tigers led by Hank Greenburg who just returned from military service won their first championship since 1935. The Cubs failed to win its first World Series since 1908.*

Naturally, Danny and Mickey were excited to be back at spring training. Both were anxious to play ball and hopeful that their 1946 Phillies and Senators could match the Cubs recent success and they would fulfill their biggest childhood dream - to both play in the same World Series. It was something they talked about ever since playing together in American Legion ball.

Danny had a whirlwind journey to complete in order to attend the Phillies' 1946 spring training. He shipped out from Tokyo in February, spent a few weeks at his home in Chester, and travelled to the Phillies training camp in March. The spring training workouts and games passed by quickly. He was not comfortable facing fastballs thrown by pitchers, having only switched within weeks from carrying a rifle to swinging a baseball bat. His hitting average was poor. He was also beginning to have occasional nightmares that woke him up in his hotel room with a cold sweat. He didn't tell anyone. The dreams were all pretty much the same. It was always a bright sunny day and he was standing in a foxhole in a forest. He couldn't move his feet and his arms hung uselessly at his sides. Suddenly multiple objects were racing faster and faster towards his head. He couldn't move or raise his arms to protect himself. No sounds came out of his mouth. Just before impact, he would wake up, sweating and frightened. He knew that there was a connection between this dream and his inability to hit the ball consistently. He was determined to get pass these dreams.

The two pals both played well enough and they both headed north to start the 1946 season with their teams. Mickey was playing regularly and hitting as though he had never left the team but Danny was struggling. In late May, Danny was on the road with the Phillies when he received some bad news. He was traded from the Phillies to the St. Louis Cardinals.

He called home. Sitting in his hotel room, Danny was speaking on the telephone to Kate who was home in Chester. After only a two weeks into the season, he was moving again. "Nope. I don't like it either, Kate. I thought I was here to stay."

Kate was disappointed and surprised by the unexpected news. "You didn't get a chance to show them anything. They know that you need more than six games to get your swing back. You tried so hard. It's not fair."

"I know hon. It doesn't seem fair but they don't pay us to try hard, they pay us to hit." He paused. "And I'm not hitting." He sounded discouraged. "Ben Chapman and the Phillies want to win, just like everyone else."

Kate was never comfortable having so many of their important conversations over the phone. She appreciated, especially since the war, that speaking on the phone was much better than waiting for letters that took long to travel between her and Danny. Letters that you cherished receiving but that you couldn't talk back to, and expect an instant reply. Nevertheless, it was always very difficult to handle the tougher moments between them without them being able to see each other. There was so much more comfort in seeing and touching. "Danny, when do you report to St. Louis?"

"That's the hardest news. I'm not going to St. Louis. They're sending me down to their minor league team in Rochester."

Her voice rose and then softened with added disappointment. "Oh! Danny I'm so sorry. I wish I was right there next to you."

There was only silence on Danny's end of the phone.

Very near to tears, Kate offered a thought that she had previously kept to herself. "Maybe you need to take time away from baseball. Come home. Get some rest. My goodness! Last May you were marching across France and Germany and that other country."

"Hon, I can't come home. If I take a year away I won't get back at all. It's now or never. I have to stay connected to the game"

With silent tears starting to dampen her cheeks, Kate sensed that something was being left unspoken. She asked him. "Is there anything else wrong? Something else is wrong. What is it?"

Taking a deep breath and shifting uncomfortably in his hotel chair, he overcame his reluctance and voiced his biggest fear to her. "I don't want to tell anyone here but I feel awfully jumpy at the plate. I feel nervous. I think that every pitch is going to hit me. I'm pulling away. I'm fearful. I'm ducking on strikes. It's like I'm dodging bullets again."

He stopped talking, took a deep breath, and he continued. "That's not all of it. When a fast ball smacks the glove, it hurts my ears. But if I tell anyone, I'm done. They'll think I'm shell-shocked or something. I think I just need games under my belt that will help me to get all my timing back. Overcome the jitters. Get comfortable at the plate."

Frightened for him by what he was telling her, she squeezed the phone tightly. "Oh! Danny. I worry so much. Come home."

"No. I can't come home. Not yet. Don't worry. I'll be fine. I have to beat this."

"Do you think going back to Rochester will help?"

"It's got to help. It's all I have now. I have to make sure that it helps. At least no one is firing bullets and bombs at me anymore." There was a small break in the conversation as both of them felt weary.

Kate finally spoke. "Hon, you'll be back to the big leagues fast. I know it."

"I just need a few weeks to get my stroke back." was the only positive thing Danny could say.

"Do you want me to come to Rochester?"

"No. Stay home. Take care of Timmy. Say some prayers for me, for us. This is something that luck and a big bucket of prayers can fix."

"Danny, it just isn't fair to you after being away for so long and us being apart."

"I know sweetie. I've learned that things are not always fair. But I'm not going to say that life is fair when things go my way, and that life is unfair when things don't go my way. The war taught me that fear and unfairness are real. We have to fight through them. I have to fight through this. I have to change some things myself."

Kate began to hear the feisty, push-against-the odds, Danny Murtaugh that she knew so well and she smiled to herself.

Danny's voice sounded clearer as he continued. "I'm not going to Rochester to stay. I'm coming back to the big leagues. I promise."

"I know you will." She hesitated a moment. "Do you want me to tell your Mom and the family tonight that you are going to St. Louis, I mean Rochester?"

"Yes."

They continued to talk to one another about Timmy, their home, the family, and how much they missed one another. They said goodnight. It was a difficult phone call for both of them but this year they were so happy to be on the same side of the ocean and grateful that Danny was not dodging bullets and bombs.

***The Cubs extended their failure to win another World Series championship into 2015, increasing its gap of 107 years since its last appearance in the World Series. The last time the Cubs won the National League pennant was this pennant in 1945.**

1946, Hitting for the cycle

The 1946 season started out with a lot of excitement. Many top players in both leagues returned from the war*. Among them, Ted Williams, Joe DiMaggio, and Hank Greenberg were playing well in the first two months. Williams won AL batting titles in 1941 and 1942 before serving for three years in the Marine Corps. In 1946, he was on-track to challenge for his third batting title in a row.

But no one was playing as well as Mickey Vernon. Early in the season, he was hitting .405 and he was leading Williams in the batting race. On May 19, Mickey made everyone in the league take notice of his talent. He was in Comisky Park in Chicago and the Senators were winning 7-1 in the second game of a doubleheader.

The play by play radio announcer for the White Sox was trying to drum some life into the game for the hometown audience. "Both clubs have played a lot of baseball today." he observed. "The Sox won the first game 4-3 but they are trailing 7-1 here late in this second game of the doubleheader. I think many White Sox fans are hanging around until now just to see if the Senators first baseman, Mickey Vernon, will bat one last time in this game. Vernon can complete one of the rare feats in baseball. And whenever there is some baseball history to be made, baseball fans want to see it done. Even rival fans."

The announcer explained to the radio listener what the fuss was about. "Vernon has a chance to hit for the 'cycle'. It's seldom accomplished in baseball. Hitting for the cycle requires that the same batter hits a homerun, a triple, a double, and a single– all in the same game. Mickey has already hit the four most difficult ones. Now he needs a single to join the few players that have done it in the major leagues."

Down on the field, Mickey walked confidently to home plate, swinging his bat from side to side.

"OK, here he comes. I wonder if he might even be disappointed if he hit a home run instead of a single." What a conundrum."

Mickey stepped into the batter's box in front of the catcher and the umpire. He dug his cleats into the smooth dirt alongside home plate. Through habit, he shifted his shoes a few times, then he put his left hand out to signal to the umpire that he wasn't ready for the pitch. "Time out, ump. Just let me get my feet set."

"My time." Called out the umpire. The ump straightened up and stepped back from the catcher who was crouched in front of him. Mickey turned his shoes some more in the dirt, smoothed some of the surface dirt, and dug his cleats into the batter's box. The announcer began again to describe the action.

"OK. Vernon is set in the batter's box. He moves his hands up on his bat. The pitcher has his sign from the catcher; the catcher looks down at the runner on first base and shifts in his crouch; then he mumbles something to Mickey. The pitcher stretches. Here comes the pitch."

"Strike!" Bellowed the Umpire.

The ball zipped past Mickey. He didn't move. He heard the strike call and looked down at the catcher, then he lifted his head to look out towards right field, and finally he settled his eye on the pitcher. Mickey also noticed that the first baseman was playing off the bag and ready for anything that Mickey could hit to him. Everyone knew that Mickey was a line drive hitter and that he often hit the ball over the first base bag. But Mickey was ready too. He had already imagined where Stan Lopat's next pitch would be thrown.

The majority of the fans still in the stadium were White Sox fans but now many were rooting for Mickey to smack a dinky single of any kind. No one wanted another homerun or any other extra base hit. This at bat was a shot at history and the record books, a chance for players and fans alike to witness history. A single here made no difference in today's game at all. The single was for the glorious, glamorous, herculean baseball feat of hitting the 'cycle'. This task might be as hard for a batter to achieve as it is for a pitcher to throw a no-hit game. In the stadium and over the air waves, fans were in rapt attention. The announcer fiddled with his microphone and his words provided eyes for the listener.

"Well, Lopat slipped that first pitch in on him. Vernon let that one go. He looks calm and he seems to know where he wants the ball. He's had a career day with five hits in seven at bats including a home run and a single in the first game. Let's see if he can get the cycle. Hit or no hit, this at bat will empty the stadium. They've all stayed to see a piece of baseball history. Here's the one strike pitch to Vernon. It's on the plate. He swings."

Crack! The sound of the bat meeting the fastball made a loud noise that seemed to be heard only after the ball had already rocketed between the first and second basemen and landed in the outfield.

The Senators dugout and the whole stadium erupted in noisy celebration. Cheers and applause were bountiful.

"Holy cow!" were the announcer's first words when the ball landed. "There it is. It's in there for a single. Mickey Vernon did it! This is a lot of fun. I don't know what they fed him in the Navy for the last few years but he ought to send for plenty more. He's got the cycle. What a night! OK, well as I said, that will thin out the home crowd. The Senators now have men on first and second. Let's see if......"

***Many major league players served in uniform during the war. All of them were anxious to trade rifles and army helmets for Louisville Sluggers. Only two of these major leaguers didn't come home after 1945. Elmer J. Gideon died in France in 1944 and Harry O'Neill died on Iwo Jima in 1945. Sadly, more than 250 hopeful and promising minor league players were killed in the war. They left not only their families with a deep sense of loss but they left the game of baseball with a void of fresh talent that was never fulfilled.**

1946, Outhitting 'Teddy Ballgame'

As the 1946 season continued, Ted Williams' Red Sox opened a big lead in the American League pennant race while Mickey's Senators struggled to play .500 baseball. The Senators race for a pennant faded before mid-season but the race for the batting title remained close between these two tall left-handed hitters. At the All Star break in July, Mickey maintained a slight edge over Williams. The writers and fans noticed and Mickey was voted to his first All Star game. Immediately after the All Star break, Mickey caught fire and Williams faded. With only two weeks left in the season, Mickey appeared to be a lock to win, leading .354 over Williams' .343. One ballplayer who stepped up big to cool Williams off was Philadelphia A's outfielder Elmer Valo. Valo made five homerun-saving catches against Williams in a back-to-back six game series near the end of the season. Williams wasn't able to get back in the lead again before the season ended. Interestingly, the Red Sox and the Senators did meet in their final set of regular season games.

During pre-game warmups before the first of these games, Mickey walked over to watch Teddy hit in the batting cage at home plate. He leaned on his own bat and watched in awe as The Splendid Splinter finished his warmup swings. Williams noticed Mickey watching him in the cage and promptly drove two identical line drives to the same spot in right field. Ted turned his head and faced Mickey. "Looks like the batting title is yours, Mick."

"Well, there's still a week to go, Ted. Anything can happen."

Stepping out of the cage, Ted shook his head and said.
"Nah, it's over. You and I know it. You and Valo make a great team. You smash the ball around the diamond and he takes the air out of my hits. At least it wasn't a pitcher that doomed me. Enjoy the ride now. I'll get you next year." Mickey stepped into the cage and started stretching. Then he swung the bat a few times, and smiled. He was finally beginning to enjoy the ride. The rest would soon be history.

Mickey won the American League batting title. He hit .357, Williams hit .340. Mickey's other offensive statistics were just as impressive. He finished with 8 HRs, 8 triples, 51 doubles, 88 runs scored, and 85 runs batted in. His salary though wasn't impressive. He was paid $9,000.

1947 Danny is back on track

Baseball was also exciting again for Danny even though he was back in the minors. He gathered all his grit and focused on playing like he did before he went into the Army. His fear at the plate gradually slipped away. He prayed as always but he also knew that he had to help himself at the same time. So he worked hard on his timing, especially at batting practice and in the games. He re-conditioned himself to get past his fear of the ball and no longer feared the ball when he batted. The 1946 season at Rochester was a success. He batted 541 times and finished the season hitting .322. He added 11 stolen bases and 62 runs batted in. He was clearly one of the best fielding and hitting second baseman in the International League, possibly in all of the minor leagues. He even showed his talent for Managerial innovation when he filled in a few times for his Rochester Manager. In one game after the Manager was tossed in the second inning of a game, Danny took over the team. He coached third base and made eight player switches. Most interestingly, he used five pitchers in the game, and won. This was an early indication of his novel and strategic approach to handling his pitching staff. He knew that a team without two or three front-line pitchers needed to get its pitching from the entire staff and that meant using a number of different pitchers in a single game, ideally in the best situations. This was in an era when starting pitchers seldom left a game before the seventh inning, and usually not at all.

All of his success led to his contract being purchased from the Cardinals by the National League Boston Braves early in 1947. He was back in the majors just as he promised Kate that he would be.

The Murtaugh family's good fortune continued into the off-season when Kate delivered their second son, Danny, Jr., on February 2, 1947. Things were good. Danny was back on track in the major leagues and he was playing with a NL pennant contender, and new teammates like Earl Torgeson, Tommie Holmes, Johnny Sain, and Warren Spahn.

1947, Nobody is perfect!

The 1947 season started with great expectations for Mickey and Danny. Mickey was anxious to begin his pursuit of a second American League batting title and Danny was now a member of the National League pennant-contending Boston Braves and he was told to report to the Braves spring training camp. This would be his ticket back to the big leagues. He was excited for himself and his family. After all, the Boston Braves finished fourth in the National League in 1946 and they were anxious to begin their challenge for the NL pennant race. The Brave's infield positions were wide open for competition and Danny was coming off a successful year at Rochester.

Though he was always serious about his game, he was not prone to sitting alone in his room reading books and magazines. It was spring training and occasionally he and his roommate would drift to the horse races or a teammates-only card game. Sometimes he missed the team curfew.

One night in Florida, Danny and a teammate were out so late that they decided that the only way they could be back on-time for practice would be to go directly from the card game to the ball field. They wouldn't have time to go back to their room at all.

The next morning, shortly after players began arriving at the ball field, Braves Manager Billy Southworth walked onto the practice field. He passed players doing calisthenics and looked at his watch and then called over to the clubhouse boy. "Hey, Bats, as soon as Murtaugh shows up, tell him to come see me."

"Sure thing, Skipper."

Within a few minutes, Danny and his roommate arrived at practice. They were late but only a few minutes late. Bats told Danny that the Manager wanted to see him, so Danny placed his glove on his locker shelf and walked around to Billy's small office. The Manager was shuffling some papers across his desk.

"Good morning, Billy. Bats said you wanted to see me? I'm sorry that I was a little late this morning."

Billy Southworth was a baseball lifer who had experienced the trials and triumphs and the occasional bumps that ballplayers endure. He played sixteen years in the majors before becoming a very successful Manager. He won three pennants and two World Series with St. Louis, and another pennant with the Boston Braves. He was inducted into the Baseball Hall of Fame in 2008. Here in 1947, he was trying to prepare Danny Murtaugh and the Boston Braves for the new season and a run for the National League pennant.

Billy looked up at Danny. "I just wanted to see if you were OK, and how your night was. Did you sleep OK?"

Danny immediately felt wary. The skipper had never asked him, at any time, ever, 'how he felt'. He answered cautiously. "Yeh, fine. I always sleep well. I dropped off around midnight and never even stirred all night."

"Really?" The skipper replied, sounding surprised. "Slept like a baby, huh? Didn't wake at all?"

"No, not at all." Danny was beginning to feel nervous.

"Not even when that tractor-trailer crashed into your room after midnight?"

Looking startled and surprised, Danny half-yelled. "What? What tractor-trailer?"

During his many years around baseball, Billy Southworth had heard, hell, he was even guilty as a player of just about every excuse that a player could dream up in order to defend himself after getting caught missing curfew. Some excuses were dumb, some inventive, most were not worth repeating. Billy really wanted to hear what Danny would say in his own defense this morning. So he sat back smugly in his chair and told Danny what happened to Danny's motel room when he wasn't there.

"The one that lost control. The tractor-trailer that ran off the highway last night and wiped out your room and part of the pool's equipment shed next to your room. The tractor-trailer that would've killed you and your roomie if you fellas were in your room any time after curfew."

Danny was speechless. He blew out a rush of air and, blank-faced, he asked incredulously. "You're kidding, Billy."

"Nope. And I'm also not kidding that you are going to need a new room, and a few bucks to cover the fine for breaking curfew. Danny, you might also want to light one of your holy candles. You sure got lucky."

Fortunately, Billy had been Danny's first Manager in the minors in 1937 and he remembered and liked Danny as a person and as a player. During the rest of spring training, Danny never missed curfew and he worked harder than ever. He also continued to light candles at church whenever he could.

1947 A high-wire act

Later during the same spring training camp, Danny and the Braves travelled over to the Boston Red Sox training facility in Sarasota, Florida to play a pre-season game. The Red Sox had completed a nearly perfect season in 1946. Ted Williams returned from the war and finished runner-up to Mickey Vernon in hitting in the American League with a .342 batting average. He also added 38 home runs and 125 runs batted in. He won his first Most Valuable Player award and the Red Sox won the American League pennant with a record of 104-50. But a fairy tale ending was denied the Red Sox when St. Louis Cardinal's Enos Slaughter made a 'mad dash' in the eighth inning of the seventh game to score what became the winning run (4-3) that clinched the 1946 World Series for the Cardinals. This was the closest the Red Sox had come to winning a World Series since 1918 (led by star pitcher George 'Babe' Ruth). They would not win a World Series until 2004, having waited 86 years to do so. Certainly, the Red Sox were a team coming off the season with great disappointment but an even bigger desire to grab the title in 1947.

The NL pennant-contending Braves arrived at the Red Sox's summer camp at Payne Park baseball field in Sarasota and immediately began batting, fielding, and pitching practice prior to the game. The weather was warm and the fans began to arrive dressed in summer wear – light clothing, short sleeve shirts, shorts, tank tops, sneakers and sandals. Everyone wore a hat of varied configuration and color. Sunglasses were a new, popular accessory.

The game began with Red Sox starters Ted Williams, Bobby Doerr, Johnny Pesky and Dom DiMaggio playing in the early innings but as the game continued they were replaced by younger players who were anxious to show the Boston coaches what they could do on the playing field. Danny was not young any longer. He was 28 but he was as anxious as any young player on either team. He had been here in the big leagues in 1941-1943 and now he was trying to dig himself out of the minor leagues and back into the big leagues. He was in a more difficult situation than the rookies because he was 'older' with time working against him. Every at bat was critical to him especially here with the Braves who were a new team, Manager, and teammates for him.

He was playing well. The pre-season was tense for him but there were days when the players' moods on the field and in the clubhouse matched the sunny days and comfortable weather. That was the good feeling that was present this day in Payne Park. Danny knew most of the older ballplayers on both clubs and he was glad to be on a ball field in the sun and not tramping slowly through a German forest.

He was the next batter and he watched Red Sox pitcher Mel Parnell strike out one of the Braves' prized rookies. Danny stepped to the plate but stopped short when he heard a whistle and looked over to the Red Sox dugout. There was a friendly commotion in the first row of fans located just behind the player dugout and it only took a moment, and a lingering glance, to discover its source and appreciate the cause for the well-placed whistle.

Sitting in the front row next to the Red Sox dugout was an attractive young woman with long blonde hair wearing shorts and a pastel-colored halter top, a piece of provocative clothing that Hollywood bombshell Jane Russel might half-wear in a movie. Only this girl would make Jane look like a prim schoolgirl if she stood next to her. Danny learned later that Ginger was the name of this very noticeable woman in the exceptionally revealing halter top. It was difficult to see the top or remember the color once Ginger's scantily-covered bosom filled your line of vision. Of course, Danny was married but he wasn't blind.

The ball game was informally halted because the pitcher, catcher, and umpire were not in position to continue play. Everyone's wide eyes were fixed on Ginger. Professional and amateur photographers swiftly flooded into that section of the ballpark snapping pictures of her as she happily obliged the unplanned photo session. Danny was informed later that Ginger was a high-wire performer for one of the local circuses and she also happened to be a very big fan of Ted Williams, maybe even a casual friend.

It seemed no one in the ballpark remembered there was a baseball game to finish. Finally, Williams stepped to the dugout railing and Danny, after looking one more time at Ginger, yelled to him. "Ted, will you just look at her and smile or say something? That's why she's here. Maybe then we can play baseball."

Ted laughed and tipped his hat to Danny. That brought the umpire out of his trance and he called out loudly. "Play ball."

Danny's subsequent at bat was unremarkable, even forgettable, because he didn't remember anything about that game other than that Ginger wore a halter top. And that he might take the kids to the circus the next chance he got.

1947 Going north

Overall Danny's pre-season workouts were good enough for him to make the club and go north with the Boston Braves. It wasn't luck. Danny was displaying outstanding glove work and quick speed around the infield on defense and offense. His hitting was average and he was among the good infielders the Braves had at every position.

On April 15 Danny and the Boston Braves opened their season when they visited the Brooklyn Dodgers. Johnny Sain and the Braves took a 3-2 lead but the Dodgers came back to win 5-3. The winning run was scored by the Dodgers new first baseman, Jackie Robinson. It was Robinson's first major league game. He would play the entire 1947 season at first base. He didn't start playing second base for the Dodgers until 1948.

Bad news came swiftly for Danny. Six weeks into the season, he was told by Braves Manager Billy Southworth that he was being sent down to their AAA minor league club, the Milwaukee Brewers. This was more bad news for Danny because he was going in the wrong direction again and it was doubly disappointing because he was only twenty-eight days from having played five full years in the major leagues. An additional twenty-eight days with the Braves or any big league team would have qualified him for a pension at age fifty. He was greatly discouraged and feared that this baseball pension, the only long-term benefit from dedicating himself to the game, was slipping away from him.

1947, A reversal of fortunes

The Splendid Splinter was true to his promise. Ted Williams won the 1947 American League batting title. He hit .343. It was his third batting title between 1941 and 1947 and he didn't play for three years (1943-1945) when he was a Marine pilot during the war. Only Mickey's batting title in 1946 kept Teddy Ballplayer from capturing four batting titles in a row.

The 1947 season was above-average for Mickey but it wasn't as productive as his previous season. He was disappointed that his batting average dipped to .265. However, his run production for the Senators was steady. He scored 79 runs, drove in 85 runners, and hit 58 extra base hits including 12 triples. He also tacked on 49 walks. But it was less than what he hoped to accomplish after the previous year when he finished third in the American League MVP voting.

Further down baseball's food chain in the minor leagues, Danny completed another successful season. This time he showed his talents to the fans in Milwaukee who adopted him as their favorite player for his spirit and hustle. His name came up often in trade discussions between several big league teams, including the always-interested St. Louis Cardinals. Unfortunately for Danny, the Boston Braves executives wanted him to be available as insurance for their big league infielders. They were in the pennant race and they felt more comfortable with him in the minors. He played well at every infield position so if any one of the Boston infielders got injured, the Braves could move Danny up to the big leagues immediately. So he stayed in Milwaukee.

Frustrated at not being able to play where he belonged, Danny applied lessons and advice received from home, Chester High, and Legion ball. He put on his cap and his spikes and he played his best baseball. He led the Boston Braves farm team, the Milwaukee Brewers, to the minor league 'Little World Series'. He finished the 1947 season batting .302, scored 96 runs, drove in 49 runs, and logged a .988 fielding percentage at second base and shortstop. He was happy to be playing so well. He had now put together back-to-back highlight seasons in two very competitive top level minor leagues. Interestingly, a 1946 sports article in the Philadelphia Record signaled out both Danny and minor league infielder Jackie Robinson of the Montreal Alouettes for their overall performance in the International League. Robinson led the league in batting average and Danny finished a close second.

Danny expected that these two productive years in the high minors would result in a promotion to the Boston Braves. So he wasn't surprised when he was promoted to the big leagues, but instead of heading to Boston, he was traded to the Pittsburgh Pirates. That was a disappointment at first but he knew what was important to him and what was best for his family was that he was back in the big leagues again. Unknown to him, the perennial bottom-dwelling Pirates were putting together a team of veterans to compete for the 1948 pennant. Although they were not as glamorous nor as talented as the pennant-contending Boston Braves, they decided they were going to complete more aggressively. Not even Danny could foresee how pivotal the 1948 season would be to his baseball career. In a reversal of expectations, 1948 was a career-best year for Danny while Mickey suffered a rare and most forgettable batting slump, hitting only .242.

Fortunately, the record books and statistics were closed during the off-season. This allowed the two boyhood friends to enjoy their off-season months working out and training together. Their friendship and good natured kidding with one another kept them in good spirits and inured them from becoming either too disappointed or too elated with the previous year's performance. In fact, switching roles in hitting performances for this recently completed season brought them even closer. It was also ironic that in the short space of a week they both underwent an appendectomy in Chester Hospital. After a quick recovery, they renewed their training at the local YMCA in Chester, mostly playing handball.

Whenever the two of them stepped together onto the walled-in handball court, it always looked to be an unfair pairing as Mickey's tall, slender frame overshadowed Danny's slightly stocky and shorter physique. Seeing them simply standing in a room next to one another emphasized their height differential, and as opponents in a one-on-one sporting match, they looked like an obvious mismatch. But it wasn't. Though Mickey's size might give him an initial advantage in lateral and vertical range, Danny's hell-bent, gritty approach to winning at all costs quickly levelled the playing ground, and often-times gave him an edge. Danny also had an invisible weapon, he needled and jabbed at an opponent so much that it served as an effective distraction to the other player.

During one such match in the Chester YMCA, they were playing against each for an hour or so, taking water breaks in between games. In the middle of the last set, Danny missed a shot. "Ok. It's your serve, Mick." He said. "I'm still up on you."

No remark was ever left unchallenged when these two competed. Mickey replied. "Not for long. I'm gonna close this one out fast."

"OK. Maybe I'll let you have this set. I have to meet Kate anyway to sign some papers for the new house."

"A new house? Sounds like an excuse to me. You never mentioned it to me. Where's the house?"

Danny realized he hadn't told Mickey about it. That was only because Kate was handling all of the appointments and she was actually making the decision where they would live. After all, he was never home.

To close out the last game, Danny took his position behind Mickey and readied himself to return Mickey's serve. "It's on 12th and Kerlin Street in

Chester, just a few blocks above the high school and close to Crozier Park."

Slamming the ball off of the far wall, Mickey laughed then added. "Well as an early house-warming gift, I'll let you win this match." Danny attacked the ball and managed to speak as he grunted to hit the ball. "You and Lib should take a look, too. My sisters and my cousin are also buying houses there. The price is right."

The game continued as each player smacked the ball against the nearest wall hoping to put the ball in a position where the rebound couldn't be easily returned. The conversation continued but their sentences were strained and interrupted by the movement and effort required to play the game.

Mickey served the ball again and said. "You're spending your big league money before you get it, aren't you? You must be planning to set Pittsburgh on fire, Danny."

Danny reached for the ricocheting ball and while he was barely able to reach it, he managed to tap it off of his fingertips. The ball bounced weakly twice and it rolled along the floor.

Mickey picked up the ball and with a pause in the action, Danny said. "I am ready. It's time for me to set something on fire. I'm ready to get up there and to stay there. I don't have your hitting skills. But there's plenty I can do. I'd like to be set with a club anywhere. Pittsburgh is as good as any place for me now. I just want to be on the roster for at least twenty-eight days, enough to get the pension at 50 and be able to pay the mortgage on my new house every month."

While sharing his plan with Mickey, he was still able to slink back into a hitting position, then added. "Anyway, go get Lib and come look at the house. There's still a few more there."

"OK, maybe." Mickey relented. "But I feel like I should warn your new neighbors that so many Murtaughs are coming."

"Not all of them. Anyway, it's too late for the rest, but we'll make room for you. As long as you bring Lib."

They both struck the ball in turn as they continued to gasp through their conversation. Mick kidded Danny about living near him. "Hey, I know that you would welcome us but I'd never get a word in at the house parties. And I'd have to check my trash cans all of the time to make sure that they weren't all tied together. That's only the beginning. I'd never be safe from you and your practical jokes."

Now Mickey was distracted from the game and looking away from the wall with his arms down by his sides when Danny seized that opportunity to smack the ball quickly and hard. He caught Mickey unprepared and jokingly said loudly to Mick. "I'm hurt by those remarks."

Mickey swung off-balance at Danny's rebound and missed the ball. Danny elatedly called out. "There's my winner. You lose. I gotta go. Bye."

Of course Mickey missed the ball. He didn't have a chance on Danny's quick hit. Danny laughed and walked out through the single door along the white wall. He turned back and faced Mickey.

"By the way, Mick, I'm rooting for your Navy friend, Larry Doby. I saw the Indians got him and he looks like he can be around for a while. Though it's going to be rough, just like it was for Robinson."

"He'll be OK. I knew he belonged in the big leagues the first time I played with him in the islands during the war. That's why I told Mr. Griffith about him. I hoped that he'd get a chance to play in the big leagues."

"Yeh, well Mr. Rickey did a good thing for Robinson, a good thing for Larry, and for baseball, for all of us.'

Mickey bent over and picked up the hard rubber ball. He was remembering a day long ago. "Yep. It sure would be nice if Hank Miller was here too."

With that said, he slammed the ball against the wall, then he followed it, and smacked it again as though it was a bad guy in a gangster film. Danny and Mickey looked at one another and nodded. They were thinking the same thing. How 1937 seemed so long ago, and what was Hank Miller doing now?

1948, Danny and Jackie Robinson

Danny joined the Pittsburgh Pirates in spring training and was immediately inserted into the lineup as the starting second baseman and he played in 149 of 154 subsequent regular season games. He and the Pirates had a good, productive season. Late in September, Danny and the Pirates were playing the Brooklyn Dodgers at Ebbets Field, and with one out in the top of the fourth inning, they were leading the defending World Series champions 2-0. The Pirates and the Dodgers had competed all year with the Boston Braves for the NL pennant but now they were both finishing their season far behind the Braves. Nevertheless, these two teams were within a game of each other in the standings. Danny was having his best season and he would finish the season competing with Jackie Robinson and Stan Musial for the NL Most Valuable Player award.

Danny was batting and the count was three balls and one strike when the pitcher threw the next pitch to him. Danny gripped his bat but he didn't swing at the low and outside pitch. The umpire agreed with Mickey and called out in a loud voice. "Outside! Ball four. Take your base."

Danny tossed his bat onto the dirt and trotted slowly to first base. The Dodger's first baseman, Gil Hodges, greeted him as he stepped on the first base bag. "Don't even think about running, Danny. You're with the big boys now. Campy will rifle it to Robinson, and Jackie will tag you out. You're not in Milwaukee anymore."

Danny, never a person who left unspoken what was in his mind, said to Hodges. "There's three things that have to be perfect all at the same time. The throw, the catch and the tag. I like my chances."

Danny's speed and his aggressiveness on the base path warranted a few throws from the Dodger pitcher to Hodges who was playing close to Danny and the bag, trying to keep Danny from getting a big lead towards second base. Not surprising, on the first pitch to the batter. Danny took off running to steal second base. "He's going." Hodges shouted to Campanella, his catcher.

The batter swung at the pitch and missed it. Campanella caught the ball in his mitt and in one swift motion, he grabbed the ball out of his glove with his right hand and rifled it to second base. The ball arrived in Robinson's glove just as Danny's foot was sliding into a corner of the second base bag. The umpire was right there as Robinson applied the tag. "You're out!" The umpire shouted.

Danny was lying on the ground amidst a cloud of dust and he was spitting out dirt. He looked startled by the call.

"What? No! I'm safe!"
"You're out!" The umpire repeated and walked away.

Robinson pulled himself up after the tag and brushed off some loose dirt. He stood over Danny and looked down at him and smiled "You're out-voted, 2-1." Robinson tossed the ball to the pitcher, and signaled to the outfielders. "That's two outs."

Danny got up, brushed himself off, and headed back to his dugout. The next batter quickly lined out to left field. It was the third out. The game continued into the top half of the sixth inning and the Pirates had increased their lead to 3-0.

With a teammate already on first base and one out in the sixth inning, Danny singled. Now the Pirates had runners on first and second base. The next batter popped up and now there were two outs. Ralph Kiner, the Pirates all-time slugger, stepped into the batter's box. Danny crouched and took a short lead off first base. He was whistling loudly, trying to distract the pitcher. Whenever he reached base, this whistling habit of his could rattle a pitcher but it always annoyed the closest infielder near him. The Dodgers' first baseman Gil Hodges was no exception. "Yo! Danny. Save your energy. You sound like a birdman. You know you aren't going anywhere. Campy got you once. He'll get you again. Relax."

Smiling at Hodges and sneaking a step further off of the bag, Danny toyed with the big first baseman. "Well, if the whistle bothers you, maybe it will bother your pitcher some. The whistling makes Ralph mad too, and when Ralph gets mad, Boom! That ball will go a long way, maybe over the fence. Then I'm coming home in an easy trot around the bases."

The chatter ceased as the pitcher toed the rubber, looked over to first base, and focused back on Kiner. He gripped the ball and threw a pitch. The ball closed in tight towards Kiner's waist, but then it seemed to slow and settle out over the plate. That wasn't a good thing. *Whack!* The ball shot back rising over the infield, into the outfield, and moved much faster and higher away from home plate than when it arrived there. The ball stayed airborne until it landed in the left field stands. The score was suddenly Pittsburgh 5, the Dodgers 0.

Running toward second base, Danny looked back over his shoulder at Hodges and called out. "That's why I whistle." When Danny approached second base, he looked over at Robinson who was standing a few feet away from the second base bag. He couldn't resist needling his opposing second baseman. "Jackie, winning this game will pull our clubs even. You guys won't get any closer to the series this year." Robinson didn't say a word and he waited motionless for Kiner to trot past him too.

The score remained 5-0 in the bottom of the eighth inning. The Pirates starter Rip Sewell was still pitching. The Dodgers were making a move and they had runners on first and second base after a single, an out, and a walk to Jackie Robinson. Stan Rojek, the shortstop half of the Pirates' league-leading double play duo, turned to his infield mate at second base and said. "OK. Danny let's get two here." Danny answered him confidently. "Yep. Turning two is just what the doctor orders now. Let's keep Rip in the game."

A few outside pitches set up the next ball that rode inside and the batter hit the ball to shortstop. Rojek fielded the ball quickly and tossed it to Danny who covered the second base bag. Danny stepped on the bag, forcing the sliding Robinson out, and rifled the ball to Kiner at first base. It was a double play. The inning and the Dodger threat was over. It was Danny's turn now. After completing his throw to Kiner, he looked down at Robinson who was sprawled in the dirt. Smiling, Danny said. "Jackie, even us rabbits get caught sometimes."

The Pirates won the game 5-1. Danny finished the game with a single, a walk, and 5 putouts, 4 assists and that double play in the eighth. The Pirates finished the 1948 season with a respectful number of wins, 83. The Dodgers won 84 games but it was a disappointment for them after winning the pennant in 1947. The Dodgers would rebound and win the NL pennant again in 1949. The Pirates will take a lot longer.

Among the best

No one felt better after the season ended in October 1948 than Danny. Well, maybe Kate. She was happy for him and she knew he was relieved to add more than the twenty-eight days he needed to qualify for the baseball pension. Danny capped his dream-like season by finishing ninth in balloting for NL Most Valuable Player. Hall of Fame outfielder Stan Musial won the NL MVP award and just missed winning the triple-crown. Danny was envious. He was the highest rated defensive second baseman in the National League and he would've placed higher in MVP voting if Pittsburgh didn't have three players finish among the top ten vote-getters, depriving any one of them of the votes needed to finish first. Danny placed just behind Hall of Fame slugger, Ralph Kiner, and two places ahead of yet another Hall of Famer, Jackie Robinson.

Danny's career-best year wasn't matched by Mickey. In the 1948 season Mickey struggled. His batting average dropped to a career low .242. His offensive numbers fell off and he hit only three home runs and drove in only forty-eight runners. It was another season to forget; he would rest and prepare for next year.

However, the most momentous and solemn day of the 1948 baseball season occurred for all baseball fans on August 16, 1948. Neither Danny nor Mickey played a game that day. The Pittsburgh Pirates played the Cincinnati Reds at Forbes Field but Danny sat out the game because he played in a doubleheader the day before against the St. Louis Cardinals. Mickey and the Washington Senators had that Monday off.

This was the day that baseball fans and a large part of the nation cried. Babe Ruth died. The great Bambino, the Sultan of Swat, was 53 years old. He had been diagnosed and treated for cancer since 1947. The Babe, as he was affectionately known throughout his legendary career, was largely responsible for resurrecting professional baseball from the quagmire that it was in after the Chicago Black Sox Scandal in 1916. As a consequence of that gambling scandal, baseball was under fire and fans were disillusioned and unhappy with the professional game. Babe Ruth, first as an outstanding pitcher, then as baseball's first pure homerun slugger, brought electricity to the game and excitement to the fans for twenty plus years. His talent and personality helped to build, and paid for, Yankee Stadium and saved professional baseball. Babe Ruth was laid in state for public viewing in Yankee Stadium, the House that Ruth Built. More than 100,000 mourners walked onto the field and said goodbye. A more formal farewell was held on August 18 with a funeral Mass in St. Patrick

Cathedral on Fifth Avenue in Manhattan. The Golden Era of Baseball was coming to a close.

---

*Babe Ruth hit his final homeruns in Forbes Field on May 25, 1935. He hit three homeruns that game, No. 712,713,714. He was forty years old when he retired from baseball several days later.

1948, the Chicken Circuit

The months following the 1948 baseball season were exciting for Danny. He had worked a long time for this success and he was riding high on all of the acclamation that he received after completing his most productive season in the big leagues. As always he and Mickey were in demand for local banquets; many times sharing equal billing at the head table for sports and social gatherings, and for business and community luncheon meetings. They were a perfectly matched pair like the popular comedy team of that era, Bob Hope and Bing Crosby. There was no question who got to play the serious, good-looking half of the team, and who collected all the laughs.

Danny's stellar season was particularly helpful in attracting even larger audiences at the banquets. His success benefited Mickey because Danny received more attention and that enabled Mickey to speak less about a second poor year where his hitting was far below his career average. However, these back to back below-average years were feeding the rumor mill that Mickey would be traded. Mickey readily accepted disappointment after a single bad game at the ballpark, but he was unaccustomed with the difficulty of handling an entire year of bad games. This off-season was less comfortable than all the previous ones. Only his friendship with Danny and his friend's success lightened his mood.

Nevertheless, it wasn't surprising that shortly after the season, Mickey was traded to the world champion Cleveland Indians whose owners ironically enough included the same entertainers mentioned earlier, Bob Hope and Bing Crosby. Amazingly, after his worst statistical season, Mickey went from a last-place team to the current world champion Indians who defeated the Boston Braves in the 1948 World Series. He was also reunited with his wartime Navy teammate, former Negro League star, Larry Doby. In July 1947 just a few months after Jackie Robinson took the field with the Brooklyn Dodgers, Doby became the first black ballplayer to play in the American League. Mickey who played with Doby during the war congratulated him when he first came up to the Indians. When Doby told Mickey that he was called up so quickly to the big leagues that he didn't have enough equipment, Mickey immediately sent him a dozen of his own Mickey Vernon Louisville Sluggers. That was a kind gesture by Mickey and this was to be a memorable reunion for both players. Doby would go on to play fourteen seasons in the AL, star in two World Series, and be voted into seven all-star games. He hit 32 homeruns, and drove home 126 runs to lead the Indians to 111 wins and another spot in the World Series in 1954. Larry Doby later joined Jackie Robinson in the Baseball Hall of Fame.

Cleveland also added Satchel Paige to the team. Many writers and fans said at the time that it was a publicity stunt to add Paige to the majors. After all, Paige who was a former Negro League star player, was 40 years old (possibly older). The complaint that it was a publicity stunt was dismissed when Paige's addition to the team was parlayed into Cleveland's advantage as he won six games against one loss in only twenty-one appearances and pitched effectively in the 1948 World Series.

1949, It's a funny game

Baseball has many axioms that describe events in the game or some of its quirks. It is often expressed that 'baseball is a funny game'. It can be funny in a comical sense but this axiom refers to funny in the sense that strange things happen in baseball: in a single game, in a season, to a single player, to a team. This axiom describes a few not so funny things that happened to Danny and Mickey in the following season. Danny followed his best year in baseball with his worst year in baseball, and Mickey regained his status as a leading hitter with his new club, the Cleveland Indians but he didn't lead them into a World Series.

There are a few other old adages that may explain the turn of events that Danny experienced in 1949. One adage has to do with physical health: "You can't be good when you don't feel good". The second adage addresses mental and emotional stresses imposed by new success: 'That was yesterday. What are you doing for me today?' So a combination of injuries, and heightened expectations to repeat the previous year's performance combined to short-circuit Danny's 1949 campaign when slumped to hit .203 and appeared in only 75 games. The only good thing that happened for Danny in 1949 occurred on George Washington's birthday, February 22. A gorgeous baby girl, Kathy, was born. More importantly, there was no baseball distractions in February so Danny was home with Kate, Timmy 6, Danny 3, when his little girl came home from the hospital.

In the other league, Mickey was back in his hitting zone. He provided productive run support for the Indians. He hit a solid .292 and added 18 homeruns and 83 runs batted in. However, the Indians failed to repeat as World Series Champions and placed third in the AL behind the Yankees. Mickey put his talents on display to a larger share of the baseball world and for the first time he got close enough to smell the roses and almost feel the World Series ring sliding on his finger. But close is never good enough. He'd have to wait for next year. He came home after the season and got a new job during the holidays. He sold children toys at Gimbel's department store in center city Philadelphia and sometimes he pretended that he was giving the toys to the children for free. He smiled a lot but he knew he wasn't Santa Claus. Actually, he was a victim of Hollywood-style 'type-casting'. He was just too tall and too thin to play Santa Claus, and besides that, isn't Santa Clause right-handed?

Danny and Mickey, Ordinary Heroes

June, 1950, Korea

The 1950 season began quietly but the rumors of war were heard in the international news. The trouble this time centered far away in Korea, a country in the midst of a civil war, located near Japan and sharing a land border with China. Most Americans had never heard of Korea before 1950 and wouldn't know whether to look east or west.

Mickey's second year with Cleveland in 1950 began badly. He batted below .200 for the first time in his career and after playing in only twenty-eight games, he was replaced at first base by Luke Easter, a power hitting first baseman who had been hitting homeruns regularly out of ballparks in both the Negro League and in the minor leagues. Soon thereafter, Mickey was traded back to Washington. He played the remaining ninety games at Washington and recovered his hitting stroke and batted .306, adding twenty-nine extra base hits and driving in 65 runs. Meanwhile, Cleveland won more games than the previous year, 92, but it still wasn't enough to win the AL pennant. They finished in fourth place and Washington placed fifth. Within five years, Luke Easter would be back in the minor leagues and he would be on the same team with Danny Murtaugh.

On June 25, despite the US government's expectations to the contrary, communist-ruled North Korea invaded South Korea. Within two days, US troops, acting under the United Nations charter to thwart military aggression, landed in South Korea to halt the North Korean advance. Thus, America and the baseball community were impacted again by war. The impact would not be as severe as 1941–1945. Nevertheless, it will severely affect many ballplayers and other men and women who were called to participate in this conflict that was referred to as a 'police action'. Included among the men and women who were called to arms were baseball slugger Ted Williams and Danny's brother-in-law, Captain Dale Benny Wilson.

CHAPTER TEN
HITS AND MISSES

August 1950, Beaned

Danny was glad to see the 1949 season end. Now the 1950 season was unfolding just as he had hoped that it would. By the end of August, he was hitting .294 in 110 games. These numbers were even better than his numbers in his MVP-rated year in 1948. He was attracting attention again from executives of the pennant-contending ball clubs in both leagues. They saw Danny as a valuable player to acquire who could improve their chances of winning a pennant. He was playing at the top of his game and he knew that continuing to play well through this last month would set him up with an opportunity to be traded to a pennant contender, if not now, then certainly in 1951. Baseball was fun again.

On August 30, the Pittsburgh Pirates were playing the New York Giants at Forbes Field in Pittsburgh. The game was in the bottom of the fifth inning and the Giants with Sal Maglie pitching were leading 2-0. Maglie was pitching his normally aggressive game and the Pirates had managed only two hits so far. Danny was the lead-off hitter in this inning. He had walked in the second inning but was left stranded on first base so he was sure that Maglie didn't want to walk him again and that meant the pitcher would throw him strikes. He was focusing really well at home plate this year. Just three nights earlier he drove in six runs with a double and a homerun against the Braves. Like he said to himself a lot this year 'baseball was fun again' and he wanted to continue playing forever, or right up to the moment the clubhouse Manager came to take his uniform from him. He was where he always wanted to be. His life couldn't be any better. How could one guy be so lucky?

Danny stepped to home plate and began to dig his spikes in the dirt in the batter's box that was outlined in lime chalk. One of the Pirates players in the dugout called over to him to get a hit or a walk, anything that will get him on base and start a Pittsburgh rally. The crowd noise rose higher as fan cheers increased throughout the stadium and excitement filled the ballpark. The Pirates were playing competitive baseball.

Danny was now set in his batting stance and the catcher and the umpire were in their positions crouched behind him. He heard a loud authoritative voice come from his dugout. "C'mon Danny. Let's get on base. A hit or a walk sets up the inning." It was the Pirates Manager cheering Danny on in his bid to get on base.

Maglie was also ready on the mound. He cradled the ball in his glove and looked into his catcher who used a hand signal to tell the pitcher what type pitch to throw. Maglie didn't agree with the catcher's selection so he shook off his catcher and waited for a signal that agreed with the pitch he wanted to throw. The catcher went through the pitching signals a second time. Maglie got the sign he wanted and nodded his head affirmatively to the catcher. He went quickly into his windup and threw a pitch to Danny. The ball moved at 85 miles per hour and it was meant to drive Danny away from the plate. Before Danny could fully react, the ball was in on him, high and inside. Very high. He tried to turn away from the ball and let it go by him. But it didn't go by him. *Whapp!* He was hit on the left side of the head and fell instantly to the ground. With Danny lying face down beside home plate, the loud, noisy stadium became suddenly and eerily silent.

The catcher and the ump were the first ones to reach out to him. Danny was on his stomach but his face was turned slightly sideways so they could see that his eyes were closed. He wasn't making a sound. He was unconscious. Those close to him decided at that moment not to move him at all until a doctor or medically-trained person could determine if it was safe to do so. The hush that fell over the entire stadium was ominous. After a long stillness, players and officials started running towards home plate to assist the fallen player.

Out on the pitcher's mound, Sal Maglie and his teammates were huddling and staring solemnly at Danny's limp body. Just like everyone in the stadium, they were worrisome and stunned. As the minutes continued to stretch out longer and longer, the only sound heard throughout the stadium was an ambulance's siren approaching the ballpark.

"You'll have to tell him yourself."

Danny was transported to a local hospital and placed under medical care and observation. A few days later, he lay asleep in a hospital bed, his head propped up gingerly on several pillows. The lights in the room were dimmed and Kate and the attending physician were standing at the foot of his bed speaking in hushed tones. The doctor assured Kate that Danny was making good progress. His headaches were less severe and there appeared to be no long-term damage to his eyesight. His reactions were, of course, slower than normal but the doctor expected that they would return to normal in good time. Kate was relieved and asked her most important questions. "Is he out of danger? When can he come home?" She told the doctor, "He is already asking me if he can go home? And when can he play ball?'

The doctor was prepared for all of these questions. He knew that once a patient began to feel better, they often believed that they were ready to return to a normal routine. However, it was seldom true a person could resume their daily tasks immediately. But it was definitely not true when that patient's normal routine was to stand 90 feet away from a pitcher who is throwing the ball towards him at 80-90 miles per hour.

"Mrs. Murtaugh, not soon is the same answer to all those questions. He'll be in here for at least a few more days, maybe another week. I want to limit his physical and mental exercise and keep him under careful watch. The best place for me to be able to monitor him is here in the hospital. So he's not going anywhere just yet."

Kate expected the doctor's response but she knew that Danny wasn't going to accept it from her. "Can you please tell him? He thinks he's going home soon. He thinks he'll play ball soon."

"He has to realize that he was hit in the left side of his brain with a solid ball, like a rock, weighing 5¼ ounces, thrown from 90 feet away, and moving at 80-90 miles per hour. He's lucky to be conscious. He's even lucky to be alive. I don't want to sound dictatorial but he's my patient. It's September. He should put his spikes away until next year. I'm not releasing him to play any more baseball this year."

Kate looked resolutely at him and said. "You'll have to tell him yourself."

1951, Pirates spring training

The months following the end of the 1950 baseball season and those at the beginning of 1951 were filled with alarming news of the growing conflict in Korea. The increasing numbers of American and North Korean troops (now supported by Chinese troops) battling each other overshadowed other national and international news.

Nevertheless, winter thawed into early spring and baseball news began to fill newsreels and newspapers. Mickey was back in spring training with Washington and ready to re-gain his status as an all-star player. After spending the off-season recovering from his serious head injury, Danny was at spring training with the Pirates. He wasn't aware while he was digging out ground balls and taking extra batting practice, that his future was being discussed between the Pirates Manager Billy Meyer and Branch Rickey who had just taken over as General Manager for the Pirates.

Rickey was sitting in a dugout in Florida and finishing a conversation with Pirates Manager Billy Meyer. They were discussing their individual evaluation of Danny and his readiness to return to the lineup after the beaning in August. Branch Rickey always opened the discussions on any subject by asking the other party a question. This time he didn't agree with the answer that the Manager had just given him.

"Hell, Billy, he deserves a shot at his spot in the lineup. Damn, he even came back and played in a few games before last season ended."

"I know. I know. I was there." Meyer said. "It's your call, Branch. But you have to have another second baseman ready to play for us, and ready to play a lot. Murtaugh is 33 and he's our oldest position player. That beaning is a hard thing for anyone to come back from so soon."

Rickey conceded the Manager's point, understanding that the bottom line in any sport is to win. "I don't want to push him too hard. I don't want him hurt. And I agree that he still has to hit. Did you talk to Danny about wearing a protective batting helmet?"

"I did. But he doesn't want to wear one. None of our guys want to wear them. No one is going to wear them until the league makes helmets mandatory. All of the players think that it will hurt their hitting."

"Damn it!" Rickey yelled. "A helmet may save their lives! I've been trying to make them mandatory for thirty years now, ever since Roy Chapman* was hit in 1920. These pitchers throw harder now every year and it's going to get more dangerous for batters every year. Someday pitchers will throw the ball 100 miles an hour."

"I don't think so, Branch. But, OK. I'll ask Danny again to wear one. Either way, I'll see that he gets his fair shot in the lineup. I know he's earned it." There, it was agreed. Danny was to remain the starting second baseman in spring training and into the regular season.

After Rickey left the dugout, Meyer thought a little more about Rickey's insistence on a batting helmet. Meyer didn't like the batting helmet idea but he could see that pitchers were becoming faster and the movement of the ball was more deceptive than ever before. There just might be some value in batting helmets. Either way, Rickey was the boss and he would talk to Danny again about the helmet. Right away.

***Roy Chapman was struck in the head by a pitched ball and died in 1920. Protective head gear was recommended in almost every year since 1920. Finally in 1952, the Pittsburgh Pirates became the first MLB club to mandate that their players wear batting helmets.[2] The helmet was mandated by Pittsburgh General Manager Branch Rickey. It was created by Charlie Muse and was based on the hard hats used by coal miners. The Pirates began the season wearing protective helmets both at bat and in the field. After two months, the helmets were worn only while batting.**
Also, Rickey was correct. The pitchers threw faster every year. Major League Baseball ruled in 1971 that batting helmets must be worn at home plate by all players. At the time this book was written, it is common to see pitchers throwing between 95-101 miles per hour.

1951, Wrigley Field

On May 25, the Pirates were playing the Chicago Cubs in Wrigley Field. The game was in the fourth inning and there was a Pirate runner on base and two outs. The Pirates had just taken a 2-1 lead on Ralph Kiner's lead-off homerun in the inning and Danny was back in his familiar position at second base and he was now in the batter's box. Billy Meyer the Pirates Manager stood on the top step of the dugout and directed some baseball chatter to Danny.

"Ok, Danny. Let's get a hit here."

Danny swung at the first pitch and singled to left field. That hit placed Pirate runners at first and second base. When Danny arrived at first base, and after the ball was returned to the pitcher, the Chicago first baseman who had played with Danny in Milwaukee, nodded and smiled, then he kidded Danny. "Nice hit, old man."

"Yeh. Thanks, kid. But I need a lot more than that one. Maybe this one will start an avalanche for me."

Then the former teammate tapped Danny on the leg with his glove before stepping back in the infield to prepare for a batted ball. "Good luck with that. Right now I don't want you to go any farther than first base."

The first baseman was right. The next Pirate batter hit a fly ball to left field. It was the third out. Danny's single was one of his rare hits that year and the hit put his average just above .200. He was still having difficulty staying in the batter's box on pitches that would rise up and inside on him. He was only two months into the season but it already seemed like it was a long year.

June 1, 1951, Redemption

The Pirates moved on to play the New York Giants at the Polo Grounds in New York, Normally, a game such as this one between two teams this early in the season wouldn't generate much attention but every person here in the Polo Grounds and every person at home listening on the radio was focused on the pitcher/batter matchup that was taking place right now.

Giants' pitcher Sal Maglie and Danny were opposing each other for the first time since Maglie hit Murtaugh in the head the previous August. Maglie completed his warmup pitches, and Danny, batting leadoff for the Pirates, stepped into the batter's box. Both players appeared to be nervous. There was tension all around the ballpark as everyone waited for the first pitch to be thrown by Maglie, and the tension was also being carried through the radio into thousands of baseball fans' homes. The Pirates radio announcer relayed the scene and action.

"Fans, I've got to believe that these two ball players down on the field facing one another are both nervous. I can feel the tension all of the way up here in the broadcast booth. Murtaugh is having a rough start this season. He is hitting .200 and has been unsettled at home plate since spring training. Sal on the other hand is picking up where he left off last year, pitching some of the best baseball in the National League. And he is as aggressive as ever."

This first at-bat between them was uneventful. Danny hit a ball fairly deep to left field but it was caught for the first out of the game. The next two Pirate batters made outs very quickly. The Giants hurried off of the field to take their initial turn at bat in their half of the inning.

After three innings, the Giants had made good use of their batting opportunities and they led the Pirates, 4-0. The game settled into a lazy tempo of a not-so-interesting contest. But in the top of the fifth inning the stadium crowd once again turned its focus back on the featured matchup between Danny and Sal Maglie. Danny was scheduled to bat first again. Standing in the on-deck circle, he watched Maglie take his pre-inning warmup pitches. When Maglie was finished, the umpire signaled to Danny and he walked to home plate. Danny was more relaxed than he was in the first inning. He was still nervous but his baseball persona had taken over as it usually did once his body blended in with the flow of a game. That's why he loved baseball. He was always relaxed once the game began.

He nodded at the umpire and took his place in the box. Out on the mound, Maglie stepped onto the rubber strip on the pitcher's mound. He held the ball in his hand and positioned his fingers on the ball. He brought his arms together over his head where he joined his free hand with his gloved hand and proceeded to complete his windup and throw a pitch to home plate. Danny saw the ball speed its way toward him. He kept his eye on it and he swung and made contact with the ball. It headed out towards left centerfield in the same direction as the ball he hit in the first inning. Except this time it rose higher and kept going back, back, and back until it was over the wall and the out of the reach of the Giants rookie center fielder, Willie Mays.

The Pirates bench and the crowd erupted into a torrent of yelling and cheering. A few Pirates leaped onto the field in front of their dugout. "Way to go Danny boy! Holy shit! That's showing him." They shouted. The significance of the homerun wasn't lost on anyone in the ballpark and it was just as exciting for the fans listening at home on the radio.

Danny rounded the bases in a modest trot. He felt the New York crowds' energy and he appreciated it. As he rounded third base, Maglie stepped off of the mound with his head down. Then he took a quick look as Danny crossed home plate before he stepped back onto the pitching rubber.

Danny finished the game with one hit in four plate appearances. The Pirates lost 8-2 and Sal Maglie went on to win 23 games in 1951 and pitch in the World Series. It was Danny's only homerun of the season and his last in the major leagues.

Danny continued to struggle at home plate throughout the remainder of the '51 season. His hitting never improved and he finished with a .199 batting average. The Pirates released him after the season ended. Danny was out of major league baseball. He was going to need a job and he was too old to start again in the shipyard.

November 1951, Marcus Hook

Mickey's reunion with Washington in 1951 was the right medicine for him. He hit .293 and drove in 87 runs. The Senators lost 92 games but they didn't finish last. The even sadder St. Louis Browns (52-102) claimed that spot.

Now 34, Mickey decided that he and Lib needed to have their own home. They bought a house in Wallingford, a rural area west of Chester city and not far from Lib's parents' home in Leiperville. It was their first house and even more exciting, it was a home all to themselves. At last, Mickey won't have to listen any longer to Danny telling him to spend his all-star money for a house of their own where Mickey and Libby could snuggle without asking her parents for permission each time. Danny was convinced that was the reason he and Kate had three children and Mickey and Lib had none. Danny swore the difference was directly related to sharing a home with your in-laws. Like most things in life, Danny felt that only time would tell.

Whether he was living in Leiperville, Wallingford, or Washington, DC, Mickey's heart was always closest to Marcus Hook. After every season Mickey would come back to visit his boyhood friends and family in his old neighborhood on Green Street. The house that he grew up in sat only a few blocks from the massive Sun Oil refinery and just a few blocks away from the Marcus Hook Elementary school on Market Street. Today a bronze likeness of Mickey taking his classic left-hander's swing at an unseen baseball stands in front of the school and a few yards away is the entrance to the Mickey Vernon Athletic Complex. The youth baseball league that plays there was named in Mickey's honor in 1955. It was the first baseball league to be named to honor a major league baseball player.

On occasion, both Mickey and Danny would gather new or hardly-used baseball equipment from their respective teams' clubhouse and bring it home. One summer day while home in Marcus Hook for a short visit, Mickey passed a group of boys in his old neighborhood playing on a ball field just down the street from the house where he grew up. He watched the sandlot game for a while, then he left, saying that he'd return soon. He went home and loaded his car with slightly used gloves, bats and balls and brought them back to the ballfield and gave them to the boys. Ironically, in that same week Danny made the same type of visit and donation to boys in his old neighborhood in Chester. When Danny was informed about this coincidence, he just brushed it off and said that it was just 'two great minds thinking alike.' They were a natural pair that fit nicely together. Kinda like 'peanuts and cracker jacks', and 'baseball and kids.'

1952 Ted Williams

In 1952, baseball was 'King' again. Wins and losses, homeruns and batting averages, these all mattered to Americans again. Everyone was trying to put the difficult war years of pain and loss behind them.

Unfortunately, the United Nations' 'police action' in Korea that began in June 1950 in Korea had escalated into a full-scale war. The Korean War, as it was later called, became a larger conflict that mainly pitted the United States and China against each other as the US supported South Korea and China supported communist North Korea. Expectantly, the war adversely affected the entire United States and that included baseball. American military reservists were called back into armed service to support the need for the increasing number of troops going to the battlefields in Korea. Professional ballplayers were also called to serve but not in the same large numbers that were required during 1942-1945.

After playing in only six games through May 1952, Ted Williams was one of the ball players called to active duty with the Marine Air Corps, a branch of the US Navy. In his sixth and last game before he reported to active duty, he slammed a homerun to win the game. Fifteen months later and after flying in 35 combat missions in Korea, he returned to the Red Sox in August 1953. In his first game back from Korea, he hit a homerun in the eighth inning.

In the 37 games that he played in 1953 when he returned from Korea, Williams batted 110 times. Not surprising to his fans, he finished with 13 homeruns, 34 RBIs and a batting average at .407. Unfortunately, he didn't have enough appearances at the plate to qualify for the batting title. In all, Ted Williams' record-making baseball career was shortened by nearly five full years because of his service in two wars. The good news for Williams was that he survived both wars and he lived to enjoy fishing and baseball until he died at eighty-three years old.

Tris Speaker

The 1952 baseball season for Mickey began like most of those in the previous thirteen years. Washington Senators owner Clark Griffith always started every negotiation by telling Mickey that he would have to take a cut in his contract. Mickey and Mr. Griffith squabbled every year over the owner's offer. In the end, Mickey settled for either the same or very little more than what he was paid in the previous year. Sometimes he was even paid less than the previous year. In 1952, Mickey was paid $21,000 , the same amount that he was paid in 1951.

Spring training in 1952 was notable because it presented an opportunity for Mickey to meet Hall of Fame outfielder, Tris Speaker. Speaker who played most of career with the Boston Red Sox and the Cleveland Indians visited the Senators camp and spent some time discussing the art of hitting with Mickey and others. It was a subject that Speaker was qualified to speak about because he finished his career with a .345 batting average and smacked 792 doubles, still a MLB record. So, even at thirty-four years old, Mickey knew that it was never too late to learn something, especially from a baseball legend like Tris Speaker.

One morning at spring training, the baseball fates aligned. The sun was rising over the pristine baseball diamond and a familiar scent of freshly mowed grass floated on the light morning breeze as the clubhouse attendant approached Mickey who was sitting in the dugout tightening the webbing on his first baseman's mitt.

"Hey! Mickey, Tris Speaker is looking for you. He's over at the batting cage." Mickey looked out onto the field. "OK. I see him." Then he walked to the batting cage where the Hall of Fame centerfielder was handling an old Louisville slugger.

"Good morning, Tris. Are you ready to give me some of your hitting secrets? Maybe your tips will help me get into the Hall of Fame someday."

Even at sixty-five years old, Speaker still made an impression on the young ballplayers who gathered around him. He was nearly six foot tall and he hadn't strayed too far away from the long, lean look of a tall Texan that he actually was. He greeted Mickey with that wide-open welcome that made you suspect that you knew him from someplace else before you ever met him for the first time. "Well, Mick, I've been thinking some since our talk yesterday. Seeing as you are getting to be my age, I thought it might be a good time for you to try a lighter bat." He laughed but Mickey winced.
"Thirty-four ain't old," Speaker continued, "but it ain't twenty-five either. A lighter bat, same length, will let you get around like you were twenty-five again. Wanna try it? It's like putting a lift in your shoe when your leg bones start to shrink."

Mickey laughed this time. "Sure. I'll try it. Using a lighter bat, that is, not the shoe lifts." Pausing a bit, he added. "I've always used a 35 ounce bat but I guess using a lighter bat makes sense. I just don't want to get out too far in front of the ball." Tris agreed with Mickey's concern. He knew all ballplayers were creatures of habit and routine. They were nervous about any change with their batting style and equipment. "That's right. But you aren't going to change your swing or your stance. Here, just swing this bat and get the feel of it. With just a little less weight, you'll pick up your original bat speed again."

Tris placed the Louisville slugger in Mickey's hand. Mickey held it separately in each hand, then gripped it with both hands and took a swing at a phantom ball.
"OK. As long as it worked for you, I'll try it."

"Whoa! Hey, wait a minute, Mick". Speaker said, "Worked for me? Hell, I never tried it. But then I never hit below .300." He smiled at Mickey and added. "You don't change nothing when everything is working." Then he handed Mickey another bat and said. "Here's an even lighter bat. Let's get started."

*The Korean War ended when an armistice (peace treaty) was signed in July, 1953 at Panmunjon, Korea on the border between the newly established nations of North and South Korea.**

*Ted Williams received the highest salary in 1952, $85,000. Stan Musial $80,000, Jackie Robinson $42,000, Yogi Berra $33,000, Willie Mays and Mickey Mantle, $7,500 each. Tris Speaker's highest salary was $25,000 in 1921.**

1952, Branch Rickey's plan for Pittsburgh

Danny's playing career was over. He never got comfortable at the plate during the entire 1951 season. Now, aged 36, his body, especially his legs, had slowed down considerably. His spirit was still fiery and competitive, but neither his speed nor his physical energy were readily available every day.

The Pirates new General Manager, Branch Rickey, was very familiar with Danny's relentless nature and perseverance. Rickey was aware of Danny's success in the St. Louis Cardinals farm system that Rickey first organized when Rickey was General Manager for the Cardinals. He also remembered Danny's role as the leader and spark plug for the Cardinal's minor league Milwaukee Brewers when they won the Little World Series in 1947. He had been watching Danny for a long time. At one point just in the past season he considered having Danny replace Billy Meyer as the Pirates Player/Manager but he decided that Danny needed some managing experience. Mostly, he didn't think it would help Danny to be suddenly responsible for all his teammates when he might find himself in the middle of his own batting slump.

The 1951 campaign was over and it was all old history now. Rickey wanted to talk with Danny about his future in baseball. That was the purpose for inviting Danny to meet with him today in Rickey's office at Forbes Field.

Danny arrived early and spent a small amount of time talking with Pirate employees and groundskeepers before walking upstairs to meet with the General Manager.

Knocking on the slightly open door, Danny poked his head around the door. "Mr. Rickey. Am I too early for our meeting?"

"No. Not at all." Rickey bellowed, and motioned to a chair. "Pull up a chair. Danny. I want to talk to you about a job. I know you can help the both of us, and the Pirates, too."

Danny moved into the room and sat in a chair directly opposite Mr. Rickey. "Yes, sir. What job? I had an awful year. I hope the job isn't collecting tickets. But I just might take it right now."

Rickey laughed, "No. You don't have enough experience to do that job." Then he just as quickly he shifted into a more serious tone. "Danny, I want you to help the Pirates climb to the top of the National League, even beyond that."

This time it was Danny's turn to laugh. "Sure. That's what I've been trying to do these past three years."

Mr. Rickey smiled at Danny's honest response, then said. "Well, this is a different assignment. I want you to go to New Orleans and be the player/Manager for the Pelicans. There are some good players there. But I need them to get better and to learn to play harder and smarter. I want them to be gritty, to learn how to play against the odds, to fight the bigger foe, and win."

Danny wasn't sure why he was asked to meet with Mr. Rickey but he was sure it wasn't something as dynamic as building a baseball dynasty in Pittsburgh. He didn't say anything. He continued to listen.

Rickey continued. "I want to pull the Pirates to the top like I did for the Cardinals and the Dodgers. I have the plan but I need the men. I know you have the stuff. But you have to go back to the minors and get some experience managing a team. That's my offer."

Danny was still quiet. He shifted his feet. Then he smiled.
"Yes, sir. I'll take the position. Baseball is my life… outside of my family."

"Mine too." Rickey replied. "And good people are its fuel." The General Manager thought for a moment. He hesitated to speak but then spoke his mind. "I'm also glad that you said "outside of" and not "beside". Some things are more important than baseball." He added plainly. "You will start right away."

"Thank you, sir. I'll do my best."

"I know you will. I'm counting on you to do that. I also know you will be a better Manager than you think you will be. OK. That's all for now. Enjoy the crayfish in New Orleans."

Both men got up from their chairs and shook hands. Then as Rickey sat back at his desk, Danny nodded farewell and turned and walked out of Rickey's office, back into his life in baseball.

March 1952, A New Orleans Pelican

Danny left his family back in Chester and arrived in New Orleans as the player/Manager of the New Orleans Pelicans. He had a lot on his mind as he focused on this new chapter in his life. He was still going to be on the field and in the game. He also might regain his confidence and his stroke and that's why he agreed to be a player/Manager with the Pelicans. There was always that possibility that it all might come back and he'd be in the majors again. Now he understood why boxers always wanted to get back in the ring. They always thought they could win the next fight and wouldn't be knocked back onto the canvas.

One morning shortly after spring training began and after he had acquainted himself with the team, he called for an informal meeting in the locker room. "Fellas, as I told you on the first day that I met you all, I'm glad to be your teammate and your coach." He let that soak in some, then added. "Earlier this morning, a local sportswriter asked me if I had decided who is going to play at each position on this team. I told him that right now I'm only certain that I know who is going to play second base, and that's me."

All of the Pelican players laughed. Even after only a short time with Danny, both the young rookie players and the veteran minor league players knew that Danny had a sense of humor and a respect for fairness. They were comfortable laughing with him, and because it was contagious, they now all laughed with each other.

Danny continued. "I know that my being a player/Manager might be difficult for you and for me sometimes, especially if I'm not doing my share of playing good baseball. We'll going to work that out together."

A veteran player raised his hand and when Danny pointed to him, he asked. "Coach, does that mean that if you hit below .300, we get to vote on whether you should keep playing or not?" Danny thought about the question for just a moment and a sly smirk crossed over his face. "Yea. OK. The players will all get to vote on it. But only the Manager can make the final decision." Danny was the only person in the room who was pleased with that response. "After all," Danny offered. "Hitting .300 might be too much to expect from the present starting second baseman." Everyone laughed, except the backup second baseman.

Now it was time for Danny to tell them he knew the challenge that lay ahead of them. He started his career in the minor leagues and he had been sent back several times. He was back again.

Danny and Mickey, Ordinary Heroes

"I want to tell you that I understand how you feel about being here in New Orleans, five hundred miles or so from where you all would like to be right now, and that's on a major league team."

"I'm sure there's not one person in here, player or coach, who couldn't say at one point or another that you think you've been screwed. That you shouldn't be here. That you should be in the majors. Well, that may be so, but that's passed. That's not why you are here right now. You're here to play baseball and to show how much you want to keep the game in your life. This is a place that gives you a chance to prove you belong elsewhere. There is a lot of pressure. But most importantly, you are playing baseball, a game that you love, and you are playing for money. You are getting paid. Maybe not a lot. But you're lucky to be paid to do something you love to do. So, enjoy it!"

He looked around the room at his players and shared one last thought. "Let's all play hard and have fun with one another. Let's all stay lucky. Understood?"

All of the Pelicans responded at once. 'Yes, sir.' was the loud response. Some voices were louder than others, a few were pensive, most all were excited.

Danny acknowledged the response and started to leave the room but he turned back to face the players and spoke again with a calm, mischievous look on his face. "Oh! I gave it more thought. There isn't going to be any voting on the starting second baseman's performance. Not this year." He smiled and walked out of the locker room.

July 25, 1952, Gay Anne

Mickey accepted Tris Speaker's advice and he used a lighter bat throughout the 1952 season. But this 'lighter bat' experiment was not good. Mickey hit only .251 and although he hit ten homeruns and he drove in a highly respectful number of runs, 80, he wasn't thrilled with his low batting average. The Senators won more games than they lost (78-76) but they still finished in fifth place.

The best news for Mickey came on July 25th. Mickey and Lib celebrated the birth of a beautiful baby girl, Gay Anne. Mickey and Lib lived in Washington DC during the baseball season so Gay was born in Garfield Hospital less than five miles from the White House. Mickey and the Senators played at Cleveland that Friday night but Mickey flew to the hospital immediately after the game to see Lib and his new baby girl.

Garfield Hospital was a well-known medical institution in the District of Columbia dating back to the nineteenth century. In the early hours of the following morning (July 26), Lib's mother, Catherine, was sitting in the hospital room next to Lib who was holding and fussing over her baby girl. Lib had awakened only minutes before Gay was brought into her room. Though Lib was tired, she was so very happy to have this time to snuggle with her tiny daughter. Lib's mom sat back and watched the Mother and baby exchange, through their touches and their eyes, the many things that they had been waiting to say to each during the past nine months of Lib's pregnancy.

A few minutes later, Catherine heard footsteps in the hallway, and heard the pace of the footsteps getting increasingly closer to the room. She knew what she expected to see and she smiled at the tall figure standing in the doorway. Catherine turned to her daughter and baby granddaughter and said excitedly. "Lib, there's someone here to see you. Both of you"

"Mom, who is it?" replied Lib. "Can they come back in a little bit while I hold my baby?"

Lib's mom suppressed a slight laugh and answered softly. "He could, but I don't think he'll wait."

Then Mickey practically ran across the room, dropped his bag on the floor, and gushed. "Hi, honey. I'm so proud of you and my little princess." He leaned over and kissed Lib but was careful not to crush the tiny doll-like angel who was nestled warmly in Lib's arms.

"Oh! Mickey. I'm so happy to see you. Oh my goodness. You got here so fast from Cleveland."

"Not fast enough.' He kissed Lib again and kissed his baby daughter. Lib carefully lifted Gay into Mickey's arms.

"Here she is. She was asking for you all night." I told her, "Gay Anne, daddy is coming to see you. So rest now because he will keep you awake for the rest of your life."

Mickey laughed and cradled the greatest gift of his life in his arms, close to his heart. "Well, I'll only do that during the off-season. Gosh, she's adorable."

Lib's mom knowingly understood that they wanted to be alone and she quietly left the room.

Mickey stayed with Lib and his baby girl for a few hours until he had to catch a return flight to Cleveland where he and the Senators would play the Indians. He arrived back to Cleveland in time for the game and he continued his celebration the same day. He smacked two base hits, walked once, and scored three runs to lead his team to an exciting win over Cleveland, 11-10, and he always considered this game as a once-in-a-lifetime first-birthday present for Gay Anne. It was also a rare win by the Senators over the 'Cleveland Flamethrower', Bob Feller, who would later be inducted into baseball's Hall of Fame in Cooperstown, NY.

Gay's birthday was the highlight of Mickey's career, maybe his life. But the baseball season still had two more long months to run before Mickey could stay home with Lib and Gay Anne. He was falling in love for the second time in his life and he wanted to spend all his time in his new home with his baby girl. It was possible that this understandable distraction may have cost him some points on his hitting average later in the season. But he would've traded a batting title to get home to Lib and Gay even a little sooner. Next year he wouldn't have to make a choice when he began a run for his second batting title.

June 1953, Training Pelicans

In mid-June, Danny sat in his small office in New Orleans preparing for that afternoon's game. He was now in the middle of his second season managing the Pelicans. Sitting on an old wooden chair in a corner of Danny's office, the clubhouse attendant was reading the morning sport's page. Danny was leaning over his desk and filling in the Pelicans lineup for the game.

The clubhouse attendant noisily folded the newspaper and said to Danny. "Skipper, it says here in the paper that your buddy Vernon is aiming for another batting title."

This wasn't news to Danny as he checked every day to see how Mickey fared in the previous day's game. But the attendant didn't know that and Danny wasn't going to spoil the young fella's fun. So he didn't look up from his desk, instead he continued to write on the lineup card and said. "I'm not surprised to hear that. What's it say?"

"It says that Vernon is ahead. He's batting .335, Mantle's at .332, and Al Rosen is close behind at .317. It says it's a wide open race."

Danny agreed with the sports writer's observation. "Well, there is a long way to go yet. But I know Mickey well and he will stay in it to the end. He loves a close battle."

The club house attendant was pleased that Mickey took the bait. Mantle was the attendant's favorite player and Mantle was also the odds-makers' favorite to win the batting title. "I don't know." The attendant replied.

"Mantle and Rosen are young guys, and Vernon's not a kid anymore. That might favor one of them over your buddy."

It was true that in sporting endeavors, age did favor the younger athlete. But Danny knew that Mickey aged slower than many athletes and that Mickey had added a new bounce in his step. "I know Mickey's thirty-five and only a year younger than me. But he's got new energy. I think that he's gonna celebrate this year for his new baby girl and win the batting title."

Snap! The young attendant heard the trap spring close. This was where the attendant wanted the conversation to take them. He got his chance to pit his baseball wits against his boss. So he smiled and said. "Wanna bet on that, Skipper?"

"Well, son, I save my serious bets for the race track and card games. But as long as Williams doesn't get back from Korea and play this year, Vernon will win."

"What? No bet at all! Geez, you don't sound too confident if you don't bet nothing."

"OK. " Danny said. I'll bet you one autographed Pelicans hat.

"Autographed by who? Joe DiMaggio?"

"No. Joe played for the San Francisco Seals, not the Pelicans. It'll be better than that. I'll make it a Pelican hat autographed by Abner Doubleday."

"He's dead."

"I know that." Danny added slyly. "He signed it before he died." Danny paused. "Now, ya wanna bet or not?"

The attendant stared open-mouthed at Danny, wondering to himself where Danny got the Abner Doubleday-autographed hat. Danny looked up at him, smiled, and walked out into the baking Louisiana sun with the Pelicans lineup card in his pocket. He was pleased with himself because he was certain that he wouldn't have to part with the Abner Doubleday-autographed Pelicans baseball, even if he did have such a thing.

1953, Al Rosen's final at-bat.

Danny's Pelicans completed their season in mid-August. The team finished in fifth place for the second year in a row but that was an improvement over their finishes in the previous five years. By mid-September, Danny was home in Chester and his friendly bet with his clubhouse attendant was not yet over. Although Yankee slugger Mickey Mantle faded in the batting race, Danny had neither won nor lost his bet. Danny bet the attendant Mickey would win the title, not that he would finish ahead of Mantle. The contest for best average came down to the last day of the regular season between Mickey and the Cleveland Indians' star outfielder Al Rosen. Mickey and Rosen had continued their furious competition for the AL batting title throughout the entire year. If Rosen finished with the highest average, Danny loses the bet.

In mid-September, the lead switched back and forth when both hitters took turns having their own hitting streaks. Additionally, the baseball commissioner announced that a bonus would be awarded to the player with the highest batting average in each league. The largest bat manufacturer, Hillerich & Bradsby, maker of the Louisville Slugger, would present a personalized, engraved, silver bat to the batting title winner in each league.

The major league baseball season traditionally ended on the last Sunday in September. The final games were generally stress-free and fans took in the final innings cheering for their favorite ballplayers and treated themselves to peanuts, popcorn and hot dogs. The final game of 1953 was an exceptional opportunity for the two leading hitters in the American

League. Al Rosen and Mickey Vernon were within a decimal point of each other from capturing the AL batting title. But their final game wasn't against each other. They were playing in cities four hundred miles apart and they were taking their final at bat in the last inning of their game at the same time of day.

In Cleveland's Municipal Stadium, Al Rosen and the Indians were trailing the Tigers, 9-3. The game's significance in a one-hundred and fifty-four game season was meaningless in the league standings and would not affect the final team positions. However, the tension and excitement felt in Municipal Stadium was not focused on who won the game but whether hometown hero Al Rosen would win the batting title. The Cleveland Manager even moved Rosen up to the lead off position so that Rosen might possibly get an extra at-bat and a better chance to win the batting title. That's exactly what happened when Rosen picked up his bat and stepped out of his dugout to take his fifth and last bat in the ninth inning of the last game of the season. A single in this last bat would lift him a decimal point ahead of Mickey and he would win the batting title.

Rosen stepped into the batter's box and loosened-up his shoulders and arms before lifting his bat and planting his feet into his hitter's stance. He heard the home crowd's cheers and applause. The radio announcer provided the fans listening at home with a snapshot summary of what this final appearance meant for their talented outfielder.

"Folks," the announcer began, "this has been some batting race. Just a few days ago, Mickey Vernon had a seven point lead over Rosen, .336 to .329. Now after games on Friday and Saturday, and after four plate appearances today, Al has narrowed the lead down to a single point, .337 versus .336. Vernon smacked seven singles in his last twelve appearances but during the same period, Al had nine base hits in his last fourteen bats, including two homeruns and two doubles. This single at bat over the whole season could be the difference between the two players."

Now, Rosen was set at home plate and he looked out at Tiger's pitcher, Al Aber. The first pitch thrown was ball one. Several more pitches were thrown including one that Rosen hit foul that just missed striking the third base bag. The count had grown to a full count, 3 balls and 2 strikes. The tension in the crowd accounted for the almost deafening cloak of silence in the stadium. Rosen stepped out of the batter's box. He took a deep breath and looked out towards left field as if he were measuring a homerun or searching for a gap in the outfield. All he really wanted to do was to find a place where the damn ball would fall onto the grass before it was caught. At that same moment a fan shouted encouragement to him. Rosen stepped back up to home plate. Aber set up on the rubber and then he threw the ball inside to Rosen.

Crack! Rosen hit the ball and sent it on one hop to third base where it was caught cleanly. Now it was a race between Rosen and the infielder's throw to first base. After batting 600 times, the batting title came down to this last play at first base.

The home crowd was at full voice, some rooted for a hit to start a rally but most cheered for Rosen to reach the bag before the ball reached the first baseman's glove. Seemingly at once, the ball smacked loudly into the first baseman's glove just as Al's left foot seemed to touch the bag.

"You're out!" The umpire shouted. This was that rare occasion where everyone in the ball park agreed who the villain was. It was the man wearing a steel-cage mask and dressed in black. The fans and both dugouts were roaring at the bang-bang play of "ball in glove/foot on bag" or vice-versa. The first person out of the dugout was Cleveland's Manager Al Lopez who practically leaped onto the field.

Yelling even before he got close to the umpire, Lopez wasn't going to let this play remain unchanged. He wanted the call reversed. It was a base hit.

"He's safe! Whaddya mean, he's out? My runner was on that bag before the ball got there." Red-faced, eyes blazing, Lopez wanted this call changed. His man was safe. Everyone could see that.

Meanwhile, Rosen's momentum from running as fast as he could carried him a few yards past the first base bag. He slowed, heard the shouting, and he turned right toward the foul line, and circled back to first base. He grabbed his Manager's arm and whispered into his ear just as Lopez bullied up to the umpire

"Skipper, I missed the edge of the bag. I'm out."

Lopez ignored Rosen and continued to argue that the call should be reversed, that Rosen was safe. He wanted this last hit for Rosen even more than Rosen wanted it. Five minutes of animated discussion ended just before the umpire was ready to toss Lopez out in the ninth inning of a meaningless game on the last day of the season. The call remained unchanged. Rosen was out at first base. The batting title was still not settled. Four hundred miles away in Washington, DC, Mickey prepared to end his season with his last turn at bat.

1953, Mickey's final at-bat

In the nation's capital, the Senators were trailing the Philadelphia A's 9-2 in the bottom of the ninth inning. Like the Cleveland game, this final season game would not change any team's position in the league. The sole interest for the home crowd was whether Mickey would hit well enough today to win the batting title. The top of the Senators' batting order was scheduled to bat in this final inning. Mickey would be the fourth batter in the inning, so he would only bat if any one of the first three batters got on base.

While the three scheduled Senator hitters were picking up their bats and getting ready to bat for the last time this season, the Senators Manager, future Hall of Famer Bucky Harris, checked with the press box and was told that Rosen made an out in his final at-bat and the Cleveland game was over. The same news source told Bucky that Mickey had a .0005 lead in the race. Mickey didn't need to bat.

Bucky walked over to Mickey who was sitting on the bench and told him that the Cleveland game was over. Rosen would finish second to Mickey - as long as Mickey didn't bat again. He told Mickey that he intended to send out a pinch hitter for him if a Senator got on base. Mickey said no, he wasn't going to sit. He wanted to win the title on the field. He also told Harris that he wouldn't bunt for a hit. He wanted to win the title on the field and he didn't want to pass up his regular turn in the lineup. Bucky continued to discuss it with Mickey but he wasn't able to convince him to sit down. The irony of the situation was that Rosen needed to change his batting position in the lineup to have that extra bat to win it, while Mickey needed to sit out his last bat to win the title. It was simple math spread out over 154 games and nearly 600 at bats for each player. Regardless of the math, Bucky and Mickey knew that if Mickey batted, and made an out, Rosen would win the batting title.

With Mickey's insistence on batting if a teammate got on base, Bucky devised another plan. He walked to the on-deck circle and spoke to Kite Thomas, a veteran utility player he selected to pinch hit and who would lead off the inning for Washington.

"Look, Kite," Bucky explained. "I don't want Mickey to come up this inning. We aren't gonna get eight runs in the last inning of our final game. We're staying in sixth place. So make an out. All three batters will do the same. Mickey's moment is our shared glory today."

Thomas' reply was simple. "OK."

The umpire didn't want the season to last one minute longer than it had to, so he called out to Thomas. "OK. Let's get a batter in here."

Ray Murray the A's catcher was standing on the batter's side of the plate a few steps away from the umpire. Thomas stepped closer to the catcher and whispered. "Put the ball over. No walks. We'll go out 1-2-3." Murray understood what he was suggesting but replied under his breath. "Just play ball."

If he or any of Mickey's teammates got on base, Mickey's second batting title was at stake. Thomas stepped to the plate. Now, it seemed that the only teammate encouraging Thomas to get on base was Mickey. Mickey was always a team player first. "C'mon Kite. Get yourself a hit."

Thomas took the first few pitches, and the count was in his favor, two balls, and one strike. The next pitch was already headed toward home plate. *WHACK!* The ball was tagged hard and it cleared the left-side of the infield. It was a base hit. It looked like Mickey was going to get another at-bat after all and his batting title would be on the line. Just then, the A's pitcher yelled to the left-fielder. "Holy shit! Throw to second base. The runner's going to second base!"

Everyone in the stadium was stunned, and the radio announcer relayed the action to the network audience at home. "Fans, Kite didn't stop at first base. He slowed when he crossed first base, then he stared out to leftfield, and turned and started running to second base." The announcer's voice rose as he watched the A's outfielder pick up the ball. "OK, here comes the throw into second base and ... it is right on target! Kite slides, and, Oh, my goodness! He's out! It wasn't even close. The kid tried to stretch his hit into a double but he's tagged out. I admire his hustle, but it's not a smart play, trailing 9 to 2. Looks like he got too excited.

When he returned to the Senator's dugout, Thomas wasn't reprimanded or booed. Bucky Harris smiled and patted him on the back, and turned to watch the next batter, Eddie Yost, walk to home plate.

Yost hit a weak fly ball for the second out. Pete Runnels, a talented hitter who would himself become a two-time American League batting champion, was now the last batter between Mickey and the batting title. Runnels was a selective hitter and he was among the leaders on the team in walks. Suddenly, the Phillies' pitcher couldn't find home plate. Runnels looked concerned as three pitches passed by him and all three were balls. He stepped out of the batter's box and placed his bat on his shoulder. A few seconds passed and the umpire told him to get back into the box. Seeming to have found a solution to his frustration, Runnels watched the next pitch approach the plate, and though it was off the plate, he swung his bat. He tapped a slow ground ball to the second baseman who fielded it and tossed the ball to first base for the final out of the game. The season was over, and the 1953 AL batting race was over. The Senators lost the game, 9-2. But the dugout reacted as though they had won the game because they all knew Vernon wasn't going to bat again this season. So, Mickey didn't bat. He ended the season waiting on deck. Now, the bigger question remained. Is Mickey the 1953 AL batting champ?"

He did. He won the 1953 batting title in one of the tightest batting races ever in the major leagues. As it turned out, it wouldn't have mattered whether he got a hit, walked, or made an out, he would've still won the batting title, by less than one thousandth of a point, .0007.

In addition to winning his second AL batting crown (.337), Mickey had 205 hits, 15 HRs, 43 doubles, and 115 RBIs. He was the first Washington Senator to win two batting titles. Now he could go home to Lib and Gay and figure out what his baby girl was going to do with his new silver bat.

Al Rosen's final out cost him not only the batting title but he just missed winning the coveted Triple Crown* by .001 point. He hit .336, smacked 43 homeruns, and drove in 145 runs. He won the 1953 AL Most Valuable Player trophy.

***The hitter's Triple Crown title is awarded to one player in each league who finishes that season with the highest numbers in the three major offensive categories: highest batting average, most homeruns, most runs batted in. Roger**

Hornsby and Ted Williams are the only players to win more than one batting Triple Crown (2 each).The pitcher's Triple Crown is likewise awarded to one pitcher in each league who leads in the three primary pitching categories: number of wins, most strikeouts, lowest ERA, (earned run average per game). Grover Alexander won four pitcher's triple crowns; Sandy Koufax and Walter Johnson won three apiece.

December, 1953, When family calls

Success has its rewards and its responsibilities. The next five months after capturing his second batting title were a whirlwind for Mickey. Following the World Series, he traveled with an All Star team headed by his boyhood hero and Philadelphia Athletics' Hall of Fame slugger, Jimmie Foxx. Mickey finally got home before the holidays but only long enough to relax a little before he went to spring training in late February.

Things were also going well for Danny. Immediately after the season, the Pirates renewed his contract to manage the Pelicans for a third year. Branch Rickey was pleased with the Pelicans improved play, and more importantly he liked how Danny was managing, and how he taught the game to the players and provided leadership for the team. Danny was also learning more about the strategy of the game. Unfortunately, the promise of the approaching holiday season was interrupted with sad news.

Early one evening in mid-December the phone at Danny's home rang. Kate was in the downstairs foyer walking past the phone when it rang. She lifted the black receiver from the phone's cradle and placed the audio end to her ear and spoke into the speaker. "Hello." She recognized her sister-in-law's voice on the other end of the phone. "Oh! Hi Peg. It's nice to hear from you. Sure. He's right here." Kate signaled with her right hand to Danny who was sitting in the parlor. "Danny, it's your sister Peg." Then sensing that Peg was upset, she asked her. "Is everyone OK?" There was a pause, then Peg asked for Danny again. "Yes, Peg. Here he is." Kate handed the phone to Danny who had heard enough to know that this was not going to be a normal 'how is the family' update. He took the phone from Kate and hoped that his worry was unwarranted.

Peg and her husband Bennie and their three children had moved to Utah shortly after an armistice was signed in July 1953 ending the Korean War. Bennie was on active duty as a Captain in the Air Force and he was stationed on Hill Air Force Base near Salt Lake City. The Murtaugh family, Danny and his four sisters' families were all close and always communicated with one another, but long-distance telephone calls from Utah were usually reserved for the weekends, mostly on a Sunday and always in the late afternoon. This call was out of the ordinary. That's why Danny was concerned as soon as he heard Kate say his sister's name.

"Hi, Peg" he said. There was no immediate reply but he waited for a few seconds before saying anything else because he could hear Peg trying to speak but her words were muffled and interrupted by small sobs. His shoulders suddenly stiffened and he felt a cold chill pass through him. "Peg?" he paused again then asked. "What's wrong?"
He waited and he could hear Peg trying to speak. When she did speak she was barely audible. Danny's initial fear was correct. Peg told him that Bennie was dead. Stunned, Danny at first was over-whelmed. He gathered himself, and said, in a soft voice. "Oh no. Peg, I'm so sorry. How? When did it happen? Where are you now? Where are the kids?"

The questions spilled out from him. He realized that he was speaking too fast and he stopped talking. On the other end of the phone line, Peg began crying more but she was able to tell him that an Air Force officer was with her and the children. "OK. OK, sis. Let me talk to him."

Peg put the officer on the phone and the officer told Danny that his brother-in-law died earlier that day in an airplane crash while on an assignment thirty miles north of Salt Lake City. The accident occurred during an abortive landing and the crew was killed. Danny was able to get more information about the accident from other authorities who arrived at his sister's house. He was assured that Peg and her son and daughter would be cared for by friends and neighbors. He told Peg and the attending officer that he would arrive in Salt Lake City on the next day. It was very difficult when it came time to say good night to his sister. After speaking briefly again with the officer and placing the phone down on the cradle, he felt helpless, as though he was abandoning Peg and her children for the rest of the night at a time when they needed him the most.

Several hours later Danny and Kate were sitting alone at their kitchen table. They were reviewing what they needed to do so Danny could fly out to Utah and bring Peg and his nieces and nephew back home. Danny had just spoken on the phone with his sister, Madge.

"Kate," Danny explained to Kate. "Madge told me she and Art have some money on hand they intended to use for Christmas shopping this weekend. They can loan us the money for the plane trip so I can leave for Utah right away. You can withdraw money from our bank on Monday and repay them." Kate understood and nodded, but she repeated again the thoughts that filled her with sadness. "I can't believe it. Poor Peg and those little kids."

Danny flew the next day to Utah and later he brought his sister and her three young children: Mary Ellen (9), Betsy (7), and Ben (3) to his house. Danny and Kate made immediate plans to move Peg and her children into their house on Kerlin Street in Chester. Timmy, Danny and Kathy were going to have two new sisters and another brother.

Danny and Kate's family grew instantly from five to nine, and it was a loving arrangement that lasted two years until Peg purchased a new home of her own in Milmont Park, a few miles north of Chester. Danny and Kate's kindness was returned years later when Peg generously shared her own new home with Danny's family while Danny and Kate were waiting for a home to be built in the same Milmont Park neighborhood. As Mickey always fondly recalled, these Murtaughs never settled too far from one another and a helping hand was something you never had to ask for, it was usually already there. __________

Danny and Jackie Robinson, 1948. Note glove on field. Many players left gloves at their field position when they batted.

Tim, Kate, Kathleen, Danny,

Lib, Gay, and Mickey Danny, Jr.

Ted Williams and Mickey
ready for 1947 season.

Mickey and Lib at
Griffith Stadium

Chester, PA on the Delaware
It was a busy port through two
World Wars.

President Eisenhower gives a
Silver Bat to Mickey for his
AL 1953 highest average.

CHAPTER ELEVEN
IKE LIKES MICK

1954, Ike likes Mickey

Mickey's second batting title brought him a lot of attention and great personal satisfaction. However, in the following pre-season he found himself again in tough contract negotiations with Clark Griffith, the Washington Senators owner. Griffith wanted Mickey to accept $21,000, the same amount that Mickey received for the 1951 and 1952 seasons. Mickey requested $35,000 after winning the batting title. The pressure to get a raise was always on the player's end. That was because in the fifties players didn't have agents. They negotiated directly with the baseball owners or their executives. Player agents didn't become a common part of the growing business of baseball until the mid-seventies with the advent of free agency that resulted from St. Louis Cardinal's star outfielder Curt Flood's legal battle with Major League Baseball*. So Mickey negotiated alone and the salary discussions went back and forth between Mickey and the team owner. The negotiations concluded just before the regular season began. Mickey accepted $30,000. It wasn't easy to get it.

It was also a baseball tradition since 1910 that the President of the United States toss out the first ball at the Senators' first home game. William Howard Taft was the first President to throw out the first pitch from the stands to the catcher who would stand on the field a few feet away from the President. Once the catcher caught the ball, the home plate umpire symbolically shouted, "Play ball!" and the game began.

On this opening day, the stadium was packed as the Senators hosted the New York Yankees. After meeting Mickey Vernon, Bucky Harris, and several other dignitaries, President Dwight D. Eisenhower threw out the ceremonial first pitch from a private seating area beside the home team dugout. The game started and the Senators 1954 season was underway. Mickey began his quest for a third batting title.

The game moved steadily along and after nine innings, the game was tied 3-3. The Yankees made three outs quickly in their half of the tenth inning. Now it was the Senators chance to win the game in extra innings.

The sun was present on and off in the early innings but a cloud covering hung over the stadium during the final half of the game. Here in the bottom of the tenth the shadows were lengthening and it appeared that darkness might fall sooner than normal on this early spring day. Regardless, not very many people had left their seats, including the President. Ike, as the President was affectionately called, was reported to be a big Mickey Vernon fan and he certainly acted like it. He was determined to stay long enough to see Mickey win this game. But it didn't look like this was going to happen today. Mickey was having a very bad day. He was hitless in four appearances, and most unusual for him, he committed an error at first base. He was scheduled to bat third in this inning. To add even more difficulty for Mickey, Yankee starter and fire-baller, Allie Reynolds, was brought in to the game to relieve the Yankee pitcher. Reynolds was coming in to pitch this one inning primarily to pitch to Vernon. Yes sir. The Yankees really wanted to impress the President.

Eddie Yost was the first batter and Reynolds walked him. The next batter, Tom Wright, struck out. Now Mickey stepped up to home plate. Bucky shouted from the top step of the dugout. "All right, Mick. Let's move Eddie around the bases."

Yankees' catcher Yogi Berra heard Bucky's remark and added his own two cents from behind the plate. "Yeah, Vernon, right now it looks like you're trailing everybody for the '54 batting title." That was Yogi's style behind the plate. He rode every batter who came to the plate whenever he was catching. Whether they were veterans or rookies, it didn't matter to him. He never stopped talking. Even the umpires couldn't shut him up. Mickey was used to hearing this from Yogi and he had learned to put up with Yogi's antics for the past eight years. So Mickey simply replied. "Yep. This would be a good time to come out of my early season slump." But no one ever got the last word in an exchange of baseball chatter with Yogi. "Mick, you'd have a better chance if you were facing somebody else but Allie. He's fresh and fast."

The umpire signaled to the pitcher and admonished the two players in front of him. "All right, fellas. Save your chatter for after the game."

Berra was correct though. Reynolds was firing the ball like he always did but he was staying away from Mickey. Mickey took two pitches away for ball one and ball two before fouling off the third pitch. Bucky was still yelling encouragement to Mickey. "OK, Mick. Two balls, one strike. Time his fastball. He's gonna come in on you."

Yost had taken a short lead off first base. Reynolds pitched from the stretch and delivered the 2-1 pitch to home plate. The ball moved fast but it stayed up and out over the plate. Mickey saw it and he prepared himself to hit it to any place on the field where there was no fielder. With his eye on the ball, he delivered his classic hitter's stroke. *WHACK!* The sweet spot on Mickey's bat met the fast ball just in front of home plate. It was a solid hit and it quickly cleared the infield and continued to rise.

Someone in the dugout shouted. "Holy crap!' That ball is gone! Mickey got all of it."

Mickey took a quick glance at the ball as it travelled swiftly to right center field, and he watched it climb easily over the stadium's thirty foot wall. He trotted around the bases chasing Eddie Yost. The game was over. Mickey's homerun won it for the Senators, 5-3, and nearly everyone including the President of the United States was on their feet cheering.

Mickey crossed home plate then walked slowly, surrounded by his noisy teammates, to the dugout. Just as he reached the top steps of the dugout, a tall man in a dark suit pushed past the other players and sidled up next to Mickey. The tall stranger was a US Secret Service agent assigned to protect the President. He flashed an official-looking metal badge, and said with polite authority. "Mr. Vernon. The President would like to personally congratulate you. Please follow me."

With no time to refuse the invitation and no chance in hell that he would've refused, Mickey followed the agent to the President's box along the first base side of the infield. The President was overjoyed with the exciting finish and with the Senators win over the Yankees. He told Mickey that the homerun was "a wonderful sports moment". Of course, Mickey was happy to win the game, but he was more excited about having the President personally congratulate him. In a flash, Mickey's mind went back in time and space to an island in the South Pacific, and then it jumped forward again to this moment nine years later in Washington, DC. He knew that the President who in 1945 was the Supreme Allied Commander of American Forces would fully appreciate that single introspective thought. But what a season already! Only one day completed in the new season and the Senators were in first place and the Yankees were in last place. He was leading the league in homeruns (1) and runs batted in (2). The only downside was that the reigning batting champion was barely hitting .200.

---

*Curt Flood played 12 years for the St. Louis Cardinals. He was a three-time All Star outfielder who won seven Golden Gloves and batted over .300 six times. He and the Cardinals won the World Series in 1964 and 1967. His was traded on Oct. 7, 1969 to the Philadelphia Phillies. Unhappy with the trade, he believed he had "a right to consider offers from other clubs." When MLB Commissioner, Bowie Kuhn, denied his request, Flood sued Major League Baseball, alleging that MLB's reserve clause violated antitrust laws as well as the Thirteenth Amendment (This Amendment outlaws slavery, and involuntary servitude).

The MLB reserve clause was part of a player's contract that stated upon the contract's expiration that the rights to the player were to be automatically retained by the team. This meant the player was not free to enter into another contract with another team. Therefore, once a player signed his first contract, he was owned by that team forever, unless the team and only that team traded, sold, or released him. The player himself could not initiate any moves on his own. The player in essence had no freedom to market his talent and improve his salary or workplace, thus the reference to the Thirteenth Amendment. The reserve clause was overturned on December 23, 1975 and the ruling was subsequently upheld by the United States Supreme Court.

November 1954, Who is on first

Like many ball players, Danny and Mickey spent the months between baseball seasons working local jobs, appearing as banquet speakers, and just getting a few things done around the house that couldn't be done from February through October. They were in demand and many times they would appear at functions together. The joint appearances were mostly unscripted but there were a few times when the audience could be surprised. The venues for banquets and award ceremonies varied greatly.

A popular banquet hall, Columbus Center, was located between third and fifth streets on Pusey Street in the southeast part of Chester. The hall was built by Chester's Italian-American community. Though it was initially used to celebrate only the Italian community's feast days and social celebrations, it was occasionally rented out to other fraternal organizations within the city. Columbus Center stood noticeably on a slight rise just a few blocks from the Delaware River.

It was an impressive sight, situated amidst many single and multi-family homes and apartments in this clean and neat blue-collar neighborhood. Though the Center had a large double-door conveniently located at street level on Pusey Street, its formal entrance was located on a large stone landing that rose twenty feet above street level. The landing was accessed by using the two classically carved stone masonry stairways that rose from the sidewalk on both sides. The majestic features of this formal entrance were the four large Roman columns set on each corner of the rectangular stone slab. These columns supported an arched portico that extended over the wide landing, and protected visitors and guests from rainy or snowy weather. Directly under the portico were two wide bronze metal doors that stood back away from the landing. Anyone standing on the landing would be elevated twenty feet above the street and could easily greet and wave to a passing parade, or comfortably deliver a speech to a large gathering on the street below.

In November Danny and Mickey were sharing the speaker platform inside the Center for one of the many sport club award banquets that marked the completion of the baseball and football seasons. No one including Danny and Mickey could ever predict exactly what form their dual appearance would take. The Master of Ceremonies for this occasion was Matt Zabitka, a popular sportswriter and columnist for the local newspaper, The Chester Times, whose readership included Chester and all of the surrounding communities in Delaware County.

As always, the Center was nearly full and most attendees were now seated. At the front of the hall, stretched across the front of the stage was a long table. This was the seating area for the honored guests and the officers of the specific organization that sponsored the banquet. It was succinctly referred to as 'the head table'. A podium stood in the center of the stage just a few feet behind where the guest and officers sat. This is where Master of Ceremonies Matt Zabitka stood earlier to make his welcoming remarks and introduce the guests seated at the places of honor before dinner. When dinner had ended, and coffee and dessert were being served, he began the program and introduced the featured speakers.

"Welcome everyone to the American Legion Sports Banquet. We've introduced our honored guests. Now we are fortunate tonight to have two guest speakers." To add some levity, he playfully ad-libbed. "We are fortunate because we aren't paying either one of them."

Danny was seated at the head table next to Mickey and he called out to Zabitka. "Wait, Matt! I know you aren't paying Mickey, but I didn't know that you weren't paying me. I mean I'm a Manager. Mickey's a player. Who gets paid first, the boss or the worker? Ike or Nixon?

Someone in the audience shouted. "Yeh! Murtaugh or Vernon?" Everyone laughed.

Zabitka pointed over to Danny and spoke up. "Stop right there, Danny. I didn't even introduce you yet." He laughed and said, "I may not even bring you up here, now."

Then Matt Zabitka formally began again, keeping a cautious eye on Danny. "Ladies and Gentlemen, Delaware County is proud of our athletes. We are here to honor many of them tonight for their accomplishments this past year. To help us celebrate we are especially proud to have two men from Delaware County who love the game of baseball, and who earn their living playing baseball."

He continued. "First, let me introduce the man you've already heard from tonight, Chester's own Danny Murtaugh. Danny played nine years in the major leagues and he just completed his third year managing the New Orleans Pelicans way down in Louisiana. He piloted this year's team to second place, winning 92 games." The audience applauded and Danny acknowledged the applause with a short wave and a big smile.

"Our other guest speaker is Mickey Vernon, the pride of Marcus Hook. Mickey is a four-time American League all-star first baseman for the Washington Senators, and a two-time American League batting champion, winning the title in 1946 finishing ahead of Ted Williams and winning on the last day in 1953 over Al Rosen. Mickey finished this past 1954 campaign with another set of exceptional hitting statistics. His batting average was .290, he hit 67 extra-base hits that included 20 homeruns, 14 triples, and 33 doubles, and he drove in 97 runs. Please welcome them both to the podium, Danny Murtaugh and Mickey Vernon."

The crowd responded with applause, cheers, and a few whistles as Mickey surprisingly dashed to the podium and grabbed the microphone like it was a laurel wreath awarded for an Olympic race.

"Ladies and Gentlemen, please excuse my rush to get up here but I've been around Danny for so many years now that if I want to say anything, I know I better do it before he gets the microphone. Sometimes at these functions, people will compare the two of us to Hope and Crosby. That's OK but it's not exactly correct. Danny is not funny, and I can't sing." He paused to enjoy the laughter. "There is one other difference. At least Hope lets Crosby sing a song or two. For a fella who says he doesn't talk much, Danny never lets me get a word in. He tells me that's because I can't sing and that nothing I say is funny."

As if on cue, Danny got up from his seat at the table and walked to the podium and stood next to his pal. "Mickey, wait a second. I have to speak before you because everyone always wants to hear what the All Star and batting champion has to say. Then after you finish, the crowd thins. Guys pretend to go to the john but never come back. That's why Hope tells his jokes before Crosby sings. Give us little guys a chance to tell our short stories."

Not willing to be short-changed again by his clever Irish foe, Mickey replied. "Every time you tell a short story, it lengthens. Then I get the short end of it and I only get a few minutes to speak."

Danny looked away from Mickey and out to the audience. He spoke to the audience as though it was a single 'third person' in the room and he was going to share with them what he thought was the reason for the current misunderstanding between the two good friends. It was just poor communication.

"Uh Oh!" Danny began. "That sounds like there is a problem of communication between the player at first, and the player at second."

Mickey looked puzzled, but as if on cue, he asked Danny. “Huh! What’s the problem?”

“No.” Danny said assertively. “Who is the problem.”

“Who?” asked Mickey.

“Yes, you. That’s Who.”

Now more puzzled than ever, and trying to decipher Danny’s comment, Mickey asks earnestly. “What is the problem?”

“No.” Danny quickly replied. “Like I said. You are.”

Becoming more frustrated, Mickey’s voice rises and he asks loudly. “Wait a second. I’m who?”

“Yes. That’s correct.” Danny answered, pleased that his friend now finally agreed with him.

But Mickey’s mind wasn’t clear at all. “No. I mean who am I?”

“Yes. You are Who. That’s right.” was Danny’s simple reply.

“And you are who?”

“No. What! I’m What.”

Really confused, Mickey cried out. “You’re what?”

“Yep. I’m What, and you are Who.

Mickey, thinking Danny is asking him a question, is even more exasperated and finally exclaims, “I don’t know!”

Definitely on cue, several voices in the audience, recruited earlier by Danny, respond loudly and all together. *"No, he's on THIRD BASE!"*

Instantly, the center erupted in laughter, including Danny and Mickey. There was great applause as the skit ended. It wasn't as smooth as Abbott and Costello, or Hope and Crosby, but it was a hit.

MC Matt Zabitka stepped to the microphone as the laughter subsided. Then he invited the audience to ask Danny and Mickey questions about the events of the past year as well as their predictions for the coming season. Afterward, the many awards and trophies were distributed to the worthy recipients. Neither Danny nor Mickey ever admitted to any preparation for their Abbott and Costello monologue.

"This is how we always communicate, and we get along fine." was Danny's stone-faced reply.

December 1954, "Where's Charleston?"

The Murtaugh house was unusually quiet just before this Christmas holiday. The reason was easily explained. While Danny and his family were in New Orleans during the past season, Unkie passed away. It was unexpected. He hadn't been ill but his heart stopped beating one evening when he was at his home not far from his sister Nellie's house. It was a difficult time for Danny. Unkie was always at the center of his life from his first minutes of his birth to his current struggle to remain in baseball. Danny's Mom and Dad and his sisters were of primary importance to him but he and Unkie shared a unique bonding. They seemed to breathe the same air whenever they were together. They didn't share it like two people taking turns breathing the air. They breathed it simultaneously, and enjoyed the warm relationship of an uncle and nephew who seemed to be so much more at times: like a father and son, a big brother and a little brother. Tim Mc Carey was not an easy person to like, and not a sentimental pushover but he was among the best things in Danny's life. Now he was gone and Danny missed him at Christmas.

There was also something else that was bothering him. Something he had to tell Kate regarding New Orleans. He wasn't going to go back to the Pelicans. He was angry at the way many fans disrespected and behaved toward his family at home games because they thought that one decision or another by Danny had adversely affected some games during the season. Despite winning the most games in a single year than any Pelican team in the previous decade and finishing near the very top of the league, the most rambunctious fans resorted to demanding more than Danny or the players could deliver. So Danny had seen and heard enough. He was finished with the Pelicans' fan base in New Orleans even before the season ended. What should have been a happy time for everyone connected to the team instead became a nightmare in expectations that his team could not fulfill soon enough. Danny could improve the team and the players but he no longer wanted to win for the fans. Too many had done irreparable damage to his family's sense of safety. He knew at the end of the season he wasn't going back to New Orleans but he never spoke a word about it to Kate. He wanted to have a wonderful holiday season and handle baseball questions after the New Year began. However, he had just received a positive response to his request for an interview with the owner of the Charleston Pirates, an independent team in Charleston, West Virginia. The owner wanted to interview him for the Manager position on the day after Christmas.

The kitchen table was the one place that seemed to attract the family's most meaningful conversations whether at a meal or late in the evening. It was late in the evening when Kate joined Danny at the table. Danny told Kate that New Orleans was no longer the place where he wanted to work and Kate wasn't greatly surprised. She knew that Danny was wrestling with something because he just didn't seem focused on the things that were right in front of him. His mind seemed to be concentrating or concerned with something else. She told him the same thing that she always told him when he had to make a career decision, and she meant it.

"Hon, you know the kids and I will go wherever you want us to go."

Danny expected Kate to say exactly that but this time he didn't want her to make it too easy for him to leave her and the kids too far away from him. "I know that you always do whatever I ask. Now, I think it's my turn to think less of myself and do more for you and the kids. You need to be closer to home. West Virginia is a lot closer to home than Louisiana."

"Is Mr. Rickey upset that you don't want to go back to New Orleans? You have that team playing winning baseball now."

"He's not upset. He understands. He just told me to keep managing somewhere. He's certain that I'll move up, but I have to stay in the game to be visible when a team is looking for a new Manager. I can't stay home. He reminded me of an old adage. "Out of sight, out of mind".

Kate listened. She didn't want him to be far from home but she didn't want him to take any position just to be closer to home. They both knew that his future would be connected to winning. She didn't know anything about Charleston. "Danny, is Charleston a good organization? If they aren't, stay in Louisiana. Wait for the call there."

Danny was firm in his reply. "Four years in Louisiana is one too many. Branch Rickey might retire. Joe Brown could move up to General Manager. I'm not sure how Joe feels about me. This will get us closer to home, then maybe the majors. It's now or never."

The next words out of Kate's mouth were the same words that you would've expected to hear from a Pittsburgh sports writer who might be sitting in front of her Danny. The exception is that she reached out and put her hands into his hands. Politely, warmly, she took a quick breath and asked the million dollar question that all athletes and coaches know the fans want to hear answered in only one way.

"Have you met the team owners and the players?" "Can you win in Charleston?"

"I didn't meet any players. This came up so fast that I only met the owner in the late summer. The team isn't very good. But they are in a Class AAA circuit, that's the last step before the major leagues. It will be tough to win a lot of games. But if I do, it might mean a fast train back to the big leagues.

"What do you want to do?" Kate asked.

They were still holding hands across the table. Danny released her left hand and ran his right hand through his hair, then said. "There isn't much else that I can do besides baseball. It's my life, it's our life. I can't build ships anymore. I paint houses too slowly. Even the milkman doesn't trust me to help him carry the milk bottles from his truck. You can ask Eunice about the broken milk bottles that covered her front steps the last time I helped. Charleston brings us closer together and that's a good thing."

Kate let go of Danny's other hand and stood up and walked around the table. He stood, and like they always did, they embraced.

"Let's go! Danny." Kate smiled as she continued. "Let's pack for Charleston, West Virginia." Then she paused and pulled away to look into his eyes. She said with uncertainty. "Exactly where is Charleston, West Virginia?"

December 1955, McGovern's Men Store

A bird's eye view of Chester shows a city with an amoeba–shaped land mass bounded on the east by the Delaware River, and with vague, ill-defined boundaries on its west, and its north and south. Without its posted city-limit signs, you would be unaware exactly when you left the city and crossed into a neighboring community. However, the commercial downtown section of the city is mildly organized.

The numbered streets run east to west from the river's edge while the named streets run north to south from the city's northern end, next to Eddystone borough. This crisscross pattern of numbered and named streets forms a slightly crooked rectangle in the center of town. The majority of the city's retail stores lie within this rectangle. In the middle of downtown, at 7th and Market streets, is a small triangular piece of land occupied by a small newsstand slightly larger than several large broom closets. Most cities would place a statue of a great person here, or possibly an art sculpture, maybe even a fountain. But Chester is a riverfront city, an industrial city. News is far more valuable and meaningful to its businesses and its residents. This nearly century-old newsstand was covered with a gazebo-type roof that protects its customers from rain and snow while they purchase its newspapers, magazines, and tobacco. Roder's, as the newsstand was originally christened, is still a city fixture and a synonym for newsstand in Chester. Surrounding this small oasis were numerous retail businesses - restaurants, movie theatres, jewelry shops, and dress shops. Nearby were places of worship representing the city's diverse religious communities – Catholic, Protestant, and Jewish.

One of the most successful businesses here in the center of town was McGovern's Men Clothing Store, a men's fashion shop that was a popular stop for men and women in the second half of the twentieth century. It was also a place of employment for Mickey and Danny during several off-seasons. They were hired by the store's namesake, Jim McGovern, because he was an astute businessman and knew their celebrity and welcoming personalities would attract customers and fans who would need dress pants, a suit, or any other quality clothing. Mr. McGovern was also a baseball fan. Mickey and Danny were good salesmen and often worked with Mr. McGovern, who along with his other tailor, performed all of the fittings, sewing tasks, and provided answers to his customers' fashion-related questions regarding style, color and fabric.

It wasn't often that Mr. McGovern wasn't in the shop but this day he had scheduled a lunch meeting with a business associate. Though he felt confident when either Mickey or Danny were minding the store, they weren't tailors. They were responsible for an increase in sales because of their popularity and polite service, not for their sewing skills. However, he told them many times that all measurements for suits and trousers will be done by him or by one of his other tailors. In fact, just before leaving for lunch today, he reminded them, especially Danny, to leave the white chalk alone and tell any customer who wanted or needed a measurement to wait until he came back from lunch. He wouldn't be very long. Otherwise, Danny and Mickey should get a name and a phone number from the customer and Mr. McGovern would arrange a later appointment for a measurement. His last words were. "Have them wait if they want to wait. Sell them something else why they're waiting. I'll be back in an hour or so."

A half-hour passed and a small number of customers had come and gone. The store was empty when the bell over the entry door rang. Danny and Mickey were standing at the sales counter when the bell alerted them and they watched a middle-age man enter the store. Mickey was closest to the door. "Good afternoon, sir. How are you today? Can I help you?"

"Yes, you can. I need a suit. A dark one. I need a couple shirts; maybe two ties."

"Sure." Mickey volunteered. "I can help you. Come on over here."

Danny was behind the sales counter as the man passed by him. Danny smiled and said. "How are you doing, sir?"
The man didn't respond verbally but he nodded in the affirmative to Danny, then he followed Mickey to the suit racks. Mickey stood at the beginning of the racks of suits that were arranged by numbered size. "What size are you, sir?"

"Well, I'm not sure anymore. It's been a while since I've bought a suit. My wife usually comes with me. She's working today and I'm on my lunch break. I'd like to surprise her."

This customer sounded like a sale to Mickey so he was excited and he reached inside himself for all his acquired salesman skills. "OK. Well, we can look at some suits to see what style and color you prefer. We have a fashionable range of styles here." Mickey extended his arm towards the rear of the store and motioned to a long line of light and dark suits.

There was a large selection of suits and the man realized knowing his size would narrow his search. "Can you measure me for a suit before I look at the selection you have here? I might be a size or two larger than I was a few years ago."

Mickey hesitated. He remembered Jim McGovern's instructions only less than an hour ago that no one was to be measured until he returned to the shop. So Mickey began to ask for the customer's name and phone number when Danny, with a mischievous gleam in his eye, decided to help.

Stepping from behind the sales counter, Danny interrupted Mickey's request for the man's name and number. "Of course we can fit you for a suit. We'll want to get the measurements exact. The best and newest means to do that is to perform a "Direct Continental Measurement".

Sensing that this 'help' from Danny was going to be an adventure, Mickey calmly addressed Danny. "Danny, it might be better to wait until Mr. McGovern comes back from lunch."

Fully in gear and pleased with his new plan to measure the man and enliven his currently 'ho-hum' day, Danny winked at Mickey, then looked and smiled assuredly at the customer. "Why wait. He may be gone a long time. This will only take a few minutes."

Mickey looked confused. He'd seen that look before on Danny's face and he'd heard that cocksure voice whenever Danny hatched one of his many hare-brained schemes. But he went along because when Danny was set on taking the joke as far as it can go, he didn't know how to stop him.

The man looked at Mickey, then at Danny. "OK. Measure me."

Danny was now in charge and he was determined to complete his fun. He winked again at Mickey which made Mickey more nervous. "Mickey, hand me that white tailor's chalk. Also, cut me a full body-length of brown paper and lay it on the floor between the suit racks.

"You want me to lay a large piece of brown wrapping paper on the floor?" Mickey said incredulously.

Danny said very calmly and curtly. "Yep. That's correct."
He turned and spoke to the customer. "Sir, I need you to take off your jacket and lie down over here in this open space, on the brown paper."

"Lie down? On the paper, on the floor?"

"Yep. Lie down on your back, of course, for now. We want to measure for the back part of your suit first.

"The back part of my suit?"

"Yep. That's the genius of this new European measuring technique. It's a total method, front, back, sideways. Very exact. Very European."

Danny looked over to Mickey and smiled as the customer lowered himself on his back and onto the brown paper on the floor. This time Mickey couldn't help but smile back. Even so, Mickey was anxiously watching the entrance to the store. Someone might come in before the "Direct Continental Measurement" technique was finished.

Now lying on his back in the middle of the suit racks, the customer looked up at Danny the tailor. "OK. Like this?"

Danny was standing next to the prone customer and holding a piece of tailor's chalk in his hand. "Yep. Just like that. Now close your eyes so you don't get dizzy. Now I'm going to outline your whole body while you lay still. Then you'll turn over, and I'll chalk for the front of the suit."

Just then, the store's entrance bell rang. Mickey heard it but Danny, the tailor, didn't. He was too engrossed in performing the first, perfect, European-style, 'Direct Continental Measurement' technique in McGovern's Men Store in Chester, PA. He was enjoying himself. Then Danny heard a loud, alarming voice. He realized that Jim McGovern had returned from his lunch break. The first words from the owner's mouth were loud and filled with alarm. "What happened? Who is that? Who fell? Oh, my God, what's going on?"

In that split-second after entering his store, all that Jim McGovern could see was a strange man, lying on his back, in the middle of his store. The man's eyes were closed. Mr. McGovern quickly put 2+2 together. Heart attack! He knew it was a heart attack. Worse. The man could already be dead lying in the middle of his store. He looked anxiously at Mickey.

"What happened Mickey? Did you call a doctor, an ambulance?"

Mickey didn't answer him. Danny did. In between his own laughter, Danny said. "He's not dead, Jim. I'm measuring him for a new suit."

Danny paused for a moment to give Jim McGovern time to hear what he said. Then Danny added with an impish grin. "How soon do you think you can have it ready for him?"

1955, "I can do odd jobs."

Mickey had a productive season in 1955. He averaged .301, hit 14 homeruns, and drove in 85 runs. He did this even as the new Senators' Manager, Chuck Dressen, repeatedly auditioned younger players for Mickey's job at first base. Dressen's plan as early as spring training was to use Mickey sparingly because he thought Mickey was too old to play every day at age 37. It wasn't an unexpected or unrealistic opinion or evaluation of a 37 year old athlete in any sport. Mickey, always a team player and supportive of fellow teammates, willingly tutored his replacement at first base. Julio Becquer was a young black Cuban player struggling to learn the position and to learn a new language and culture. Mickey accepted the opportunity to work closely with Julio. He had never forgotten that day in 1937 when Hank Miller wasn't invited to join him and Danny in the tryout session in Chester. That memory still bothered him and he was glad to see such injustices erased and watch as players of all races and nationalities were given opportunities to play baseball at all levels of the game.

Mickey had seen a lot of changes in his eighteen years in baseball. Most of them benefited the players and the game of baseball. Soon though he became personally familiar with a difficult aspect of professional baseball, an aspect of the professional game that many players including Danny had already experienced. Mickey became a baseball nomad. He spent the final four years of his career playing in three different cities for three different teams. This was before players gained some control over their careers with the advent of 'free agency' which wouldn't come until two decades later. However, prior to the mid '70s, team owners handled their players in the same manner as they handled pieces of capital equipment and tools. The players were bought, sold, traded, punished, or mothballed whenever the owner wanted to do so. Thus, Mickey and others were shuttled from one team to another based on an owner's need for players, for cash, as a punishment, or for whatever reason they wished.

Elsewhere, Danny experienced a low point in his managing career. Before mid-season, the Charleston Senators were already a disappointment. The club was losing money and the owner was going bankrupt, and players who could go elsewhere left the team. Morale was low. Miraculously, Danny won nearly half of the games he managed before bowing out voluntarily. His decision to move to Charleston wasn't a good one and he soon realized that the owner was broke. Danny's straight-forward nature allowed for an amenable gentleman's agreement between the owner and himself. Danny willingly accepted the owner's decision to "fire" him at mid-season because he knew that the owner could no longer afford to pay him. The only positive outcome from all this was the opportunity for the Murtaugh family to spend most of that summer together on their first family vacation at the New Jersey beach. In other years, they were invited to spend two weeks at the shore with either their friends or family but there was never a summer when Danny was home. Now he was home, unemployed, and out of baseball. He welcomed the opportunity to be with friends and family by the sea.

1954 More chicken

That off-season Danny and Mickey appeared at the usual city and county sport functions and dinners. These were commonly referred to as the 'chicken circuit' because the dinners were all the same: chicken, potatoes, green vegetables, and ice cream, maybe a sundae, for dessert.

On one occasion, local athletes were being honored by the most active and successful sport's organization in Chester, the Lloyd Athletic Club. The club sponsored football, baseball, and basketball teams for boys and men, and promoted boxing events at Lloyd Field in Chester. After dinner was served, Danny and Mickey decided to each tell a story of their own from the past baseball season. Also, just a few days prior to the banquet, the Senators announced Mickey was traded to the Red Sox and would play in Boston for the 1956 season.

Matt Zabitka was again the emcee of the program. This time he reasoned that the only fair way to decide who would speak first was to flip a coin. Zabitka was out-witted by Danny again since the coin was provided by Danny. It was no surprise that Danny won the coin toss four times in a row, and was 'lucky' (?) to be the one who would speak first.

Danny appreciated the audience's welcoming applause and after acknowledging the honored guests and his audience, he began speaking. "I'm not going to talk long this evening. I know that the big news this week is that my friend, Mickey Vernon, will be playing baseball next year with Ted Williams and the Boston Red Sox." He paused a moment and the audience response was long and loud. Danny let it ring throughout the banquet room for a few seconds and continued. "I'm sure everyone is anxious to hear what Mickey has to say about having to share headlines in Boston with the Splendid Splinter." He added wryly. "I wonder if anyone in Beantown will even notice that Mickey's there. Boston is a tough town and most Boston fans think they have a one-man team."

This remark made a few attendees groan but most of the audience laughed and Mickey who was the target of the humorous remark smiled. Switching gears, Danny focused on himself. "First, I want to thank those few wise guys here tonight who sent me sympathy cards this past summer when it was announced that my own ball club, the Charleston Pirates, closed down due to bankruptcy."

There was laughter then a few comments were shouted from the audience: 'it's a raw deal', 'who needs them', and so forth. Danny waited for the supportive comments to pass, then continued speaking.

"It was a tough, and thankfully, a short season this year. The good news was that Kate, the kids and I got to spend a day or two on the beach in the summer. I wasn't sure how to get there. I haven't been on the Jersey beach since I was a teenager. We aren't usually home during the summer. That's also the only reason I'm thanking the wise guys for the sympathy cards. They were the same people who loaned us the beach house. You have to take the bad with the good, sometimes."

He continued. "Overall, the experience wasn't so bad at Charleston and I did learn something. Money was tight, sure, and I learned not to squander any valuable assets. For example, I always encouraged hitters to stay alive at the plate, foul off pitches until you get the pitch you could hit. But this year team funds were awfully low. How broke was the team? Well, I should've stopped those batters from hitting so many foul balls into the stands. Balls cost money, about $3 apiece. I should've made a team rule – when you swing the bat, you must either miss the ball or you hit it fair, no fouls. I should've fined them two bits for every foul ball instead of paying to replace baseballs. I could've used that money to buy a couple of players. Then maybe I might've been able to turn the season around and increase attendance, and still be managing."

He stopped talking and waited for everyone to understand that he was kidding them. He said. "But, I didn't. Now I'm home." Flashing his wide Irish smile, he ended his short monologue. "Thanks for listening. By the way, I can do odd jobs. Call me."

The audience laughed and applauded, and whistles accompanied Danny as he stepped away from the podium. Once he was seated, Mickey walked purposefully to the podium and pulled the microphone up to its full height and began speaking. "Good evening everybody. I'm glad to be here with all these athletes, and with Danny, too." He stopped for a moment, grinned, and looked down the table to Danny.
"Yes, Danny. I'm excited to be moving over to the Red Sox. The chance for me to appear in a World Series is now much higher on paper than when it was when I was with Cleveland. Though I'd rather go to the Series with you. You and me, side by side. That was always our promise to one another." The audience applauded.

Mickey adjusted the microphone. "I'm going to miss my friends in Washington but I'm looking forward to the new experience of playing in the lineup with Ted Williams. As many here may know, Ted is a fierce competitor. Hitting is his life's skill and his intense dedication to hitting is legendary."

Shifting his feet a little for balance, he decided to tell a story that showed a glimpse of Ted's intensity and wit.

"In a game this past season against us, Ted was batting against a rookie pitcher for the Senators named Pedro Ramos. Ted rarely strikes out but this kid struck out the mighty Ted Williams, and the rookie knew how big this was. So, immediately after the strike out, the catcher threw the ball back to Ramos. Pleased with himself, Ramos motioned to his own dugout, and with the fans looking on, he innocently rolled the ball gently to his pitching coach in the dugout. Of course, he wanted to save this ball forever.

After the game was over, Ramos walked across the ball field to the Boston dugout and approached Ted and asked Ted to sign the baseball. Ted immediately erupted into a cascade of brightly colored, teamster and longshoreman-type profanities. The kid was shocked and red-faced and he was nearly in tears when Ted noticed and relented. So Ted signed the ball and Ramos left the dugout. It was amazing that the kid survived the instant rage and that there was no confrontation with 'Teddy Ballgame.'

A few people in the audience, thinking that the story was over began to applaud, probably saluting Williams' gesture of signing the ball and ending it peacefully.

Mickey raised his hand to halt the applause and he said.

"No, wait. There is more to the story. About two weeks later, Ramos faced Ted in another game. This time, Ted wasted no time or pitches. He sent the kid's first pitch deep into the right field stands. As Ted was rounding first base, he called over to Ramos and he said, "Hey, kid. I'll sign that son of a bitch, too, if you ever find it."

The laughter was instantaneous, raucous, and enduring, and Mickey was pleased with himself. Having learned the old show business adage that it's best to leave them laughing, he had only one last remark. "That's my new teammate. I'm happy and excited. I'm sure that I'll have more stories like this one next year. Thank you."

Mickey stepped away from the microphone and he left the audience still laughing and rising to their feet. In Chester and Delaware County, Danny and Mickey struck again. Hope and Crosby should be thankful that they didn't have to follow that act.

***Mickey's banquet story excerpted from 'The Teammates', David Halberstam.**

1955, "Still a promise."

Shortly afterward, Danny and Mickey were eating lunch at a local restaurant on Welsh Street in downtown Chester. Business was slow at the clothing store so they took their lunch break together while Mr. McGovern minded the store. Jim McGovern didn't leave Danny alone in the store anymore.

They ordered as soon as they sat down and the waitress delivered two bowls of soup, and saltines. Danny as always was the first to pick-up his spoon and he began eating.

"Well, Mick, congratulations on going to Boston." he said in between tastes of soup. "The World Series is getting closer for you. Boston is overdue. They're smart to add your bat and glove." Munching on a cracker, Danny added. "With you and Williams hitting back to back, they might have gotten themselves a sure pennant."

Mickey played with his spoon and moved his bowl a bit. The trade was something he knew could happen but it was tough for him to move into a new locker room and dugout. He had done it once with Cleveland and back again to Washington, and he didn't like it at all. He knew he would be able to talk about this with Danny. After all, Danny had been through this 'nomad' treatment plenty of times.

"Yeh! I hope so, Danny. When I heard that I was going to Boston, I felt bad about leaving Washington again. But I'm glad that I'm going to a winner. Going to a team that has a great shot at a World Series makes it hard to complain about it to anyone."

Danny continued to enjoy the soup but he was animated about Mickey's move to Boston. "They didn't just trade you to Boston, Mick. The Red Sox wanted you and they paid the right price. They expect that you'll be the final piece that gets them into the World Series."

The conversation ceased long enough for the two friends to eat the soup and the saltines. Danny was crushing a single saltine at a time into his soup. It was a habit picked up in his mother's kitchen from watching his dad putting saltines in any kind of soup that he ate. 'Added nourishment' his father would say and laugh. His Mom wasn't so approving.

During the pause in conversation, two local businessmen walked into the restaurant. The first businessman was wearing a dark gray, three piece suit and he looked like a banker. His companion was younger and was probably a co-worker. He was also wearing a suit but it was navy blue and he wasn't wearing a vest. The two men walked up to Danny and Mickey, and greeted them. No one stood up. They knew one another and a formal greeting wasn't necessary. Besides it was lunch break and every minute counted.

The banker spoke first. "Hi, fellas. Soup looks hot." Then he looked at Mickey. "Mick, good luck in Boston."

"Congratulations, Mickey." said the younger man. "The Yankees are in for a real battle now. Williams and Vernon, back to back."

"Thanks fellas." Mickey was never comfortable with praise but he knew that he would hear comments and good wishes from friends, neighbors, and strangers an awful lot in the next few weeks. He understood how excited they were. He was excited too. There wasn't much more he could say without letting his soup get cold. The businessmen walked away and sat at a table across the room.

Danny hardly slowed down his eating and he was on track to have a second bowl of soup before Mickey had eaten even half of his first bowl. Naturally, Mickey was getting attention from fans all over the country but he was concerned about his buddy. Other than the war years, this would be the first time in seventeen years that his friend would not be earning a living on a baseball field. He and Danny talked recently about baseball jobs but nothing had come to Danny yet. Nevertheless, they both knew that the baseball buzz never stopped. Someone, somewhere was looking for somebody on the field or in the dugout to make their team better. Danny understood that he had to pay his telephone bill and keep his line open. If he could've arranged it, he would have someone next to his phone all of the time so he would never miss a call. But who could afford that expense. After all, you can't leave a message on a phone if there is no one there to answer the phone, at least not in 1955.

They finished their soup and crackers and ordered a second cup of coffee. Coffee was always the final piece of the lunch ritual. Mickey took a taste from his cup, then he asked Danny a question. "Have you gotten any phone calls?"

Danny did receive a call last night and he planned to tell Mickey after lunch. "Yes. Joe Brown called me last night and offered me a Manager's position with Class A, Williamsport. I didn't tell you this morning because I planned to tell you here at lunch."

Mickey remained silent. He knew that Danny had more to say.

"But it's a step back from the talent level at New Orleans and Charleston."

Baseball like businesses and military organizations had its own hierarchy with a structured path on which players and managers and executives moved from one end of that path to the other end. Williamsport was a Class A level league that ranked lower than Class AA and Class AAA. Houston and Charleston were higher levels leagues that groomed more promising or polished players and managers. Danny understood that some people might interpret this Class A assignment as a signal that he was falling behind in his baseball career.

"That's OK." Mickey said. "It's baseball. It keeps you in the game. Joe wouldn't come back to you if he thought you should stay out of the game. The way I see it, Danny, is that he and Ricky want you around. Take the job. Things happen."

"Yeh. I know they do." Danny answered but he didn't sound like he believed it himself at that moment.

Mickey remembered the one idea that he thought was promising. "How about the sporting goods store? Have you thought anymore about opening a store downtown?"

"I did. But now I'm not sure that's for me. I can't sit in one place any more, same place, every day, every week, all of the time."

If anyone understood how Danny felt, it was Mickey. He didn't have to think about 'life outside baseball' because he was always in demand. But when he did think about it, he knew he would be restless sitting in one chair all day long. He said forcefully. "Then, take the Williamsport job. It's not far from home, about 180 miles away. You'll be closer to Kate and the kids. I know that I'm getting tired myself of being away from Lib and Gay."

Danny chuckled. Boston was three times further away in distance than Williamsport but a lot closer to Philly via rail. "Well, now you can catch a fast train from Boston to get home. If the Red Sox win the next World Series, you can stop playing baseball whenever you want. What's left?"

"That sounds good Danny but you and I know we will always have baseball fever. Remember when we promised to share the World Series glory if either one of us ever got close? Carry one another's bats. Play for free. Even drive the bus. Do anything to be in a World Series together."

Danny's eyes shined at the memory. "Yep. I do. It's still a promise." Then Mickey lifted his coffee cup and tilted it towards his friend. "Yep. Still a promise."

That was how their coffee chats always ended. Always on a happy note regardless of what good news or bad news they shared. Positive thinking was the strongest part of their common nature and cemented their lifetime friendship. Humor and baseball were abundantly shared and they held within themselves the missing part of each other that they provided to one another when difficulty or decision confronted them. It was like a perfect marriage that enabled two entities to become the best of themselves.

February 1956, "Dad, it's for you."

The winter months at the Murtaugh house on Kerlin Street were generally quiet. The mid-week evening hours were the quietest after dinner had ended and the kitchen was cleaned. Timmy, Danny, and Kathy always finished their homework before dinner so they could watch that evening's favorite television show. The biggest benefit of this fascinating new TV technology was that when the show came on the television, the entire family gathered in the same room and watched the show together. It was also very common that the prime shows were over by 9 PM or sooner and the kids were all sent to bed immediately afterward with instructions that all lights were to be turned out.

There were few interruptions or unexpected visitors after dinner. So whenever the doorbell rang or even when the phone rang, everyone's ears perked up. That's what happened when the household phone rang one evening in February.

The phone sat on a small table centrally located in the entrance foyer between the living room and the dining room and just a few feet from the steps that led to the second floor bedrooms. A small chair was positioned next to the table to provide comfort for anyone who might be on a lengthy conversation. Kathy now seven years old was the first person to reach the ringing phone. She picked up the phone and offered her practiced greeting. "Hello, Murtaugh residence." She practically sang those three words into the telephone. Kathy listened to the voice on the other end. "Yes." She said. Then she held the phone out to her Dad who was sitting in the living room, and who had a full view of his daughter and the phone. "Dad, it's for you."

Danny was sitting in a soft cozy chair across the room. He stood up and walked over and took the phone from his daughter and placed it up to his ear. "Hello. Who's calling?" He paused to listen for the reply. "Oh. Hi, Joe. Fine, thanks." He paused again and listened. "Tomorrow. I figured I'd get into Williamsport before noon." Danny waited and listened to the person on the other end. "Uh Huh. Yes. Sure. OK. I'll talk to you tomorrow. Yep. I'll be here. Call anytime. Yep. 10 am is fine. Alright. Goodbye, Joe."

Danny hung up the phone and walked into the kitchen where Kate was just finishing making school lunches for the kids.

Danny and Mickey, Ordinary Heroes
Kate heard the phone ring and she heard Kathy tell her Dad that the phone call was for him. She thought that Kathy answered the phone perfectly and she was pleased that she spent time teaching her daughter how to answer properly like a young lady. She tried to not listen in on the conversation but Danny's short cryptic answers heightened her natural curiosity. "Who was that?" she asked.

"That was Joe Brown."

Hearing that Joe Brown was calling Danny the night before Danny was leaving to drive to Williamsport made her nervous.

"What did he want?" Then she asked the most fearsome and obvious question. "He didn't want to change his mind on Williamsport, did he?"

Danny moved closer to Kate and kept his eyes down. She saw this and was afraid of what he would say next.

"Yes. He did. He changed his mind on Williamsport. He doesn't want me to go there tomorrow. He doesn't want me to go there at all."

Kate turned to Danny with a worried look on her face and sighed lowly. "Oh! Danny."

Now he straightened up, lifted his face to hers and with his eyes sparkling, he smiled and said. "It's OK. He wants me to go to Pittsburgh instead. He wants me to be a coach for the Pirates." He let that sentence settle softly between them, then he added. "Kate, we're back in the big leagues."

"Oh my Lord! Is that true? Are you sure it was him? It was Mr. Brown?"

"It was him, alright. He's gonna call me at 10 am tomorrow and give me all the details. I'm not reporting to Williamsport at all."

"Then who goes to Williamsport?"

"I don't know. But I hope that it's someone who will be as happy to go to Williamsport as I am to go to Pittsburgh."

Danny and Kate reached out for each other and embraced. Danny kissed Kate and lifted her off the kitchen floor and swung her around once. Kate's legs just missed hitting Kathy who was standing nearby the whole time listening to everything, just like her mother would do. Kathy ran out of the kitchen and into the small hallway. She raced up the steps to her brothers' bedroom and told her big brothers that they're all going to Pittsburgh. "We're all back in the big leagues." she said.

At exactly 10 am on the next morning, Joe L. Brown, Pittsburgh Pirates General Manager, called Danny and told him to go directly to Florida instead of Pittsburgh. He wanted Danny to join the rest of the Pirates in spring training. Danny was going to replace a coach who decided to leave the team. The Pirates Manager, Bobby Bragan, a former teammate of Danny's on the Phillies, requested that Danny be the replacement. Unknowingly, all three - the Pirates, Bobby Bragan, and Danny - were closing in on their shared destiny.

Over in the American League, Mickey and the Boston Red Sox didn't get into the 1956 World Series and they didn't get into the 1957 World Series either. But Mickey performed better than expected as the Red Sox number four batter in the Boston lineup just behind Ted Williams. At 38 years old, he had a stellar year. He hit .310, slugged 15 homeruns, and drove in 85 runs. He was selected to the AL All Star Team for the sixth time. But none of this was enough to replace the disappointment of not winning the pennant. The mighty Yankees won the pennant and the World Series. In the following year, 1957, Mickey was less productive and batted .241. The only memorable piece of baseball history for Boston in 1957 was that Ted Williams, the Splendid Splinter, won his last batting title. He made his last run at hitting .400, he fell short, but hit an unforgettable .388. It was his sixth and last batting title. He and Mickey were both 39 years old.

1957, "I'm better than you think I am."

Danny completed his first year as an assistant to Bobby Bragan and coached the Pirate infielders. It was a difficult year for the team but he was in the big leagues again. The Pirates finished with 66 wins and 88 losses. The following season in 1957 was not much better and by July they were headed towards 100 losses when Joe Brown was trying to decide if he should fire Bobby Bragan and change Managers in mid-season.

Joe Brown was in his office on a rare day off. Clyde Sukforth, one of Bragan's coaches, was talking to Joe.

"Joe, I know he can make them a better club. He's got grit. He's feisty, he's a battler. The players respect him." Sukeforth was standing in front of the GM's desk and he was pleading with Brown who had replaced Branch Rickey as the new Pirates General Manager.

Joe decided to remove Bragan and he offered the interim Manager's position to Clyde who was a veteran coach with many years of experience. Clyde refused the assignment only minutes ago but he had the ideal candidate for the Pirates, Danny Murtaugh.

Brown wanted Sukeforth to convince him so he asked for more information. "OK. OK. But what about his game knowledge? His strategy?"

Now, Clyde had a frustrated look on his face. "Joe." He said. "He won for you for three years in New Orleans. That wasn't a talented team. He understands pitching, young and old players. He respects the game. He plays to win. He's patient. He uses everybody's skills."

Joe had heard enough. Maybe he heard too many positives. He asked Clyde one last question. "He can't be perfect. What don't you like about him?"

Clyde thought for a moment and replied. "That's easy. I don't like his taste in cheap cigars. They smell awful. Oh! He doesn't curse enough for me. Hell, he doesn't curse at all. He's the poorest example of the typical Irishman that I've ever seen. He doesn't even drink. Not beer; not whiskey. But the biggest reason I have for not liking him is that he always beats me at pinochle, and he takes my money." Clyde waited, he thought some more and said, "That's about it."

Joe knew all these things too but he was playing the devil's advocate and he wanted someone experienced in the game to say out loud the same things that he was thinking.

"Well, I like him, too. Branch likes him. But I need you to stick around. Guide him when you can." Joe closed his eyes and for a flash of a moment he thought that he had gotten a glimpse of the future. "OK, Clyde. Let's take a shot with him. Go down on the field and bring him up here."

Clyde went down to the practice field and brought Danny back upstairs to Brown's office. Clyde knocked lightly and opened the door. Danny entered first, then Clyde followed and closed the door behind them.

The GM was seated at a large desk in the far end of the room facing the door. The desk was flanked by a window on each side of the back wall. Joe stood up as Danny approached the desk. Joe didn't make a motion to shake hands instead standing up to acknowledge that Danny was welcome into the room.

"Hi! Danny, have a seat." He motioned to a chair nearby.

"Hi! Joe." Danny sat, still uncertain as to the reason he was sitting here.

All three men were seated now. Joe sat in a plush leather chair behind his massive mahogany desk. Danny and Clyde sat in cushioned chairs on the employee's side of the desk.

"Danny, I'm going to get right to the point. I'm replacing Bobby as our Manager. The team is sinking lower than last year. I want to win. But worse than not winning is losing 100 games in a single season. It's an ugly mark, a stigma. That's where this team is headed now, 100 losses."

Joe stopped talking. Then he motioned with his hand towards Clyde. "Clyde thinks you can stop this slide. That you can make the team play better. He's convinced me that you can help the team. What do you say? Can you make the team better?"

Danny wasn't overwhelmed or surprised at this offer. He read the papers and lived in the clubhouse. Bragan was leaving. That is what Managers do when they don't win even if they don't have the tools to win. Danny felt that he could do as fine a job with these players as anyone in the organization. Maybe better. He knew most of the players from having coached or played against them in the past five years. He was nervous of course but he was ready.

He shifted very slightly in his chair. "Well, Joe, I think the boys can play better. I'd welcome the opportunity to show them how to do that and win." That's what Brown wanted to hear. If Danny could do it. Good. If not, then that was on Danny. At the least, the GM had put a plan in action.

"OK." Joe explained. "There are fifty-one more games to play. The team has 67 losses and anything more than 32 losses would be disastrous. It's too late for a pennant and I'd like to see a winning record but that's not likely. Just keep the Pirates away from 100 losses. Understand, Danny?"

"Yep. I do. I plan to stay away from 68 losses. If that fails, then my goal is to stay away from 69. If I start out to settle for 99 losses, it will lead to 100 very quickly. I promise to have the team play better than that."

"Clyde will be your right-hand man. He thinks a lot of you. So did Branch. Do what you can. Also, understand that this is an interim position for you through the remainder of the season. Good luck, Danny. Come directly to me for anything you need."

Joe got up from his leather chair and walked around the desk and shook hands with his new Manager. Flushed with excitement and nervousness, Danny also shook hands with Clyde, then he turned away from both men and walked to the office door. As he reached for the door knob, Danny turned back and faced Joe. He took in a full breath of air, smiled at Joe, and said. "Joe, I want you to know that I'm a much better Manager than you think I am."

Then Danny turned away, opened the door, and left. He walked back down and onto the field. He knew that only wins count. To win, he needed to make the players better and he needed to get them to play like a team. It was his team now and he had eight weeks to make it a winning one.

*** Branch Rickey retired due to poor health in 1955 after 52 years in professional baseball. He had been a player, a Manager, an executive, a part owner, and most importantly, an innovator of baseball's farm system and a trailblazer in the development and use of batting helmets for players. He is a member of the Baseball Hall of Fame.**

CHAPTER TWELVE
MANAGER OF THE YEAR

August 1958, "Go west."

It was difficult in 1958 to believe that any baseball news could be more surprising than the lowly, perennial, second-division Pittsburgh Pirates were being touted as a favorite to win the National League pennant. It was true but there was even bigger news. The 1958 baseball season ushered in the biggest geographical change in the staid, traditional, arena of major league baseball. In May 1957, a majority of team owners in both leagues approved the move of the Brooklyn Dodgers and the New York Giants from New York City to the West coast. The Brooklyn Dodgers were moving to Los Angeles and the New York Giants were moving to San Francisco. The separate owners of the two New York teams had been planning their moves for several years. The success and the drawing power of the mighty Yankees had been too powerful for the other two New York teams to compete against. Baseball in New York was dominated by the New York Yankees. The Yankees won and made money. The Dodgers and Giants were neighborhood teams who won and had loyal fans but didn't make as much money as the Yankees.

The lure of new stadiums and increased revenues out West cemented the final decision. This announcement foreshadowed baseball's immense growth across the country. Several teams had relocated a few years earlier (St. Louis Browns, Philadelphia Athletics, Boston Braves) but this east-to-west coast bombshell hastened the expansion of major league teams in both leagues into cities west of the Mississippi, and south of the Mason-Dixon Line. Between 1960 and 2015, the number of major league teams would expand from sixteen to thirty. During these 55 years, it seemed baseball teams changed cities and names more often than Babe Ruth hit homeruns, or Rickey Henderson stole second base. The Pittsburgh Pirates were one of the few teams that would remain unchanged. The Cincinnati Reds, Philadelphia Phillies, and St. Louis

Cardinals were several others who stayed in place. The Washington Senators embarked on the longest and wildest journey, travelling to several new cities and adopting several new identities. Although they were one of the earliest baseball franchises, there was a period of 33 years when Washington, DC did not have a team in major league baseball (1973-2005).

1958 Manager of the Year

Outside of this maelstrom of change, and in advance of the 1958 season, Danny received a formal contract from Joe Brown to manage the Pirates. Brown now saw what Branch Rickey saw several years earlier. Danny was a winner. Danny finished 1957 with more Pirate wins than losses: 26 wins and 25 losses. The Pirates lost a total of 92 games. But it will be twenty-eight more years before the Pirates ever lose more than 90 games in a single season, thanks in large part to Danny Murtaugh's legacy, a legacy begun mid-season in 1957.

The Danny Murtaugh-led Pittsburgh Pirates finished the 1957 baseball season playing over .500 baseball. Joe Brown and Clyde Sukeforth looked smart, and Joe Brown looked even smarter when he re-signed Danny for the 1958 season.

That decision paid off for the Pirates when they started the new season as one of the hottest teams in the National League and continued to play well. There was a pause in their happy mood in mid-season when Danny's mom, Nellie Mc Carey Murtaugh, passed away on July 25th. Danny left the team and spent more than a week with his family. With his Mom and Dad both gone, Danny was needed at home. He was the only son and he wanted to be near his three sisters and the large Murtaugh clan through this difficult loss. The Pirates baseball club was concerned that the team would lose their winning ways while their skipper was away. Fortunately, while Danny was gone, they kept winning.

When August arrived the Pirates played a big series against the former New York Giants, now relocated as the San Francisco Giants. Two wins in this three-game series with the Giants would put the Pirates in second place, a rare spot for Pittsburgh. The first-place Milwaukee Braves could hear Pirate footsteps. One big reason for the Pirates success was big first baseman Frank Thomas. Frank was the club's leading slugger who replaced Ralph Kiner. He was Pittsburgh's only long-ball threat and this year he hit 35 homeruns and drove in 109 runs. He played in his first All Star game the previous month. Frank, like many players on this Pirates team, was showing much improvement. Murtaugh's approach with the team was reflected in his players' improvements and in his coaches' attitudes. There was an air of relaxation for everyone in the clubhouse that contributed a healthy intensity to their performance on the field. It was what all sport fans in Pittsburgh had waited so long to enjoy. The Pirates were becoming a winning team that reflected the grit and perseverance of the people who lived in the Steel City. Crowd noises, cheers, applause, and joyful stomping were common parts of Pirate baseball games. When the 1958 season ended, Danny's club had won 84 games and finished in second place behind the Braves. Danny's season as Pirates Manager was as highly satisfying as his 1948 performance as a player. He was voted as the National League Manager of the Year and won the award in his first full year of managing a major league team.

December 1958, Shoemaker Hill

Elsewhere, Mickey salvaged what started as a strange season for him. The year began when Boston traded him back to Cleveland. This was his third team in four years. Cleveland had signed Mickey to be their insurance as a backup for their young, heralded, first baseman, Vic Wertz. But when Wertz was injured in spring training, Mickey, now 40, played in 119 games for Cleveland. He hit .293 and was selected to his seventh and final AL All Star game. Most notably, by the end of the season, Mickey played in his 2,227th game at first base, breaking Yankee Hall of Famer Lou Gehrig's record for the number of career games played at first base

(2,137). It was another memorable season for Mickey but he wasn't as fortunate when he was home during the 1958 off-season.

On an evening early in December, Mickey was driving from work in downtown Chester to his home in Wallingford located just northwest of the city. He was only a few blocks from work when it began to snow. Just as darkness blanketed the city, the snow began to fall rapidly and the city streets and sidewalks were quickly covered with a slick coating of freezing snow. Mickey drove cautiously while the snow continued to deepen on the streets. Mickey had reason to be more careful than usual. He had recently purchased a brand new vehicle, a German-built car, a Volkswagen. Volkswagen is a German compound word meaning 'the people's car' in English. It was strikingly small and it seemed to be missing its engine until you were informed by the engineer, most likely a German, to look for the engine in the rear of the car. The engine was intentionally mounted inside the back end of the car where the trunk would normally be located. Fortunately, the German car designer realized the need for storage space so he put the rear trunk in the front of the people's car. Consequently the small, round, lady bug-like appearance earned the car an instant and iconic American nickname, the 'Beetle'. Its biggest claim to fame was its economic and strategic benefit of reportedly being able to go farther on a gallon of gasoline than anything built on four wheels in the automobile industry. It could go 25 miles on a gallon of gas when most American cars travelled 8-10 miles. With gas predicted to rise from 23 cents a gallon to as much as 30 cents a gallon by 1960, the Beetle was an economic boon for its owners.

Unexpectedly the snow-covered roads provided the first winter test for Mickey and his new car. Mickey had barely passed the 'can he fit' test when he initially bought the car. His long athletic body did not easily conform to the Beetle's tight interior. He always took several minutes to wrestle himself into driving position behind the wheel. So far his drive home was uneventful as he prepared to exit the city but the continuing snowfall presented an increasing driving hazard. The city's final intersection on the northwestern end of the city is at 24th Street and

Providence Avenue, and this four way intersection sits at the top of a hill commonly referred to as Shoemaker Hill. The cross street at the intersection is 24th Street where Providence Avenue runs out from downtown Chester and descends from the top of the intersection down to the bottom of the hill, then the road continues over a small bridge and begins its rise up to the crest of a hill that leads to Wallingford, Mickey's home. It was an average graded hill to traverse in fair weather but it was a more difficult challenge on a snowy night.

Mickey approached the intersection, crossed over 24th Street and began to move in traffic slowly down Shoemaker Hill and out of the city. He was following a city transit bus and a car down the hill, and several more vehicles were following closely behind him.

Suddenly there is a loud *HONK!* Then another *HONK*, and a loud *THUMP*! These noises were accompanied by the sound of breaking glass and crunching metal amidst the quiet snow that was still falling on the road. In a rapid tempo, there was a repetition of identical crashes, one after the other. The rear ends of cars were being smashed by the front ends of cars directly behind them. It was a chain reaction accident, like a series of echoes from a canyon. The source of the crash was the city bus at the front of this parade of vehicles that descended the hill. The bus slid on the snowy surface and the driver tried to stop suddenly on the slippery descent but this caused the car in front of Mickey to hit the rear of the bus. Likewise, Mickey's Volkswagen slid and smashed into the car in front of him. A series of crashes continued until a total of five vehicles were involved, and Mickey and his Beetle were sandwiched in the very middle of the collisions. The noise stopped as abruptly as the noise began. For a few seconds, that seemed more like minutes, there was no sound.

The first person out of his car was the driver of the car directly behind Mickey. His car struck what appeared to be Mickey's rear-end trunk but what was really now Mickey's new engine. He exited his car and he said to no one in particular. "I couldn't stop."

The driver of the car in front of Mickey stepped gingerly out of his car and added his voice. "The bus tried to stop, then it started to slide. Its brakes must've locked. I almost slid under it."

Soon, everyone was out of their cars including the bus driver. Everyone except Mickey. The driver who hit the rear end of Mickey's Volkswagen looked into the front window and he immediately saw that Mickey couldn't move. The impact from his car caused the front of the Volkswagen to push into the car in front of him and the trunk that was where Mickey's engine would normally be collapsed easily back into Mickey's body. He was alert but he was hurting. The other drivers gathered outside his driver-side window and started to assist him.

Mickey waved them off. "I'm OK. I just can't move my legs and arms enough to get out of this little car of mine."
He was soon able to escape the car and he was seated in one of the other cars. The snow kept falling until the police and ambulance arrived and soon the cars were redirected on their own, except Mickey's Beetle. It was towed away. Mickey was the only person injured in the accident. He suffered cuts and bruises and aggravated an existing knee injury and recovered at home over the winter months. His people's car was crushed. His new Volkswagen became his last Volkswagen and it was quickly replaced by a larger American automobile. The 'people's car' was not the right car for Mickey.

May 26, 1959, on the same field

Mickey fully recovered from his car accident and opened the regular season with Cleveland visiting Kansas City. However, after the second day of the season, Mickey was traded to the Milwaukee Braves. He wasn't happy but the good news was that he was still going to get another shot at playing on the biggest stage of all, the World Series. The Braves were the defending National League champions and considered to be the front-runner who was expected to appear in their third straight World Series in October. After just missing American League pennants with Cleveland and Boston, Mickey, at 41 years old, was excited for the opportunity to be a part of a National League contender for the World Series. This would be his third opportunity to fulfill every ballplayer's dream. But Mickey and the Braves would battle a familiar but new fierce competitor for the National League berth in the coming World Series, the Pittsburgh Pirates. The only way Mickey could get to the World Series this year was to help the Braves prevent his lifetime friend Danny from leading the Pirates to the same pennant. Only one of them would be able to go into the World Series this year. The other one goes home. That's not how they planned it so long ago.

In the spring of 1937, Danny and Mickey both signed professional baseball contracts but this was the first time in 22 years that Mickey and Danny faced each other in the major leagues. The Pittsburgh Pirates were a new addition to the short list of contenders for the pennant. In many local and regional sport columns, the Pirates were being predicted to win the 1959 pennant over the Braves and advance to the World Series for the first time since 1925.

This two-team race for the pennant began early in the season and included a memorable game on May 26 at Milwaukee. Ironically, it not only pitted the Braves and the Pirates against one another, but it placed two boyhood friends in opposing dugouts to be witnesses to perhaps one of the best pitched games in baseball history.

An hour before game time, the two men, still boys at heart, casually strode from their opposite dugouts toward the batting cage. They wore different uniforms and there was a clear physical difference in the men. One was tall and athletic, the other was much shorter and maybe a few years from being in playing shape. But they were thinking the same thing. How lucky are we now to be here on this field together. They came together, smiled widely, and shook hands with feeling.

Mickey spoke first. "Your guys are hot, Danny."

As closest of friends as he and Mickey were, Danny never let up his competitive guard against an opponent, and today Mickey was an opponent like every other person who got paid by a team other than the Pirates. Danny knew his club was playing well, very well, but he kept his reply simple.

"Yeh. Just in time, too. Our bad start in April didn't give us any room to stumble too long."

Putting his left hand into his pocket, Mickey grinned and said what almost sounded like a wish. "Well, it's early but one of us might get to the Big Series?"

"Only one of us? That wasn't our deal." The Pirates skipper replied.

"No, it wasn't. We're supposed to get there together. Maybe that's what happened to me in Boston and Cleveland. I jinxed them because I wasn't meant to go to the Series without you."

Then Mickey winked at Danny and added one request. "Don't tell Williams."

Chewing his trademark tobacco and watching his players loosen up on the field, Danny folded his arms like a General surveying his troops. "You know that we can still get there together, later. But you can't wait for anyone. You gotta catch that gold ring when it's within reach. Like we said when we were kids, we wanna go together but if we can't, don't pass up the prize."

"Guess we gotta get there first."

"Well, tonight's as good as any time to start the chase." was Danny's spirited reply.

"I don't know about tonight, Danny. Maybe tomorrow will be better for you and your guys. Burdette is going for us tonight."

There were no surprises in baseball. Every team had scouts watching the other teams. Danny knew how well Burdette was pitching this season. "Yeh, Lew is rolling along, all right. But we don't want to skip a night. We want to win tonight and tomorrow."

"No chance.' Mickey was starting to pile his confidence on top of Danny and treat him as an adversary, not as his friend. "Burdette, Mathews, Adcock, Covington, and Aaron? You might have to start a new winning streak again next week."

Danny smiled, shook his head and turned to walk back to the Pirates' dugout and said over his shoulder. "We'll see, buddy."

Then just like he did when they were just two kids from the sandlot, Danny who had already been given a copy of the Braves starting lineup barked out a wise-crack remark to his friend.

"Oh, Mick. Watch out for splinters in your backside, bench-jockey."

They both laughed. And not surprising at all, Danny had the last word.

May 26, 1959, A game for the Ages

They were both correct. This game delivered one of the best pitching duels in baseball history. Lew Burdette proved Mickey to be a soothsayer as he and Pirates left-hander Harvey Haddix pitched the best games of their careers and engraved their names into the golden ledger of baseball lore.

Danny and Mickey, Ordinary Heroes

The short walk to home plate that Danny and Mickey took before the game was soon forgotten. Almost four hours had passed and the game continued.

The radio announcer took a much-deserved long drink of water and welcomed newly tuned-in baseball fans to the large number of listeners who were already enthralled with this classic pitching duel.

"Well, fans, this has been a real nail-biter all night long, and it's been a long, long night. If you are just tuning into the game because a friend called you to tell you something special was happening in baseball, then you've come to the right place. We have a scoreless tie here in the bottom of the thirteenth inning. The Braves are batting. Mantilla, Mathews, and Aaron will face Haddix this inning. It's just unbelievable. Neither pitcher has wavered from their command of the game. Lew Burdette has completed thirteen innings and though he has given up a barrel of hits, twelve hits so far, no Pirates have scored. But it's doubtful that he will come out for another inning. What a pitching performance by him.

But right now, the man of the evening is the Pirates' Harvey Haddix. Amazingly, he has out-pitched Burdette. Tonight he is crafting a game for the ages. He has a perfect game through twelve innings! No walks. No hits. No runs. No errors. Not a single Braves runner has reached first base. No major league pitcher has ever done it. Haddix has retired 36 batters in a row. This is thrilling."

The announcer pulled himself away from the microphone and took a much-deserved drink of water. Haddix stood on the mound in the bottom of the thirteenth inning. The crafty left-hander completed twelve innings and not one Braves player had reached first base. Now he waited for Felix Mantilla, the 37th batter to face him tonight.

In the Pirates dugout, Danny and his pitching coach, Bill Burwell, were having the same conversation they've had for the last six innings. They jointly arrived at the same decision each time.

"Danny," Burwell said, "leave Harvey in right now. He isn't done. No one is hitting anything off of him."

Danny was not prepared for this. No one in baseball was prepared for this. A perfect game for twelve innings and the pitcher doesn't seem tired. Danny actually looked more tired than Haddix. Besides, the only way that Haddix could get credit for the perfect game was to finish the game as the closing pitcher. If Danny removed Haddix now it would mean Haddix pitched a remarkable game but he wouldn't get credit for a hitless or perfect game. The rule was very clear, a pitcher has to finish the game in order for him to be credited as the pitcher of record for a shutout, no-hitter, or perfect game. It was also a baseball taboo and bad manners to remove a pitcher when he has a no-hitter, and more important, a perfect game was a masterpiece that you don't interrupt. It is something that only God should touch. So, Danny decided to let Haddix pitch until the Braves got at least one runner on base or until the Pirates won.

"OK. He still looks strong." Danny said admiringly, shaking his head and chewing his tobacco. "I don't know how he's doing it. Let's get him past Mantilla and Matthews, then we'll decide on Aaron."

Felix Mantilla was a veteran player with good speed. He stood in the batter's box, waiting for the first pitch from Haddix. He had already decided he would swing at the first pitch and he hit the ball sharply to third base. Don Hoak moved quickly to his right to field the ball but the ball ticked off the end of his glove. Though the ball was slowed a little when it caromed off Hoak's glove, it still managed to roll all of the way to the left-field corner. Bob Skinner raced across to the leftfield corner and got to the ball quickly, his strong throw back into the infield forced Mantilla to stop his advance to second base and he returned to first base. The Pirates called time out.

Even after thirteen innings, a scoreless tie, and a night game, the stadium was still filled. Hardly anyone had left. All eyes now looked out to the scoreboard where runs, hits and errors were posted manually by a man seated behind the scoreboard. On those occasions where a ball was misplayed or was difficult to handle, the official home scorer was the sole arbiter who determined if the ball was a hit or an error based on the scorer's opinion on the range of difficulty of the play. On difficult plays, it was common for the home scorer to award hometown players with base hit rulings and award the opposing players' borderline hits as errors. Neither hit nor error was posted yet.

The Pirates bench coach spoke for all of the Pittsburgh fans. "Damn it! Hoak just missed catching it. Shit!"
Now there was a long pause as the crowd and all of the Pittsburgh infielders huddled at the pitcher's mound around Haddix. The decision of hit or error was in the hands of the Brave's hometown scorer and if normalcy held sway, the ruling wouldn't favor Haddix. Danny like everyone else hadn't taken his eyes off of the Hit column on the scoreboard. He knew that there was no argument possible on official scorer decisions. There was nothing to do but wait.

After what seemed to be a long, extended stretch of minutes, the ruling was posted. It was not a hit! The official scorer ruled it an error. It was decided that Hoak's glove positioning should've been enough for him to cleanly field the ball and throw out Mantilla. No one was happier for an error at that moment than Don Hoak. The perfect game was gone but Haddix still had his no- hitter.

Now Danny quickly sent his pitching coach out to speak with Haddix. Danny wanted Haddix to pitch to Matthews carefully and hopefully manage to get the batter to hit a ground ball that would get two quick outs.

Anxious to move Mantilla around the bases, Mathews hit the first pitch to the left of second base but it was hit too slowly for Mazeroski to get the force out at second base, so he tossed the ball to first base to get the first out of the inning. Mathews was called out and Mantilla moved up to second base. It wasn't getting any easier for Haddix as Hammerin' Hank

Aaron walked briskly to home plate. Aaron, a future Hall of Famer, was always anxious to bat. After all, he was a pure hitter with few flaws. He hit homeruns but he also hit for a high batting average every year. He would finish his baseball career with 755* homeruns passing the great Bambino, Babe Ruth, who previously held the record for 41 years with 714 career homeruns.

With first base open, Danny and his coaches conferred with one another to decide whether to pitch to Aaron.

While this was taking place in the Pirates dugout, the radio announcer was running through the same scenario for his audience. "First base is open and the Pirates don't have to pitch to Aaron. I'm sure Murtaugh will put Aaron on base now that the perfect game is gone. If he does walk Aaron that will put Brave runners on first and second, and set up a force-out at any base, or even better, a possible double-play that will get the Pirates out of the inning, and onto the fourteenth inning."

Down on the field, Danny motioned to his catcher, Smokey Burgess, and said. "Put him on base. Let's get a force, or get two." Then he yelled to the Pirate infielders. "Get the surest out first." Traditional baseball strategy now dictated the flow of the game even though this particular game was far from a traditional contest. Aaron trotted to first base and Mantilla remained on second base. The next batter was the Braves first baseman Joe Adcock.

After talking to his pitching coach again, Danny decided to leave Haddix on the mound. He confided his reason to one of his coaches. "Harvey's handled Adcock pretty well tonight and he's still pitching a no-hitter." Danny wanted to win the game but he's played this game his entire life and he knew that there were only a few times when an opportunity presented itself to a person in such a way that if they rose to the challenge, they would make history. This was such an occasion for Haddix and Danny was always a player's Manager. So, true to form, he decided to let Haddix pitch for all the glory after all the effort that he had shown tonight. It was even possible that everybody but Adcock was rooting for Haddix. Adcock was also determined to succeed and now he was waiting at the plate.

Haddix threw a few pitches and the batter's count was quickly 2 balls, and 2 strikes. Both Braves runners, Mantilla on second base and Aaron on first were ready to move as the next pitch spun towards Adcock. Adcock swung his bat and made contact. *Crack*! Danny knew right away where it was headed. Haddix knew it too. The ball arched high to right field and moved swiftly towards the wall. Pirates right-fielder Roberto Clemente went back, and back, and then, it was over the wall! Gone! A homerun! Joe Adcock ended this memorable game for the ages, this great pitcher's battle, with a homerun in the bottom of the thirteenth inning. There it was. The Braves won 3-0 on the three-run homer. What a finish! What a game for the history books. Harvey Haddix and Lew Burdette would became linked in baseball lore like Spahn and Sain.**

For the official record, the final score of the game became 1-0 instead of 3-0. It was a homerun but Hank Aaron mistakenly thought Adcock's ball hit the wall. He didn't see it go over the wall. So, Aaron touched second base and then trotted back to the dugout when he saw Mantilla score the winning run. He believed that Mantilla scored the single run that ended the game and there was no need to go to third or even score. The game was over.

Adcock knew it cleared the wall so he correctly circled the bases on his homerun. However, when he arrived at home plate he was ruled out at home plate because he touched third base and home plate before Aaron touched them. Major league rules declared them both automatically out – Aaron for not touching all the bases, and Adcock for passing the runner who was on base ahead of him. Fortunately, Mantilla scored before the final two outs were recorded. So, Mantilla scored, Aaron and Adcock were out, and the game was over. The final score was 1-0. How crazy was that? Later in the locker room after Adcock's complaints about the blunder riled Aaron, Hammering Hank told Adcock he would give Joe the next homerun he hit. That never happened. Aaron still owes Joe Adcock one of his 755 homeruns.

The pennant race between these two clubs continued. The Pirates accumulated injuries, then faded and finished with 78 wins and 76 losses, good enough only for fourth place behind the Dodgers, the Braves, and the Giants. They began looking immediately to add players to make a run in 1960.

1959 Close, but no cigar

Over in Milwaukee, Mickey enjoyed the entire season in a tight pennant race. He even dared to imagine himself in the World Series in October. At the end of a grueling and competitive season, the Braves and the Dodgers finished tied for first place in the National League. Unfortunately, Mickey's best chance to play in a World Series ended when the Dodgers defeated the Braves two games to none in a three-game playoff. The Dodgers went on to win the 1959 Series four games to two games over the Chicago White Sox.

In his last full year of playing baseball, Mickey appeared in 74 games but he started in only ten games. He had 91 plate appearances and finished with his lowest season batting average, .220. He ended the year with 20 hits, including 7 extra base hits, and 14 RBIs. Most disappointedly though, he missed his third 'almost certain' opportunity to play in a World Series – first Cleveland, then Boston, now Milwaukee. He came close three times. He was familiar with the baseball adage that 'three strikes and you're out.'

***Barry Bonds is the current leader in career homeruns with 762**
****In 1956, Braves had only two quality pitchers. Their fans summed up their strategy for winning games in a playful rhyme, 'Spahn and Sain, and pray for rain.'**

CHAPTER THIRTEEN
OFF SEASON MOVES

Yankees or Pirates?

After the 1959 World Series and prior to the beginning of spring training for the 1960 season, America was focused on its national rite of civic pride: the election of its 35th President of the United States of America. The candidate speeches and the political party rallies would continue for thirteen months, finally ending on Election Day, Tuesday, November 8th.

The 1960 Presidential campaign was especially noteworthy for at least two reasons. Firstly, there would be a new President in the White House because Dwight D. Eisenhower had completed two full terms as President and he could not run for re-election for a third term as agreed in the Twenty-Second Amendment to the US Constitution. Secondly, it was possible that the new President would not be a member of the social class that was traditionally elected to be President of the United States of America. That social class was informally referred to as WASP. The acronym stands for White, Anglo-Saxon, and Protestant and it describes the race, nationality, and religious faith that was commonly shared by nearly all of the men who had been previously elected as United States Presidents.

The two major candidates for President in 1960 were the incumbent Vice-President, Richard Nixon, representing the Republican Party, and John F. Kennedy, a young Senator from Massachusetts, representing the Democratic Party. Senator Kennedy was one exception to the social order. He was an Irish- Catholic and he was only the second Catholic to seek election as US President. Al Smith, a former Governor of New York, was the first Catholic to run for President and he was defeated by Herbert Hoover in 1928. Richard Nixon who was born in California was the second exception to the rule because he was a member of the Quakers, a smaller and even lesser known religious sect.

However, in October, 1959, the presidential election was the farthest thing from the minds of both Danny and Mickey and most baseball fans. With spring training on the horizon, Mickey and Danny were both confronted with new challenges. Danny was tasked to strengthen his Pirates ball club and to get them ready for a pennant race while Mickey was at a crossroads in his career. He was 42 years old and he was recently released by the Milwaukee Braves. This was the first time that he had not been contacted by any team and it looked like there were no offers forthcoming. It looked like he would not be on a major league baseball field for the first time in twenty-one years, exempting of course his wartime service in 1943-1945.

He was sitting in his home in Wallingford preparing to travel the next day to New York City to interview for a position as a scout for the New York Yankees. His good friend Danny was aware of the interview and called him the day before and asked if he could come over to Mickey's house to discuss an idea that he wanted to share with him. Mickey said sure but he said that he hoped that it had nothing to do with he and Danny opening a men's store of their own. Mickey couldn't imagine either one of them going to 'tailoring school'.

In less than an hour, the two friends sat in Mickey's kitchen drinking a hot beverage: tea for Danny, coffee for Mickey. In the next half hour, Danny laid out his idea to his buddy.

"So that's my proposal, Mick. You don't need to go up to New York. You'll be right on the field with me. What do you say?" The idea and offer was straight-forward. Mickey would be added to Danny's coaching staff with distinct responsibilities.

Mickey liked it, but his thoughts were on the World Series. "Danny, you know the Yankees are tough to turn down. It might be the only way I get to the World Series without buying a ticket."

Danny folded his arms in the manner that he did when he was buttressing himself for a serious comment or conversation with an umpire. "No. Mick. I don't agree with you. Not this time. This year you can walk in with me and the rest of the Pirates without a ticket. We'll be on the team together. You can get your World Series ring."

"That would be great, Danny. But, who has the best odds to be in the series? The Pirates or the Yankees?"

The chair that Danny sat in was starting to get too tight for him as he got increasingly excited about his vision for the coming year. "Mickey, the odds aren't "now or never" for the Pirates, They're now. We've added some strong pieces to last year's bunch. I feel real good. And you can help us, help me. What do you say?"

Mickey was getting swayed by his friends' energy but the Yankees were hard to turn down. "I don't know. Are you sure? I mean I've been on three teams with shots at the series and they all missed. I could be a jinx."

"You're no jinx. You're my lucky piece. Come with me. Let's do this together. You and I, just like American Legion 1935. What do you say?"

Mickey knew where his heart wanted to go but he wanted to think clearly on the facts. Yankees versus Pirates. The facts were the Yankees go to the World Series just about every year whereas the Pirates have practically forgotten how to spell World Series. So has Mickey.

Sensing that his buddy was at the precipice of a decision, Danny said firmly and calmly and more like a father than a friend. "OK. So, you can go to the World Series with the Yankees next year. But this is the year that you and I go to the Series together."

That single emotional negotiation based on friendship and a promise finally wore Mickey down. His strong insistence on hard facts lessened and he agreed with his friend. "Well, the Legion was a long time ago. But it worked. Maybe that is what I was missing, you. Maybe we need to be together again on the same team." He paused, then added. "OK. Yes."

Slamming his hand on the kitchen table and whistling loudly, Danny jumped up from his chair. Then he patted Mickey on the shoulder and grinned. "Good. Joe Brown already sent you the contract that I already told him to put your name onto. Hey, pack your bat and glove too. That contract lists you as a player/coach. You might get to play some."

Mickey felt like a weight had been lifted off his shoulders because he knew he was on the right ball team.

Danny was set to travel to Bradenton, FL that same night. "Tell Lib that now she and Kate can shop together in Florida and Pittsburgh. And, Mick, when you call the Yankees back, tell 'em from me that you and I will see them in the World Series, if they can get there."

Danny shook Mickey's hand, said goodbye, and walked out the front door. He was whistling a familiar tune all the way to his car. It was a celebratory rendition of 'Take Me Out to the Ball Game.'

Golf Outing

It was a rare sunny and mild day several weeks before Christmas. Mickey, Danny, and Mickey's close friend, Joe Seber, decided to play one last round of golf before winter placed a firm grip on the golf course. They arrived at the first hole and were ready to tee off after agreeing to a friendly wager whereby the winner of each hole would collect fifty cents from each of the other two players. The grand winning total for a perfect performance, winning all 18 holes, would be eighteen dollars, the maximum payout for each player would be nine dollars. Both amounts were a tidy sum in 1959, especially for these three golfers. The term friendly was stretched in some of these matches.

Joe was a friend of Danny's from Chester. The biggest connection for the two friends was that Joe's wife, Doris, and Danny's wife, Kate, were close friends in high school. Joe also played baseball but he never participated beyond the semi-professional leagues. He did play more golf than all three of them because Danny and Mickey were never home long enough to find time to play much golf. So it wasn't often that the three played a round of golf together.

Joe took a few practice swings to loosen up. Then he took a tee out of his pocket. "I'll hit first, then you Mickey, then Danny.

"That's fine with me." Mickey answered.

Danny agreed but like always he added something to the match. "Fellas, let's spice it a little. Let's make it Single Ball Challenge Golf."

Mickey had never heard of this Challenge Golf. He was OK with playful variations to sporting games but he asked Danny for more clarification on it.

"Well, it's simple." Danny explained. "Each of us gets one chance to substitute one of our strokes with our choice of throwing, tossing, or rolling a ball from anywhere on the course. You can do this only once during a match, at any time. Also, there are no mulligans in the match. Agreed?"

Joe had played Challenge Golf with Danny before. He simply said. "Sure. I'm in."

Mickey thought a moment and agreed. "That's a new twist to me. But I'm fine with that. So it's one time only. You can do it any time, but you don't have to use it. Correct?"

Joe and Danny both looked at Mickey and together they replied. "Correct."

They settled into the round of golf and continued for four hours in the cool morning sun. The three golfers evenly exchanged quarters and dollar bills throughout the match and there was no clear overall winner. Now the match was nearing an end. On the 18th tee, Danny proposed that the winner of this hole would be crowned champion, and that a two dollar bonus will be paid by each losing golfer to the winner of the final hole. They all agreed.

Joe stood at the 18th tee box. "I don't think that I've been first to hit off the tee since the 1st hole. How about if we change the order just for this last hole."

Again, that was fine with Mickey. "OK. Joe. You're first, Danny is second, then me."

All three drives landed somewhere near the fairway and the second and third shots were randomly scattered. Amazingly, the players' fourth shots all avoided the sand trap and the small pond on the edge of the green. Now they were all positioned around the pin for their fifth shot and first putt. Joe was away at sixteen feet from the pin; Danny was on the opposite side of the pin at ten feet; Mickey was a short three-foot putt from the hole.

Mickey was hitting his ball last since he was closest to the hole so he volunteered to take out the flag. Joe reminded the others. "First man in the hole wins?"

"No." Danny stated. "But you won't even be third man in the hole anyway."

Joe took a deep breath, positioned his putter and tapped his ball with a short push. It glided nicely along the green grass, but faded to the right, still a few feet short of the hole.

Now it was Danny's turn to get his ball into the hole. If he missed from ten feet and Mickey putted his ball in from three feet, Mickey, the perennial All-Star baseball player, would get all the glory. Danny paused before striking his golf ball. "Fellas, I'm gonna use my Single Ball Challenge."

That announcement surprised Joe and Mickey. They had forgotten all about the quirky ad-lib that Danny had inserted onto their match back on the first tee.
Mickey looked over at Danny and asked him. "Wait. Are you going to pick the ball up and throw it into the hole instead of taking a ten foot putt?"

Danny answered. "Well the agreement was that we can throw a ball, toss a ball, or roll a ball, correct?"

"Yep. That's what we agreed." Was Joe's short reply.

Now Mickey understood what Danny was going to do but he was confused as to why Danny would take such a risk now. He wondered aloud. "OK. We agreed. But, Danny, putting from ten feet might be easier than doing anything else."

"Not if I had a three foot putt like you have, Mickey." Danny paused. "Hmmm. Let me think."

Then Danny stepped back and looked at his ball lying ten feet short of the hole. Talking to himself, he walked towards his ball with his putter in his hand. But he didn't stop at his ball. He walked past his ball and then past the pin. He stopped in front of Mickey's ball. In one motion, he bent down, picked up Mickey's ball, and threw it into the nearby pond.

"What?" Mickey looking stunned, shouted unbelievingly. "That's my ball!"

"I know. OK. Mickey, it's your turn." Danny said no more and he folded his arms.

Joe smiled at Danny and he looked pityingly over at Mickey who still hadn't moved and who still hadn't closed his mouth. Mickey's ball was at the bottom of the pond and Joe knew it was a legal move in Single Ball Challenge Golf because Danny used his one free ball toss. Only he tossed Mickey's ball, not his own. Mickey's only play now was to take a penalty stroke and wait for his next turn which came after Joe and Danny's sixth stroke would likely put their balls in the bottom of the tin cup.
That is exactly what happened. When Mickey dropped his last putt into the cup, it took one more stroke than Danny. He was checkmated and he lost his first and last game of Single Ball Challenge Golf.

Joe placed the flag back into the empty hole. He looked at Mickey's face and saw the same flummoxed look that he had seen on so many other faces after their first and only round of Single Ball Challenge Golf with Danny. After all, Joe played this Single Ball game with Danny many times. Now all he could do for Mickey was to pat him on the back and comfort him with the truth.

"Danny never loses in Single Ball Challenge. He's lucky, I guess." They all laughed, and Mickey was now all the wiser.

Danny still wasn't finished with being himself. Once they loaded their car with their golf clubs, Danny turned to his golfing partners, grinned mischievously and said.
"OK. Fellas. Pay up!"

December 1959, "Maris is as good as ours."

With rumors swirling that Leo Durocher would replace him in the Bucs dugout, Danny was told personally by Joe Brown that Danny was the Manager they all wanted to see at spring training in February 1960. Joe made a point to tell Danny that he was pleased with him as the Manager of the Pirates and that he liked the nucleus of the ball club. A few changes were made to the roster. Danny was pleased all of his players were healthy, and even more experienced after contending for the pennant in the previous two years. Forecasted by many sportswriters to finish third or fourth this coming season, the Pirates were increasingly creating a camaraderie and a winning attitude on and off the field. Nevertheless, there were a few pieces that the Pirates wanted to add to the team to improve their chances of winning the National League pennant. Pitching was at the top of the list and adding a left-handed power hitter to the lineup was a close second.

The 1960 winter baseball meetings were held in December in Miami, Florida. After four days of team and league meetings, General Manager Joe Brown asked Danny to come to Joe's suite in the Fontainebleau Hotel. Joe wanted to discuss team business, particularly to update Danny on the progress of several player trade offers.

Joe met him at the door to his spacious suite. Danny walked into the suite and sat on one of the two chairs in the sitting room. Joe sat in the second chair.

The General Manager began with the single most important deal that the Pirates had been working on for months.

"Danny, Maris is as good as ours.' Joe sat back and looked like the cat who swallowed the canary. "It took a while," he said "but Kansas City will make the trade for Groat." He continued. "Each side will throw in a couple more players. But we got our left-handed power hitter."

Joe expected Danny to start whistling at this news. But he noticed that Danny looked down at his own feet before he said anything in response to this good news.

"Joe, I've been thinking a lot about this deal. I like Maris, a lot. He's a slugger with good fielding and throwing skills. Just what we want, maybe even better than we hoped for. But..."

Joe sat up a bit higher in his chair. "But what? What do you mean but! This is what you wanted. We agreed on this exchange."

This was a bad moment for Danny. He knew that Joe and his scouts had worked tirelessly on making an offer that would loosen Maris from Kansas City. Danny wanted that bat, that player. But He'd had time to evaluate his club and he now thought the price might be too high for the Pirates.
"I don't know, Joe. I just don't feel good about it anymore. I don't want to lose Groat. He's become the core of our team, on and off the field. He's the leader."

Brown's temper was approaching blast-off when he gathered himself and calmly asked Danny what he thought was the central question and was a sure way to measure the value of the trade through his skipper's eyes.
"OK. Let's make it very simple." He paused and looked intently at Danny and asked. "What do you think is better for the Pirates? Us adding Maris or keeping Groat?"

That was it, Danny thought. Joe was good. He pared things down, removed the gloss, the trim. This was why they got along so well. They were fundamentally similar and honestly direct with one another. This question required a simple answer. He didn't ask Danny who he thought was the better player, the better person, the better teammate. Who was the best player for the Pittsburgh Pirates? Danny liked this man.

"Joe, this year...I think it's better for the team to keep Groat. We can win with Dick leading them. Maybe Maris is better for the long haul but not better for the Pirates this year."

"Are you telling me that you don't want to make the deal?"

"Yes. I don't want to make the deal. It's not a religious fervor that's come over me, Joe. It's not like God spoke to me. I just don't want to let Dick go."

"You know that means that we may go into the season with Stuart as our only power hitter in the lineup every day."

"Yeh. But I like your recent pickups of Rocky Nelson, Hal Smith and Gino Cimoli. We can move them around and get power production from all three and it may possibly equal one full-time batter. Plus it will give the other players some rest once in a while, even cover for injuries. We'll be ready for the end of the season when it counts the most to be healthy."

"OK, Danny." Joe exhaled. "I'll nix the deal, damn it. Do you wanna stay here in the room while I call Kansas City?"

This is one time when Danny didn't want to be in the same room with his boss. "No! I think I'll go out, take an alka-seltzer tablet, maybe light a candle in church, and hide in a corner for a day or so."

Brown was acting solely on Danny's gut feeling. He trusted Danny's feel for the game, and he really respected his handling of the team inside the locker room, and how his team performed on the ballfield. Even so, he had a few final comments before his skipper went out the door.

"Fine. Do all that. Except you only get an hour to hide. We've got to start looking immediately around the league for another power hitter and a starting pitcher."

March 1960, just like old times

The Pirates went to spring training ready and determined to win a pennant, and the bigger prize, a World Series. It was a busy and anxious time for Danny and his coaches. But it was also a happy time for Danny and Mickey. Like everyone else in their selected profession, they've always dreamed to reach the top. Now they have an opportunity to share that dream together on the same team.

The Pirates were touted as a solid contender in 1960. Roberto Clemente continued to display his burgeoning all-star skills; Dick Groat, a two-time college All-American basketball star at Duke, was a forceful team leader; and Mazeroski, Virdon, and Skinner all added superior defense and timely hitting to the every-day lineup. Vernon Law, Bob Friend and star reliever, Elroy Face, anchored the pitching staff, supported by Harvey Haddix and a bevy of experienced relievers. Haddix had been acquired from Cincinnati in January 1959 along with Don Hoak and Smokey Burgess in exchange for the Pirates' slugging first baseman, Frank Thomas (35 HR, 112 RBIS). Earlier, in a special Canadian League Players draft, the Pirates selected Rocky Nelson, a veteran hitter, as insurance for Dick Stuart at first base. Three more players were added in December 1959: Hal Smith, Gino Cimoli, and pitcher Clem Labine. All of them were expected to play well and improve the team.

In the opening week of spring training, the Pirate infielders and outfielders were gathered at their respective positions either on the infield dirt or on the grassy outfield. Pitchers were outside the first and third base foul lines loosening their arms and tossing a ball to one another. Mickey and Danny were also out on the field soaking up the sun but they also had the extra warm feeling of being together for the first time in Florida with highest hopes to grab the big prize this year.

The coaching positions were filled by the Manager and the Manager generally assigned a coach to fit the same position that he played in the big leagues or in the minor leagues. There were few exceptions. Danny wanted Mickey to be the exception. He planned to have Mickey serve multiple roles for the Pirates: first base coach, hitting coach, and trusted adviser and confidant. Danny, of course with a smile on his face, made it clear that Mickey would only get paid for one of those jobs.

Mickey always came to the ballpark carrying his first baseman's mitt. He passed by Danny and told him what he planned to do each morning. "I'm going to work with Dick and Rocky on some first base infield drills. So they won't be at the gab session this afternoon. Is that Ok with you?"

Danny made it clear numerous times in pre-spring training meetings that whatever his coaches thought that they needed to do to make their position players better was fine with him. He just wanted to know when any drills and meetings were going to impact his general team meetings.

"You're their position coach. Mick. Work them out to get them where you want them to be. Oh. Spend some time with them around home plate too. Coax some additional hits out of those two and anyone else that you think you can help."

Then Danny added. ""Funny, you know that I always envied that you only had to travel less than 100 feet from the dugout to play your position at first base. Do you even know what outfield grass feels like?"

Mickey heard him and he knew this time Danny had walked right into a left hook. Now the unusual was about to happen. Mickey would get the last word this time, not Danny. With a deadpan look on his face, Mickey faced his friend and asked him a two-word question.
"Do you?"

Not a word. That was Danny's cryptic response. Danny had been a lifetime infielder and although he played all four infield positions in his career, he never played in the outfield. Not once. Not even in high school. He had forgotten Mickey had major league experience in the outfield.* Danny didn't lift his head so Mickey wasn't able to see him smile as he walked away heading for the pitchers' workout area and the bullpen

*** Mickey did play one positon in his major league career other than first base. He played four games in the outfield in his last season with the Milwaukee Braves. He was 41 years old.**

CHAPTER FOURTEEN
DANNY AND MICKEY AND THE PIRATES

March 1960, Rule No. 1

The Pirates road record in 1959 was a dismal 31 wins and 46 losses. Danny wasn't sure what caused the poor road record but he was determined that it would not be repeated in the new season. This concern led to his decision to make an announcement late in spring training. He wanted to evoke a new No.1 Rule for the season. He was convinced that the eventual fruit of this rule would be a National League pennant for his team, and subsequently, a berth in the World Series. Until, this meeting, only he and Mickey had discussed it and they were still discussing it quietly in the back of the locker room when the players, coaches, and staff started to take their seats in the clubhouse.

Mickey knew that Danny had thought about it a lot, probably since mid-season last year. He supported the idea and reassured Danny. "If you feel strongly that this will work. Do it."

"I will." Danny continued. "It's not going to be popular. I know the wives enjoy travelling with us to the different cities spending some time with their husbands. They get to see the sights, do some shopping and so on. The husbands pay attention to them and show them around town. The wives really enjoy themselves. It's only normal. That's the good part. I also know they don't make every road trip. Some have kids at home. But when they do come, the guys get tired. They don't rest between games. We lose too many of those games. That's the bad part. I don't enjoy losing games in those cities. So I'm positive that this new rule will make a difference for us. What do you think?"

"Yep. It makes sense." was Mickey's reply.

"Yep, Mick. It will show everybody how serious we are about winning every game. They'll see how strong we feel about capturing the pennant."

Mickey nodded his head in agreement again. He noticed the room was filling up.

Danny continued. "But, you know, I think that it will go over better Mick if you announce it as your idea. Maybe say that it was something that was done at Cleveland or Boston; you know, something practiced by winning pennant teams."

"Me? My idea?" Mickey didn't like the sound of this.
"No. I'm the newest fella on the club. I'm not that smart to think of it anyway, and I'm certainly not that stupid to announce it as my idea. Do you have something easier that I can do that won't make them all hate me before the first regular season pitch is thrown?"

"No, I don't." was Danny's response. "But I think this rule is easier than asking them to give up playing cards and drinking beer."

Mickey laughed. "Yeh, but it's not my idea. And banning cards and beer is impossible. But announcing "no wives" on road trips is dangerous. It's not the players I fear. It's the wives. I like the rule but not half as much as you do. You do it. You'll be an innovator like Branch Ricky."

Laughing now, Danny tells Mickey that he was just testing him to see if he would jump into a hornets' nest for him. "That's OK. I wouldn't want you to say anything that you don't want to say."

"Good." Mickey was relieved. The subject was closed.

Once everyone was seated, Danny and Mickey walked to the front of the room and greeted the players and the coaches. No visitors, no press, no family or friends were admitted to these team meetings. Danny began. "I called this meeting to go over our team rules. Fellas, you all know we had a rough time on the road last year. We lost 46 games in the other teams' ball parks. That's sixty percent of our away games."

He stopped and canvased the room, looking at every player and even checking the faces of his coaches.

"We can't let that happen again if we want to win the pennant. So I've thought about what we can do and consulted with some of the best minds in baseball. One of them is here in this room. Mickey Vernon."

Standing next to Danny, Mickey was suddenly unsure where Danny was going with his comments to the team. Danny continued. "Mickey has suggested what I think is the single most effective idea to improve on last year's poor road record. It will be Team Rule No. 1."

Mickey was stunned and he stood there speechless as Danny continued to deliver Rule No. 1. Mickey shouldn't have been surprised that Danny struck again. He closed his mouth, then he closed his eyes, then he saw his golf ball disappearing again into the pond.

Danny continued. "So Rule No.1 begins on Opening Day. Wives will not be allowed to accompany players or coaches on road trips. I think that will improve our road record and launch us into the World Series."

There was murmuring and mixed responses on Rule No. 1 and there was discussion on team curfews, fines, and other standard team rules regarding game behavior before the meeting ended. The players weren't very upset at Rule No. 1. Some wife/family trips were tiring, and some interrupted the players' daily card games. But there was no doubt that their wives would have more to say. They would be certain to discuss it with the genius who suggested it so they were going to be looking for Mickey Vernon, Danny's new coach and confidant.

"You gotta give to get."

Danny, Mickey and the Pirates started the season playing winning baseball through May 1, winning 12 of the first 15 games. Near the end of May, they were in first place. But Danny, who knew that a team could never have too much good pitching, had already asked Joe Brown to find more pitching. Now June was overtaking May on the calendar and Danny wanted to find out if Joe had found any acceptable candidates. During the Pirates latest home stand, he arrived at the ballpark early and went to talk to Joe.

Danny rapped lightly on Joe's office door. Joe was expecting him. "Come on in, Danny." Joe called out. He was sitting behind his desk and he was pleased with his team's position in the NL standings. "I guess we got everybody's attention, huh? They know we're in it."

"Yep." Danny smiled. "We have their attention. But we want to knock them down a little farther. Joe, as always, we need pitching."

Taking a seat, Danny gave Joe a summary of what Joe already knew, but nevertheless it was a summary that needed to be repeated. "Law, Friend, and Haddix are delivering the goods for us now but it's a long season, Joe. We need a fourth starter and another fella that can pitch both middle relief and start a few times when the schedule backs up later in the summer."

The first words that came out of the GM's mouth were not surprising. "Everybody wants to add good pitching. The other side of adding is subtracting. Who can you give up in your dugout that we can trade?"

This was something that Danny and his coaches had wrestled with in many informal meetings without having too much success. Danny's answer was swift. "No position players. I can part with several pitchers for somebody who can help us for the next few months."

"Danny, I've tried. Nobody wants the pitchers we have to give. But I did speak to St. Louis and they can part with Mizell."

This news was the best thing that Danny had heard. He knew Mizell. "Fine. I like Mizell. A left-hander. He'd fit in for us real good." Then he asked Joe the million dollar question. "What does St. Louis want?"

"A big ticket item." He gave Danny a few seconds to think about that, then added solemnly. "Julian Javier."

"Ouch!" was all Danny could say.

It wasn't a secret in baseball that Julian Javier was a top prospect in the Pirates farm system. Pittsburgh knew that he would likely come up next year and that he would be around for a long time. They had great plans for him. It was evident that St. Louis did their homework on Javier. They liked him and they knew how desperate the Pirates were for a left-handed pitcher who could step in immediately and help the Pirates get to the World Series this year. Naturally, Danny didn't want to see Javier move over to the Cardinals.

Stating the obvious, Danny told Joe what Joe already knew. "He's our best minor-league player." Then turning his poker face into a frown, he asked Joe. "Is there anyone else we can offer them? Maybe a multi-player package without Javier?"

"No one that they want. They want only Javier. Right now he's a big piece of our future and a shortstop with all the right skills. He can also be a big part of the Cardinals' future.

Couching a big decision into a succinct question was a knack that Joe Brown did so well. It allowed him to simplify even the most critical decisions. Joe first asked Danny plainly. "What do you want to do?"

Before Danny could reply, he asked Danny another question that required choosing one of the two most rudimentary responses in human language, yes or no. "Danny, will Mizell make the difference that we need to win the pennant?"

Holy crap, he thought. Here we go again. My friend the GM is loading this on me. How fast can I send a prayer to heaven and how quickly can I expect an answer. Danny made that his prayer.

"Joe, I'm this year's Manager with this year's first place team. Javier will help us in a year or so, and for many years after that one. But Mizell will help us this year. He isn't a certainty but without him or someone like him, we probably fall short this year."

Joe didn't see his Manager flinch or sweat while delivering this plea. He knew that Danny would carry himself the same way through the rest of the year. "All right. Hell, I'll work on it. Let's go for broke!"

Feeling himself breathing normally again and almost hearing his blood running through his body, Danny sensed that he had just come through a storm and he was now on the calmer side of it. "OK, Joe. The sooner, the better." Pressing his luck, Danny added. "If you can manage it, get me another experienced pitcher with some life and guts in him." Then he locked eyes with Joe. "And, Joe, I'm sorry about Javier."

Danny got up out of his chair and started toward the door until Joe stopped him.

"Oh, Danny. One more thing."

'What's that?"

"Until we get Mizell, stay in first place, or very close. I don't want to lose Javier, and the pennant."

"Uh huh. And after I do that, is there anything else?" They both laughed.

Danny and the Pirates continued to win while Brown worked on a deal for Mizell, always leaving Javier on the edge of multiple offers to the Cardinals. Finally, on May 27, The Pirates traded Julian Javier to St. Louis for Wilmer "Vinegar Bend" Mizell. The Pirates knew that Javier was a prized player but the trade was mutually successful, and it was made just in time. In July, after Danny used thirty-two pitchers in a span of eleven games, the Pirates acquired another pitcher, Dodger's Clem Labine. He was the final piece added to the 1960 Pirates roster.

Julian Javier moved up quickly to the major leagues and became an all-star shortstop for the Cardinals, playing in three separate World Series for them. Danny always considered that Javier was a key and unseen contributor to the Pirates success in 1960.

July 24 "Play Gino more."

July faded and the hot and muggy dog days of August signaled that the final eight weeks of the season had arrived. Most of the teams entered the recent annual mid-summer All-Star break with tired and injured players. The Pirates were no exception. They were in a mid-season slump having lost seven of their last eleven games. As part of Danny's daily post-game routine, he always called Kate from either the empty clubhouse or his hotel room.

She picked up her ringing phone. "Hi, Hon. I heard your game on the radio. I'm sorry. It was a tough loss. But your guys rallied some in the late innings. That was a good sign. They just fell short of a hit or two."

"Thanks hon." Danny was in his hotel room. He was more tired than usual and barely able to disguise his disappointment so he was glad he could lay out his true feelings for only his sweetheart's ears. "Yep. The season has weeks like this. It just bothers me because it moved us out of first place because the Braves won both games of their doubleheader tonight."

"You'll get back to first place."

"I know that too but the pressure gets higher on everybody when you slip a little. We have the Cardinals tomorrow. Our pitching is holding up and Elroy is blazing hot. But our fellas do need to get those couple of hits a game that we've been missing."

They spoke a little about the kids and the summer heat. But Kate could hear her husband's fatigue so she decided to end the conversation and let him rest and relax in his hotel room. "Well, Danny, eat something light and get some rest. And, hon, take that cigar out of your mouth. I can hear you puffing it between words."

"Alright, Sarge."

Kate's final words were always the same. "I miss you and I love you."

Danny's singular reply was also always the same. "I love you too." Right before she hung up the phone, Kate broke her routine. She whispered. "Oh, I almost forgot. Play Gino more this weekend."

"Thanks, coach Kate. Goodnight."

"Goodnight, hon."

Sept. 25 Clinching it

The Pirates won their next game, 4-3, and immediately went back into first place. They swept the Cardinals and began a new hot streak, winning 22 of 30 games through August 25th. 'Vinegar Bend' Mizell won his eighth game against two losses since joining the Pirates from St. Louis in June, and the Pirates stayed in first place for the rest of the season. There was one serious set-back when Dick Groat's wrist was broken on September 6 after he was hit by a pitch thrown by Lew Burdette. As late as September 25th, it was still uncertain if he would be back in the lineup for any post-season play. Fortunately, Dick Schofield filled in for Groat and played shortstop at an all-star level. The Pirates held onto first place.

Danny was still worried and tonight his team was losing its third straight game to the Braves. He could use some good news and it came late in the Pirates game when he learned that the second place Cardinals had lost to the Cubs. Now it was official. The mathematical number to clinch the title was zero. Danny and the Pirates won the pennant. It was the first Pittsburgh pennant since 1927.

The players were silent as the game ended. After all, it was a loss. They ceremoniously shook hands with one another as they exited the playing field. But as soon Danny walked into the privacy of the clubhouse, he launched one of his loud, piercing whistles and set-off a wild celebration. Loud whooping and hollering, hugs, laughter, even tears, filled the clubhouse. Danny with his arm around Mickey was already being interviewed by a local sportswriter. The sportswriter maneuvered himself in between the two close friends who couldn't look any more different together than day and night.

"Congratulations, Danny." The reporter began. "This is a great moment for you, the team, and your city. You're the champs. How does it feel to be going to the World Series?"

Danny like Mickey had waited for a long time to hear anybody ask him that question. "Great! Just great. I'm happy for my players, and my coaching staff, and Pittsburgh, and especially for Joe Brown and for our owner, Mr.Galbreath."

"Danny, does it bother you at all that some people say that you lost these three games to the Braves and backed into the pennant instead of capturing the pennant on a day when your club wins the game?"

This question was not one that Danny expected to be asked at this moment of celebration but he didn't hesitate in his modest reply. He knew that his sidekick standing next to him had the same answer that he would give. "Well, you know I'm careful with swear words but Mickey here is less strict at times. I'll let Mickey answer that question."

The sportswriter stretched his microphone in front of Mickey, and Mickey bellowed loudly and firmly in his gentleman's voice. "Hell, no!"

Then Danny augmented Mickey's answer. "No! We didn't back in. We've already won 92 games. That is more than anyone else in our league and we aren't done yet. We have a few more to win."

With champagne bottles popping and players using them like water guns to spray bubbly on one another, the sportswriter continued asking questions. "What about the Yankees? The Bronx Bombers are a power-loaded team with Mantle, Maris, Berra, and Skowron. What are your plans?"

"We plan to show up and play our best in the World Series. Everyone knows the Yankees are good. But the Yankees haven't faced our pitchers and hitters this year."

A spray of sparkling champagne landed on Danny's hair and his cheek and he signaled that he was done with the interview. "Right now, I'm going to celebrate. Where's my soda?"

"Danny." The writer asks. "You're not even gonna sip some champagne?"

"Soda got me here. I'm not changing now. I'll have a soda and smoke this here fresh cigar a little later."

At that moment, Elroy Face, just about the shortest player in the room, poured an entire bottle of champagne over the tops of Danny's and Mickey's heads. He yelled as he poured it. "Skipper, close your mouth. You don't have to drink it, but you sure deserve to wear it."

Everyone in the clubhouse let out a roar, then hollered and cheered as Danny grinned from ear to ear. Danny's head, face, and fresh cigar were all dripping wet with champagne.

September 1960 Mickey's fourth decade

In the few remaining games, Mickey was activated onto the expanded team roster. An expansion of a team's roster was an annual league-wide practice and it was allowed only in the closing weeks of the regular season. It was generally an opportunity to reward minor league players with some playing time in the majors and to use the extra players to give the tired veterans some rest. Mickey's activation and subsequent appearances as a pinch-hitter in these regular season games placed Mickey among a very few select professional baseball players. He became only the fourth player since 1900 to play in four decades. He played his first game in 1939 and his last game in 1960 and 2,407 games in between.

His former teammate, Ted Williams, became the fifth player to do so when Williams announced his retirement a few months later. There are presently only twenty-two players who have played in four decades between 1900 and 2015. Nine are pitchers.

Joe E. Brown, Joe L., and Danny clowning around.

Danny and Casey Stengel

Mazeroski's homerun. Scored tied 9-9, 9th inning, No. 9 at bat. Final score 10-9.

Game 7, Bill Mazeroski races home

After shocking the baseball world
with a World Championship in 1960,
the Pittsburgh Pirates dominated
the NL East in the 1970s, taking
six division titles and winning Fall
Classic crowns in 1971 and 1979.

Trophy case in HOF at Cooperstown, NY

Pittsburgh Pandemonium, 1960 World Series

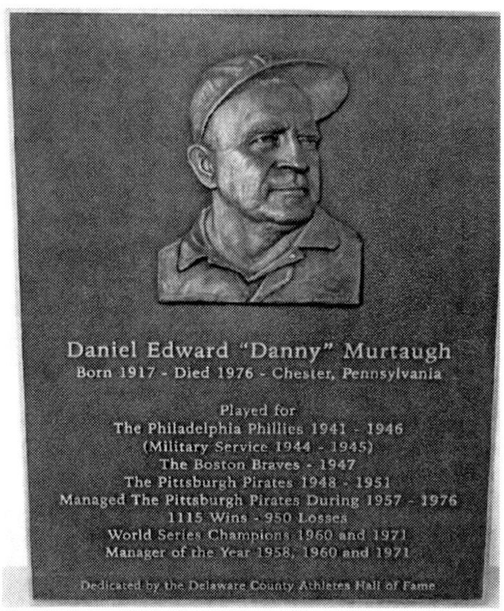

Daniel Edward "Danny" Murtaugh
Born 1917 - Died 1976 - Chester, Pennsylvania
Played for
The Philadelphia Phillies 1941 - 1946
(Military Service 1944 - 1945)
The Boston Braves - 1947
The Pittsburgh Pirates 1948 - 1951
Managed The Pittsburgh Pirates During 1957 - 1976
1115 Wins - 950 Losses
World Series Champions 1960 and 1971
Manager of the Year 1958, 1960 and 1971
Dedicated by the Delaware County Athletes Hall of Fame

Danny's Hall of Fame numbers

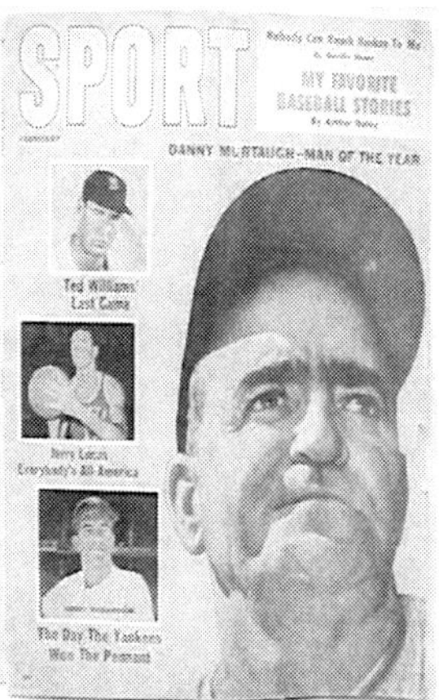

1960 Man of the Year

Mickey Vernon statue
Marcus Hook, PA

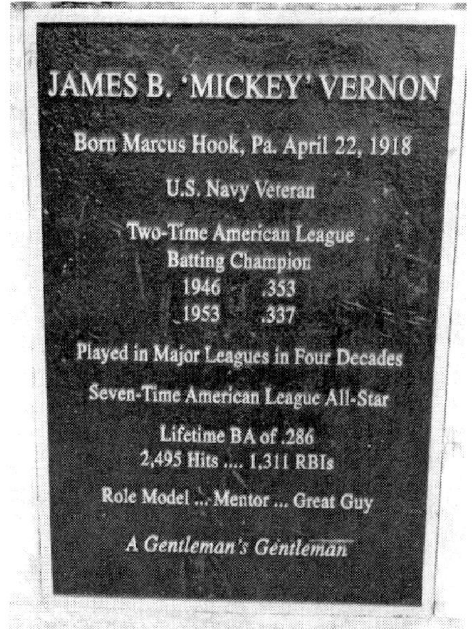

JAMES B. 'MICKEY' VERNON
Born Marcus Hook, Pa. April 22, 1918
U.S. Navy Veteran
Two-Time American League
Batting Champion
1946 .353
1953 .337
Played in Major Leagues in Four Decades
Seven-Time American League All-Star
Lifetime BA of .286
2,495 Hits .... 1,311 RBIs
Role Model ... Mentor ... Great Guy
A Gentleman's Gentleman

Mickey's Hall of Fame
numbers

Danny and Mickey, 1959. One year before Danny convinced Mickey to pass-up the Yankees and join him in Pittsburgh

Bill Mazeroski scores. Danny (40) and Mickey (42) make sure Maz touches home plate

CHAPTER FIFTEEN
WORLD SERIES, Games 1 through 6

October 2 Sunday, "No broken yolks."

On Sunday morning, three days before Game 1 of the World Series, Danny, Kate and the children returned from attending 10:00 am Mass. The phone rang and Timmy, Danny's oldest teenage son, answered the phone. It was a national sportswriter who wanted to do a quick interview with Danny for the next day's morning newspaper. Danny recognized the writer's name and Timmy handed the phone to his Dad.

"Good morning, Danny, I just want to get your feelings on all the excitement that's floating around you now. How do you plan to spend your Sunday, handle the pressure, that sort of thing, before the big series."

Polite but short in his response, Danny explained. "OK, but not too many questions. I'm getting set to make breakfast for my family. I don't get to do that often and there's more pressure on me here now on breaking the yolk in an egg than there is in sending a runner from third base in a tied game."

The sportswriter laughed and said. "Sure. I'll make this fast." There was a slight pause while the sportswriter positioned his pen and paper. "Danny, you always seem to have a calm approach to the action going on around you, yet when you played you were a feisty, noisy, restless infielder who was constantly in motion. How were you able to put away your nervous nature and even your noisy trademark whistle?"

"Well, I still get nervous about things, you might call it nervous energy, but now I'm too old to squander any energy that I still have. So I mostly let Dick Groat and Don Hoak handle that hectic part of the game. As for whistling, geez, I still whistle. My Uncle Tim taught me to whistle before I could speak. Whistling is fun. It always kept me busy. I'm not scared when I whistle, I like the song in 'The King and I'. But sometimes whistling doesn't always fit. I didn't whistle so much in the war, not on the battlefield anyway. And I never feel like whistling when I'm losing."

Continuing at a fast pace, the sportswriter asked another question. "You were always fearless on the field. Is that what helped you get through the war?"

Danny laughed. "Fearless? Never fearless. But not reckless, either. Just mostly calm and careful. In the war, I was scared like most soldiers. But since I got through the first battle I figured I might stay that lucky again. So I did my best to survive. After the war I said to myself 'When I get home, I'm never going to worry about anything again'. I mean I won't worry over a lot of things like they are all as serious as life and death. War was real life and death. Baseball is a game."

"Danny, One last question. Do you have any prediction on the series?"

He heard the question and he hesitated to answer it. He didn't want to provide any fuel to the fire before the Series began. He laughed lightly and answered the last question with a smile in his voice.

"Well, I do have a favorite team and they haven't been in the series in a long time. I think that they're going to make the most of it and win at least four games."

The sportswriter chuckled. "Thanks for taking a few minutes to talk with me." He wished Danny and the Pirates good luck in the series. Danny hung up the phone and Kate quickly handed him an apron and a dozen fresh eggs for cooking. She gave him only one instruction "No broken yolks."

October 3 "Who has the Pirates in the pool?'

The city of Pittsburgh had a grand outdoor party just after midnight on the September 26th as nearly 100,000 fans greeted the Pirates when they arrived at the Pittsburgh airport and were driven to the stadium.

A week later the Pirates ended their regular season with back-to-back wins over the pesky Braves and received good news and bad news. The good news was that Dick Groat was back in the lineup only twenty days after a Lew Burdette fast ball broke his wrist. Groat was already hitting the ball sharply and looked quicker than ever in the field. His final base hits of the regular season were enough to allow him to come back to win the National League batting title. The bad news was that Vernon Law, the Bucs' pitching ace, injured his ankle on the evening of the team's pennant celebration. His ankle remained swollen and he didn't have enough days off to be fully healed for the Yankees.

Monday night Danny and his coaches gathered in the team clubhouse for a short meeting to review the status of position players and pitchers, and to go over their plans for winning the World Series.

Danny spoke first. As always, he took things serious but never so serious that he couldn't find some humor in the moment. "OK, fellas. Who has the Pirates in the pool?"
"Not an awful lot of people outside of Pittsburgh." Hitting Coach Lenny Levy replied. "That's for sure. Maybe nobody outside Pittsburgh?"

Third base coach, Frank Oceak, chimed in to defend the Pirates team honor. "Guess we'll have to fight or run."

Then it was Mickey's turn to join the discussion. "Anyone who's seen us play, knows we'll fight."

"So, do you think we should fight? Or run?" someone asked.

Mickey knew that it was a rhetorical question. Of course they would fight. He made his answer fit the game of baseball itself to add a little humor. "We should only run when we have a man on second and when the ball is hit to the right side. That's about how much running we'll do. This club is ready."

That was what the skipper wanted to hear. He wanted everyone to be alert and be together in mind and spirit.

"Yep." The Skipper said. "Our men are the best and they are keen to play anyone who is second best. And that's where the Yankees come in."

Placing his clipboard on the small table in front of him, Danny was ready to talk business, baseball business.
"OK, let's go over our injury list, our pitching rotation, and talk a little about the boys from New York."

Just before they separated into their various tasks and meetings, Danny had one last thing on his mind. He pointed to Mickey and said to everyone. "Oh, I wanted to let all of you know that Mick was right. We finished 43-35 on the road. Rule No.1 was a success. Good job, Mick. And even if the wives don't love ya, we do." Everyone laughed.

Then Danny put on his sternest face and announced to all. "So, Rule No.1 stays put through the Series. And no, this time they can't substitute girlfriends. Ain't that right, Mickey?"

October 4 Tuesday, Unkie's phone call

Game 1 of the World Series was set to begin on Wednesday, October 5 in Pittsburgh. On Tuesday morning both teams conducted a full practice session on Forbes Field. Prior to taking the field, someone posted a telegram from Branch Rickey on the Pirates clubhouse bulletin board. It said, “I would rather you guys beat the Yankees more than anyone else. You can and you will.”

Danny and his Pirates had a full and loose practice session. Now in the early evening, Danny was in his hotel room trying to rest after a busy day and before the tension and excitement of Game 1 tomorrow. He was resting in bed and beginning to doze off to sleep. After all, he was exhausted, but right before he fell into a sound sleep, he was jolted awakened by a ringing phone. He reached across the bed and picked up the receiver and placed it up to his ear.

“Hello.” He listened with great surprise as the voice on the other end of the phone line spoke to him. He was puzzled but he knew instantly who it was. “Hi! Mom. Yep. We’re all ready.” He paused. “No. I’m fine. I’ll get some sleep. I’ve had more nervous nights than this. It’s so wonderful to hear your voice. What a nice surprise.”

Danny listened for a few more seconds, then he said. “OK. I’ll look for you before the game begins. Don’t forget to wear a Pirates hat, OK? No, not a Phillies hat, a Pirates hat.” He hesitated, not wanting to say goodbye. Then he said. “I love you, too. Good night, Mom.” There was another slight pause. “Oh, sure. Put him on the phone.”

“Hi! Unkie.” Danny’s eyes lit up when he heard the familiar and comforting voice of his Uncle Tim. “Yep, this is it. Uh huh. The baseball world is watching me. Just like you said”. Shaking his head up and down, he tells Unkie excitedly. “Yep. It’s the Yankees. Who else would we want to play in a World Series?”

Danny listened to Unkie on the phone, then he laughed.
“No. I never did get to be just like Babe Ruth. But this is close. We’re playing three games in Yankee Stadium.”

After listening more to Unkie, Danny made a promise.

"Yep, I'm going to go after it. We have to win four and then you can ride in the parade with me. It will be great. Me and you, Unkie." Danny was silent as he listened to Unkie.

"My Dad? Sure I would. Is he with you now? No, I didn't get him a ticket, but I still can. Put my Dad on the…."

At that moment, another phone rang **LOUDLY** in the room.

The second ringing phone also startled Danny, and magically the phone in his hand disappeared, and just as quickly, Unkie's voice was gone. Danny looked across the bed and located the source of the second ringing noise and he reached for the black phone that was ringing on the night table.

"Hello. Yes, it is. No, not now. It's too late for an interview. No. Sorry. Goodbye." Speaking out-loud to himself, Danny grumbled. "Darn newspaper people. How'd they get my room number?"

Then he looked at the alarm clock on the night table. It was exactly 9 pm. He figured that he dozed off for about a half hour. Then he remembered his call from Mom and Unkie. He froze in place, felt a chill, and muttered to himself.
"Mom? Unkie? Dad? How can that be? It couldn't be them. It was a joke, or a dream. They're not here anymore."

He thought for a moment. "Who would play a prank like that, and on the night before the World Series?"

Awake now but still tired, he got out of bed. He washed his face and hands in the bathroom and walked back to the bed. He laid down and pulled the bedcover over himself. Like always, he blessed himself, and said a quick prayer of thanks to God. He prayed for Kate, Kathleen, the boys, and especially tonight for Mom, Dad, and Unkie. For all the Murtaugh family and friends. Then he turned out the light.

He needed to sleep. After all, tomorrow was not like any other day. It was the World Series, and the Yankees. It was a prayer answered and a dream come true.

October 5, 1960
Game 1, Wednesday - Forbes Field

The opening ceremonies for the 1960 World Series included many celebrities, a marching band, and other festivities. Pennsylvania Governor, and former Pittsburgh Mayor, David Lawrence was scheduled to throw out the first ceremonial pitch after popular singer and Pittsburgh native-son, Billy Eckstine, sang the national anthem. However, the singing of the anthem and the first pitch were delayed by the entrance of a single person who unexpectedly helped to excite the fans and loosen up the ballplayers on both teams. The unexpected third piece and first act of the opening ceremony was provided by a young Pittsburgh firefighter who parachuted out of a plane directly over Forbes Field. Despite his dual intention to get into the stadium free and to land at home plate, a gust of wind carried the brightly-colored parachute and its passenger over the third base stands and out of sight. The crowd roared its amazement and its approval. After trying for 33 years to win another pennant, Pittsburgh made a grand entrance into World Series history. The baseball world was focused on Pittsburgh. Billy Eckstine sang the national anthem and Governor Lawrence threw out the first ceremonial pitch. The 1960 World Series was ready to begin.

The Pittsburgh pitching rotation for the Series was setup for three starters – Vernon Law, Bob Friend, and Harvey Haddix. Elroy Face was available every day, if needed. Wiley Yankee Manager Casey Stengel selected Art Ditmar as his Game 1 starter instead of Yankees pitching ace, Whitey Ford. This surprised everyone. There was some talk that it was because Ford was undefeated at home in World Series games but he had never won a World Series game in an opposing team's ball park. You could say

Casey was superstitious but he liked to think he understood trends. He decided to save Ford for Yankee Stadium. It was a risk but the Yankees were good enough to take risks.

After Governor Lawrence's baseball toss, the umpire yelled "Play ball!" and the game was underway. It took less than a half-inning for the Bronx Bombers to get the city of Pittsburgh, and starting pitcher Vernon Law's full attention. Roger Maris was batting with two outs when Law realized firsthand how dangerous a hitter Maris was. Law was closing out a scoreless inning and then, **CRACK,** the ball he threw exploded off of Maris' bat and flew swiftly towards right field. It didn't take long for the ball to settle deep in the right field stands. The Yankees vaunted power was already showing on the scoreboard. After only three batters here in the top of the first inning of Game 1, the Yankees came as advertised and grabbed a 1-0 lead.

Danny looked around the dugout to make sure that everyone in there saw what he saw. Maris hit that ball on the nose and it leaped over the right-field wall in just seconds. But that wasn't all that happened. Here comes Mickey Mantle. Danny motioned to Pirates' catcher Smokey Burgess to take a new ball out to Law and to share a few words with his pitcher. Danny didn't care what Smokey talked about.

Law met Smokey at the foot of the pitcher's mound where the field was level with the infield, Smokey didn't say much. This was just to slow down any adrenalin that might be pumping furiously through his and Law's veins.

"That's what he gets paid for, Vernon. Let's get Mantle. You don't have to give him much. He'll be really aggressive now."

Just as Burgess said, Mantle was too anxious to wait for a good hitter's pitch. He wanted to drive a ball out of the park. He swung at a bad pitch and hit a long fly ball to make the final out of the first inning. The Pirates took the field trailing the mighty, and favored, Yankees.

Amazingly, the home team struck back quickly in their bottom half of the first, scoring three runs, and sending Ditmar to the shower after he had thrown only eighteen pitches. The Yankees didn't recover from that shock. It was as though the Pirates hit the Yankees in their glass jaw. The Pirates won Game 1, 6-4 despite trailing the Yankees early and allowing them to rally for two runs in the ninth off Pirates ace reliever, Elroy Face. In the scorebook, Law pitched seven innings for the win and Bill Mazeroski had two hits including a two-run homer in the fourth. The city of Pittsburgh was wildly joyous. They won round one of a seven round championship fight, baseball style. No one was afraid of the Big Bad Wolf now.

Everyone in Pittsburgh, and fans in many other Yankee-hating cities, were all wondering the same thing. Where were the fearsome, powerful Bronx Bombers? The Pirates began with home field advantage and now they still had that and a game in hand. Some Pirate fans were deliriously happy, some fans were even entertaining thoughts of capturing four in a row. Sensibly, they kept those fifteen deliriously happy Pirate fans locked behind doors where they belonged.

October 8, 1960
Games 2 & 3, Thursday and Saturday, Bombs Away

The joy in Pittsburgh didn't last more than a day. The Yankee Bronx Bombers devastated Pittsburgh pitching in the following two games, winning on Thursday 16-3 in Forbes Field. Then after both teams rested, the Yankees repeated that second game whipping with a 10-0 win behind Whitey Ford on Saturday in Yankee Stadium. Mantle hit three homeruns, two in Game 2 and one in Game 3. In Game 3, second baseman Bobby Richardson hit a grand slam to set-off another Yankee rout of the Pirates. The sports pages, TV and radio stations were filled with words like "clobbered", "murdered", and "trounced". Adding insult to massacre, the Pirates' left-fielder Bob Skinner was out of the lineup indefinitely after he injured his thumb sliding into third base in Game 1.

On a personal note, the second thrashing took place on Danny's 43rd birthday. Suddenly, the Yankees odds to win the series increased to 5-1 because the next two games were scheduled to be played in New York. The smart money was betting that the series wouldn't go back to Pittsburgh. Vernon Law, still hobbling a bit on his ankle, wasn't a sure thing to pitch Game 4 against a newly confident and charged-up Yankee lineup.

The Managers were required by league protocol to grant interviews immediately after each Series game. It was Danny's birthday and the 10-0 loss made him feel much older that night. He was trying to recover from two one-sided battles that left his Bucs trailing in the seven game series, 2-1. Nevertheless, he thought that it was safer for him to meet the press than to be anywhere near a birthday cake and a pack of matches. He made it clear that it would be a short interview session.

A young sportswriter was given the opportunity to ask Danny the first question. All the experienced writers wanted to see how Danny reacted to the kid and see which way the fireworks flew before they ventured any questions.

The novice writer started right away. "It wasn't pretty, Danny. It looks like the Yankees have revved up their bats and your pitchers have slowed down their pitches."

Allowing for the young man's innocence, Danny forced a grim smile. "Uh huh. That describes the last two games. What's your question, son?"

Not backing down at all and earning his chance to shine in his own manner, the young writer asked. "Well, what are you going to do about it? The next two games are here in New York. The series could end in New York."

Straightening up as tall as his stocky frame could rise, Danny answered the valid and bold question loud enough for everyone there to hear.

"Son, I'm going to tell you the same thing that a GI said when an Army war correspondent told him that the German Army had him and his fellow soldiers surrounded at Bastogne. "Yep." The GI said. "It looks like they got us right where we want 'em."* Danny paused before asking the young writer. "Do you know how that turned out?"

"Sure. The GIs fought back and won."

"Yep and that's what we're going to do. Law is rested for Game 4. Face is ready, too. Let's see if those Yankee hitters can hit my two guys any better than they did in Game 1."

Gaining more confidence, the young reporter slipped in a follow-up question. "Danny, did you know that your team's odds to win changed fast overnight. How do you get the players to look past that fact?"

Danny had decided to stand for this post-game interview instead of being interviewed in his trademark rocking chair. He didn't want anyone to see him in a rocking chair seeming to relax after these two nightmare losses. He fidgeted with his pouch of chewing tobacco and replied.

"Well, gambling ain't a fact. It's a guess. We don't care if the odds are in our favor or against us. We've been the underdogs all year. We just gotta win one of the next two, and go back to Pittsburgh."

Before anyone could interrupt him, the young writer proceeded with what would be his last question.
"These last two games were very impressive offensively from the Yankees point of view, twenty-two runs versus only three runs. That would worry a lot of teams."

Tired and wanting to end the post-game session, Danny provided an answer that might've come from the same GI at Bastogne. "It worries me, too. But check the rule book. To win the series, one team still needs to win four games, not score the most runs. I'm looking for a belated happy birthday present tomorrow."

"Thank you, and happy birthday." the rookie sportswriter said. Danny heard him, smiled and walked away. No more questions were asked.

***The quote was made by a US Army medic at Bastogne during the Battle of the Bulge, December, 1944. When informed that his unit was surrounded by the German Army, The medic actually said, "Yeh! They got us surrounded. The poor bastards."**

October 8, 1960 Roberto Clemente

After an early dinner following a disastrous Game 3, Pirates' right fielder Roberto Clemente and a few teammates were walking back to their hotel from Restaurant Row in mid-town Manhattan when a handful of Yankee hometown fans saw them and stopped them to chat and playfully needle the players about that day's 10-0 loss to the Yankees.

A few of this small spirited group of fans were wearing Yankee sportswear and they were excited and happy to have recognized the players. One of the fans gleefully kidded the Pirate's star right-fielder.

"Yo! Clemente. You and your buddies might want to wear batting helmets in the field for the next two games. The Yanks are hot and they're swinging for World Series hitting records."

"Yeh, wear a helmet." Another fan kidded. "You don't want to get hit by one of those rockets you can't see."

Clemente who was born and raised in Puerto Rico was just beginning to learn English, and starting to feel comfortable as a baseball celebrity. He laughed and in his improving second language assured the Yankee fan that he and his team mates weren't giving up.

"I can see the ball. I will catch the ball and I will hit it. Yankees can have the hitting records. We want four wins. We will win tomorrow. You'll see."

"No way!" The fan responded.

After all, this was New York City. The man on the street always gets the last word. "This ain't Oz, Kansas, or Pittsburgh, Clemente." He continued. "There are no magic shoes or magic bats here. You're in Yankee land now."

October 9, 1960
Game 4, Sunday - 7th inning

The Bucs were feeling the pressure in Game 4 but Danny appeared calm. Yankees pitcher Bill Terry was pitching hitless ball through four innings and the Yankees, courtesy of Bill Skowron's homer in the fourth, were ahead of Law and the Pirates, 1-0. Then in the top of the fifth, sparked by Law's two-out double, the Pirates fought back and scored three runs. At the end of six innings, the Pirates took their first lead since Game 2: Pirates 3, Yankees 1.

As Danny forecasted in his brief interview the day before, the Yankees were not able to easily duplicate their recent hitting performances against the Pirates' games two and three pitchers. The hometown Yankee fans who packed the stadium came to witness a third blow out in a row. But seeing was believing, and what they saw was another crafty pitching performance by Vernon Law. The Pittsburgh fans at home could hear the difference between the two games as it was broadcast on the radio, and some fans watched it on television, a relatively new medium for baseball.

The radio announcer was an expert at blending exciting play by play commentary, background facts, and game statistics while also relaying the crowd's and the players' shifting moods to the unseeing audience at home. "What a difference in the Yankee bats today." The announcer noted. "Law has silenced the mighty Yankee hitters. But here in the seventh, with a Yankee run in, the score is now 3-2, and the always dangerous Yankees have runners on first base and second base."

The announcer paused, and took a long look down on the field. Then he shared with the listeners what he saw unfolding on the field. "Murtaugh knows Law is struggling on that bad ankle and he's already motioned for Face to come in to the game. Yankee left-fielder Bob Cerv will bat and hope to either tie the game or give New York its' first lead of the day. It looks like Cerv will bat against Elroy Face here in the seventh."

Bob Cerv stepped into the batter's box and he squared himself around and waited for Face's first pitch.

Most of the 67,000 plus fans in Yankee stadium were rooting for a base hit or for any ball that will advance the runners into scoring position. The Yankees still needed to be careful here about sending runners home. Clemente's arm in right-field was already a big factor in this inning. He prevented runners from scoring on two different base hits. Otherwise the Yankees would be leading 4-3 with only one out. Now Face pitched from the stretch and the ball reached home plate at the same time that Cerv swung.

Smack! Cerv leaned into the pitch and drove a fly ball hard and fast to right-center field. The ball was out-racing both outfielders with centerfielder Bill Virdon moving as fast as he could. The players in both dugouts rose from the benches and held tightly onto the dugout screens. Mickey Vernon's voice was the loudest, exhorting Virdon to do the impossible. "C'mon, Billy. Flag it down. Flag it down."

The Pirates broadcaster watched it too. He almost forgot to speak into the microphone because he was completely focused on the flight of the ball. He finally managed to talk.

"That ball is smoked and it's heading for the 407 foot sign. If it's not out of the park, folks, it's against the wall!" There was a sudden pause. "No. Wait. Virdon is catching up to it. He dives, and stretches. He's got it! Oh my goodness! He caught that ball! He caught it."

The Pirates dugout and their thousand fans were cheering and hollering when the ball was caught. The Pirate fielders were all screaming to Virdon to throw the ball quickly into the infield. Down on the field, no one was happier than Danny. He nearly swallowed his chaw of tobacco. He gagged for a split second and rooted Virdon to do even more. "That's some catch, Billy. Now get up and get that ball in here fast."

All of the fans in the ballpark reacted emotionally. Some cheered, most groaned. The radio broadcaster summed it up for the listeners. ""What a catch by Virdon! That ball had hit written all over it so the runners didn't tag. Now, they'll have to return to their original bases and no one will be able to advance. That's going to keep the runners on first and second with two outs. That is the play of the Series so far. What a catch!"

Face managed to get shortstop Tony Kubek to make the final out in the seventh and the score remained Pirates 3, Yankees 2. Casey brought in Jim Coates to face the Pirates in the bottom half of the seventh and he held the Pirates hitless through the final two innings but Face battled the Yankee power hitters in two consecutive innings, retiring the batters in order in both innings, 1-2-3, to end the game. In the ninth inning, both clubs missed getting big hits that would lead to rallies. Mantle robbed Hoak of an extra base hit, then Skowron, hot all afternoon, just missed a long home run, foul by only inches. The final score was Pirates 3, Yankees 2. The series was tied again, 2 wins each. Now there was one more game in Yankee Stadium, then the series was going back to Pittsburgh. The advantage shifted back to the Bucs because two of the three remaining games would be played in Forbes Field.

October 11, 1960
Game 5, Tuesday - Skill and guts

The Yankee nation received an even bigger shock when the pesky Pirates won Game 5 Tuesday at Yankee Stadium. Veteran left-handed pitcher Harvey Haddix and Elroy Face combined to outduel the Yankee pitching corps. The Pirates won 5-2. Another relatively low scoring win by the Pirates made it clear that when the Bombers didn't score double digits, they wouldn't win.

Except for Roger Maris' solo homerun, the Yankee bats were harmless in Game 5. The amazing fact was that the underdog Pirates were leaving New York City with a three games to two games lead in the Series. No one, not even Branch Rickey, expected the Bronx Bombers to lose two of the three games played in the House That Ruth Built. There was a day off Wednesday to allow both teams to travel to Pittsburgh for the final two games to be played in Forbes Field. The Pirates would get at least two chances to win the Series. The Yankees though can't afford to lose a game. They must win two in a row in order to capture an eighth World Series title for Casey Stengel.

On the evening before Game 6, Danny and Mickey were seated at a restaurant in downtown Pittsburgh. They were alone and like always they were trying to decide what to order for dinner.

"Are we ordering appetizers, Danny? Or are we eating light with the big game coming up tomorrow?"

Danny laughed. "Let's eat like it's the Yankees last meal, not our last meal. The pressure is really on the mighty Bronx Bombers."

"Don't say 'Bombers'" was Mickey's instant reply. Then he glanced at the menu and shook his head from side to side. "It's still hard to believe that after 23 years of professional baseball, you and I are here, together, on the same team. Trying to win the World Series. It's been a long time since playing American Legion together in Chester and Marcus Hook."

Unbuttoning his sport coat and putting his cloth napkin on his lap, Danny couldn't believe it either, but it's true.
"Yep, Mickey. Just like we planned it. Except for the few hundred thousand curve balls thrown at us along the way."

Mickey could be insular most times but tonight he wanted to talk about their journey. "Did you ever think it was hopeless? You know what I mean. You had a bouncier road to travel than me. Even with all my good fortune, I did start to be doubtful after I had three chances at the World Series and missed it. Sometimes, Danny, you must've felt you were several oceans away from being in a World Series."

"That's funny. Mick. The fact is we were both an ocean away only fifteen years ago."

"Yeh, we were." Mickey recalled. "You were two oceans away, once across the Atlantic and then across the Pacific."

Not wanting to leave Mickey's question unanswered, Danny spoke solemnly to his friend. "Seriously, I didn't think this was hopeless. No more hopeless than when I was a kid on a sandlot ball field dreaming of playing in the next higher league. I was always hopeful because every time I played ball at a higher level, I felt I was getting closer to my dream. I didn't focus solely on my dream or any specific championship. I just played hard and wanted to get better. I admit that I did want to hit the ball like you, like the smooth-swinging tall kid from Marcus Hook."

"And I wanted to play the infield like you. I just didn't want to hit the dirt as much as you did." Mickey winced when he said it.

"Your skill, Mickey, and my guts. That shows that there is more than one way to grab a golden ring."

Danny and Mickey, Ordinary Heroes

The waiter passed by their table a few times waiting for an opportunity to take their order without interrupting their conversation.

Changing the subject, Danny told Mickey what a writer had asked him earlier that same day. "He asked me if I felt that Face was the hero in the series. How about that? The series isn't even over. Nobody's won yet. A darn Yankee could be the hero."

"What did you tell him?"

"I told him that all of our guys are heroes. It's true. It takes a lot of people to achieve a prize as big as a World Series, or even as little as a single game. It takes lots of people to do big and small things at different times. We know a lot of heroes. You and I. That's what I mean."

"Did he settle for that or did he switch over to bait you on Law or someone else?"

"I didn't say all that to him. Just that they are all heroes. I think he understood me. At least, he didn't follow up on that question. He did ask about Law's ankle, though."

Then Mickey picked the menu back up and before scanning it more seriously, he asked his buddy a rhetorical question. "Do you think that Casey is going to use Whitey tomorrow on only three day's rest?" Then before Danny could say a word, Mickey laughed and quickly added. "If so, who do you like? Them or us?"

"I'd like roast beef, a baked potato, and broccoli. Coffee later. Where's the darn waiter? I'm starved."

October 12, 1960, Game 6 - "Put away that cigar."

The final two games of the Series were played in Forbes Field. Normally a team playing on their own field, in front of their own fans, would be favored to win at least one game. That's all the Pirates needed to do. Win one of the two games. Not surprising though, in this Series, the visiting team, the mighty Yankees, were the favorite to win the last two games and become World Series Champions again.

The Yankee hitters had shown how strong they were at every place in the batting order. The consistent pressure that the Bronx Bombers presented to the already-abused pitching staff left little room for a miracle in Forbes Field this week. Casey and his Bronx Bombers came to Pittsburgh to finish off the Pirates.

For Game 6 on Wednesday, nearly 40,000 fans crowded into the stadium. It was another standing-room only sell out. Unfortunately for the Pittsburgh players and fans, the Yankee Bronx Bombers who showed up in Games 2 and 3 returned to form in Game 6 and reigned havoc on every pitcher that the Pirates sent to the mound. The sixth game of the series was over in less than three innings. In the most lopsided World Series game in history, the Yankees clobbered the Pirates 12-0. Whitey Ford shut out the Pirate hitters for a second time and the Yankee hitters drew baseball blood early and late in the game. The Yankees scored five runs in the top of the third and padded that safe lead with six more runs after the sixth inning. Bob Friend was rocked again and the five pitchers who followed after him were also battered. Yankee second baseman, Bobby Richardson, drove in five runs in the game and set a World Series record with a total of twelve runs batted in during the Series. Altogether, the Yankees had seventeen hits in the game and not one of them was a homerun. The only reason the Pirates didn't quit and stay home after Game 6 was that the Series was tied at three wins apiece and the seventh game was required to be played the very next day. In the three Yankee victories, New York scored 38 runs, averaging 12.6 runs per game. The Pirates scored a total of three runs, averaging one run per game.

Danny's only consolation was he knew there was still one last game to play. He knew he had his best pair of pitchers ready even though every baseball fan knew Law was hobbled by his injured ankle. It wasn't a secret to anyone, certainly not to Stengel and the Yankees. Even so, Law and Face had managed to keep the Yankee's hitting machine out of sync. Danny needed them to do it again.

Now he was back in his room and as he removed his shoes he was glad this was the last night this season he would spend alone in a hotel room. The room was comfortable alright, and large enough to accommodate his family, or invite his coaches to his room and develop some new strategy or magic potion to thwart the mighty Yankees tomorrow. Good God, he thought to himself. The Yankees certainly weren't in their hotel rooms worrying about his Pirates. No. Not tonight.

Danny wasn't fit for any company and he wasn't thinking of any new strategy. He was exhausted and he sat in a chair by the shuttered window with its drapes closed tightly. He had his shoes off and he stretched his legs over a small hassock. He had chosen the most relaxing activity that always worked for him. He called Kate and now he was speaking to her on the phone. The post-game phone calls were not lengthy but they enabled them to end their day on the phone together even if it a conversation was as short as saying "I love you" and "Goodnight". Tonight might be one of those short nights. There wasn't too much either one of them could say after a game like today.

He dialed the phone and smiled when he heard her voice on the phone. "Hi, Kate, I'm OK. I'm in the room to stay. I'm kind of like a prisoner here. There are reporters all over the lobby and the hotel exits. I can't get out. I can't even get to the church across the street to light a few candles."

It was unusual to hear distress in Danny's voice but it was there, and Kate understood. Tomorrow he would be managing his players in the seventh game of the World Series, less than a full day after his team had just lost 10-0. As usual, her voice was what he needed to hear now.

"God knows what you need. You'll be fine, hon. Play the game tomorrow, not tonight. Then you can come home and rest after tomorrow's game."

He sighed and said jokingly. "After tomorrow's game I hope I can breathe."

"Oh! My God! Danny, don't say that!" she blasted into the phone. "Remember. This is what you wanted. You're facing the Yankees and you are on the top of the baseball world."

"Me and the players." He corrected her.

Kate understood. "Of course, you and the players, and Mickey, and me and the kids."

They proceeded to talk about their children and Kate told him where she and the kids would be sitting during tomorrow's ball game. The conversation drifted into other comfortable small talk that easily made them laugh a few times. Then neither of them said anything for a few moments as they waited for the other to speak. Feeling better, Danny cheerily asked a question about an article that he saw in the newspaper the day before. He wouldn't dare ask anyone else this question except Kate.

"Kate, I read in the paper yesterday where people were talking about the top baseball Managers. So, you know, with the Pirates in the World Series and all, how many top Managers do you think there are in baseball?"

This was one of the moments where Kate loved being not only Danny's sweetheart but also his sole confidant. She knew he was a modest man, shy in the midst of public praise, but he was privately proud of his accomplishments. He liked praise as much as anyone. She also knew that only she could throw water on it and leave him laughing. So, she thought for a moment and answered him sweetly. "I don't know exactly how many top Managers there are hon, but I do know that there is one less than you think there are." He was silent. Then she got the short reply she expected from him, including the laughter. "Aw, Kate."

Kate's comforting voice drifted through the phone.
"I love you. Now, get some sleep...and put that cigar away."

She heard him laugh again and she knew that he immediately removed the cigar from his mouth. She recalled a piece of his own advice that she had heard him recite so many times.
She repeated it to him now. "You always told the kids, 'if you want something you have to move your feet and go get it'. Well, tomorrow is your day to go get it. Make all your moves tomorrow. Don't save anything. You always say that you have to play nine to win."

"Yep. That's all true. Well, just this year, these guys won 33 games coming from behind. Heck, Face might really be our most valuable player."

"No, Danny. You are." She blew a kiss through the phone. "Get some rest now. I love you. Goodnight".

"I love you too, hon. Kiss the kids for me. Goodnight."

Danny held the phone for a minute. He was just a little too tired to put it back on the phone's cradle. He couldn't stop thinking that tomorrow was what he had dreamed about doing his whole life. Now he was here. And the hardest part for him now wasn't knowing what to do in tomorrow's game, it was trying to close his eyes and sleep. He never thought sleeping would be a problem.

CHAPTER SIXTEEN
BEST WORLD SERIES GAME 7 EVER

Game 7, Thursday, October 13, 1960

Prior to the seventh and final game of the Series, major league baseball announced the National and the American League Most Valuable Players in each league. Dick Groat received the National League award and Roger Maris received the American League award. Fittingly, they represented the two teams that were playing in the World Series. Ironically they were the same players who were the subject of a near-trade in spring training that Danny decided not to make, proving an old adage, 'sometimes the trades you don't make are the best ones.' This non-trade benefitted both teams.

Two hours before the start of Game 7, Mickey and Danny stepped out of the home dugout and walked onto Forbes Field. Red, white, and blue bunting was displayed like colorful flowers all along the first level of seating around the ballpark, and even up along the second level of the stadium seating areas. Though Forbes Field* wasn't as big as Yankee Stadium, and although it didn't have the accompanying history and glamour of its iconic New York counterpart, the Pirates home park shone brightly for Game 7. It was spic and span and it looked regal with a golden tint and a halo-like appearance as the afternoon sunrays angled across the stadium.

The two friends walked quietly across the freshly-cut, green outfield grass. They turned around and looked up into the still empty stands and at the flags waving on the highest point of the stadium.

"I'm speechless." Was Mickey's comment.

"Me, too." Danny murmured.

Their eyes settled at the same time on the American flag waving over the stadium. Mickey smiled warmly at his team mate and friend. "It's a funny thing, Danny. You and I always dreamed that we would get here as players. And here we are. Yet neither one of us can win this ballgame playing on this field."

"Nope." Danny agreed as he fingered his pouch of tobacco. "Playing was all we could see then. Never thought there was any other way."

Mickey kept his eyes on the flag and said, "It seems like this is the way we were supposed to get here. What do you think, pal?"

Danny started to answer. "Well..," Then he stopped. He paused to gather his words but stood silent in the middle of the outfield. Mickey stared at him, waiting for him to finish his sentence. Danny didn't say another word.

"Wow! Danny. This is the first time that I've ever seen you speechless."

Danny turned slightly towards his boyhood friend, reached up to Mickey's broad shoulder and patted him on the back. He said softly. "OK, Hook. Let's go. Beat 'em Bucs."

***Forbes Field was built in 1909 in the Oakland neighborhood in Pittsburgh. It was named after John Forbes, a British general who captured Fort Duquesne in the French and Indian War and built Fort Pitt which later became known as Pittsburgh in 1758.**

Game 7 - First inning fireworks

A Standing Room Only (SRO) crowd (39,683 plus) filled Forbes Field for Game 7. If safety regulations were thrown to the wind, another 10,000 people would've packed themselves in to see this October spectacle. Yankee Stadium had already hosted 67,000 fans per single game in Games 3, 4, and 5 earlier in the Series.

The predominantly Pirate crowd settled into their seats just before Vernon Law finished his warmup pitches. Bobby Richardson, the leading hitter in the Series, led off Game 7 for the Yankees. This was another batting order change by the Yankee skipper and it was Stengel's seventh different lineup in the Series. He was determined to find a lineup that would be able to hit Law's pitches.

The game began under a bright sunny October sky and the first pitch of the game was a ball to Richardson. It was clear from the first batter that Law was struggling on his battered ankle but he opened strong and the Yankees went down in order in the first inning. Now it was the Pirates turn to come up to bat. Stengel sent Bob Turley out to start the game. He was hopeful that 'Bullet Bob' would throw his lively fastball past the Pirates lineup, at least through the early innings. Danny also made a few changes for the final game. He moved Bob Skinner back into centerfield after Skinner missed the previous five games with an injured thumb. On a hunch, he inserted left-handed hitter Rocky Nelson at first base in place of starter Dick Stuart.

Turley got two quick outs in the Pirates half of the inning but he missed on a full count pitch to Skinner who jogged to first base with a walk. Rocky Nelson was the next batter. He had appeared in three games in the Series and so far he had three hits in six plate appearances.

When Pittsburgh backed away in the winter from making the trade with Kansas City for Maris, Pirates GM Brown knew that he still needed a left-handed power hitter. He drafted Nelson out of the Canadian League for just this reason. Nelson was a left-handed power hitter who could come in for Stuart and face right-handers like Turley. Throughout the regular season and up to this point in the Series he had been effective for the Pirates but this was one of those moments when a General Manager's player selection becomes memorable or infamous. The Pirates GM had his cards on the table. Standing in the coach's box at first base, Mickey was talking to Skinner, then he called out some chatter to Nelson. "OK, Rocky. Take a good look at the pitch."

Turley's first pitch to Nelson was called a ball by the umpire. Turley set himself again on the mound and pitched from the stretch. The 1 and 0 pitch arrived swiftly on Nelson who swung his bat. *CRACK*!

When the sound of the bat echoed from home plate, Danny's serious face disappeared and his kid face broke out for everyone in the dugout to see. He was beaming. What an unbelievable start, he thought.

"Oh, brother! He really got a hold of that one, baby. It looks high enough to clear the fence." Then he hesitated as the ball began to curve slightly towards the foul pole on its way towards the right field wall. "Wait, it may be foul." Then Danny said jubilantly. "Nope! It's a sweet fair ball."

The ball stayed a few feet left of the right-field foul pole as it went over the wall. Suddenly, the Pirates had a 2-0 lead. What a wonderful day this was turning out to be thought everyone who lived in Pittsburgh. The next batter made the third out in the inning and the score at the end of the first inning of the last game of this wild Series was Pirates 2, Yankees 0.

It was an ominous sign for the Yankees. They had not come back to win a game in this Series after they had fallen behind the Bucs.

Game 7- Yogi's blast in the 6th inning

The Pirates added two more runs in the second inning. Bill Virdon hit a clutch single with two teammates on base. Law continued to shut out the

Yankees assisted by great outfield plays made by Clemente and Virdon. In the fifth inning, the Yankees' Bill Skowron launched a home run into the upper deck in left field. This was doubly important because it was no secret that Law was tiring. Heading into the top of the sixth inning, the Pirates led 4-1.

The Yankee batters picked up a single and a walk to start off the sixth. Danny knew that Law was finished for the day and for the Series. Law had pitched until he had nothing left. The pitching ace had a very effective Series, winning two games so far, and his pitching line today was six innings and he was charged with one run and four hits. The two runners on base now would be charged to Law if they scored in this inning. Danny walked slowly to the mound and Law handed him the ball. Patting his pitcher on the shoulder, the skipper told him. "Deacon, thanks. You gave all you got."

Danny had already motioned for 'the little man', Elroy Face to come in to the game. The signal that Danny reserved solely for his ace reliever was a typical Murtaugh 'schtick'. Affectionately, he would use his left hand to tap his lower left thigh, that motion triggered Face's entry into a game whenever Danny needed him. And in the past few years, it was often.

Elroy Face*, the best reliever in baseball, was a difficult challenge for the Yankees. He had saved all three wins in the Series for Pittsburgh. If he were to save this fourth game, the Pirates would win the championship. The challenge for Elroy in this inning would begin with the very next batter, the American League Most Valuable Player, Roger Maris.

Remarkably, Face got Maris to pop-up for the first out. But Mickey Mantle was the next batter. Face's job on the mound just kept getting harder. Trying to keep Mantle inside the park, Face pitched Mick carefully. After a few tosses, Mantle hit an RBI single to drive in the Yankees' second run making the score Pirates 4, Yankees 2. The drama only intensified as the batter that Danny viewed as the most dangerous hitter in the Yankees lineup walked to home plate.

Yogi Berra was the last Yankee hitter that Danny wanted to see in the batter's box now. Face was very good but Berra was a great hitter. Berra had also seen a lot of Elroy's pitches through the previous games. Danny knew that even Face couldn't fool him forever. Danny clenched his tobacco tightly between his teeth.

The tension didn't last long. Berra wasted no time worrying how Face would pitch to him. He crushed Face's first pitch, a normally wicked forkball, and sent it deep into the right field stands. Suddenly, the Yankees led 5-4 and all of the hometown joy was flushed rapidly out of Forbes Field. It is likely that more than one fan mumbled to themselves the raw truism often used to describe the fickle hand of fate. 'Sometimes you get the bear, and sometimes the bear gets you.' This time it was as clear as the spots on a leopard that the 'bear' got Face. Face finished the inning and managed to get the final two outs in the inning. The Pirates were coming to bat in the bottom half of the sixth, suddenly trailing 5-4.

***Elroy Face is considered to be the prototype for baseball's 'closer' that is now required on every pitching staff in major league baseball. The 'closer' is the 'last resort' pitcher who only appears late in a game where his team is tied or winning. His role on the team is to save or win the game, but not lose the game. In 1959, Face set a record for most wins in a row with 23 when he finished 1958 with five wins in a row, then won 18 games in a row in 1959 before he lost his last game of the 1959 season. He finished the 1959 season with 18 wins and one loss.**

Game 7, Eighth inning

The Pirates failed to score in the sixth and seventh innings and the Yankees added two more runs off Face in the top half of the eighth and led the Pirates 7-4. Bill Skowron's single in that inning set a World Series' record at that time for most hits by a batter in a single World Series. Bobby Richardson previously set a Series record in Game 6 when he drove in his twelfth run in the Series.

The Yankees now had a three run lead and Yankee's reliever Bobby Shantz was pitching well, having held the Bucs scoreless for the last several innings. For these two reasons, Casey decided to let Shantz bat in the eighth. Face retired Shantz for the final out in the inning. The Pirates ran off the field to prepare to bat in the bottom of the eighth inning.

The Pirate players all crowded onto the dugout bench. Danny was waiting for them. But at that moment, Don Hoak stepped off of the field and into the dugout. He glanced at Danny and made eye contact with him, and Danny nodded. Then Hoak threw his glove hard into a corner of the dugout, and stood in the center of the dugout. For a few seconds there he was, motionless and silent. Then he released a volcano of emotions that were roiling inside him.

"Goddam it, fellas! This is our game to win. We got two innings to do it. Let's start now. Hit the damn ball hard, run hard. Don't save any energy or guts for the next game or the next inning. Use it all now. We're a comeback team. Have been all year. That's why we're here today. Skipper knows what we have inside. C'mon let the Yankees and everyone else see it. I want this game! You all want this game! Let's go get the damn thing."

The players and coaches erupted in a loud roar of agreement and support. Everyone jumped off the dugout bench, milling frantically around the dugout.

"Gino." Mickey called out. "You're batting for Face. Let's start it off the right way. Pick a pitch, hit the ball, and get on base. Whaddya say?" The Pirates were desperate.

Meanwhile, there were some puzzled looks on Yankee fans in Forbes Field when Shantz batted in the top of the eighth inning. The Yankee radio announcer told the Yankee fans at home why he thought Shantz batted. "Casey is convinced that Shantz is the answer to keeping the Pirates scoreless. He kept Pirate runners off the bases in the past two innings. I'm sure that's why Casey let Shantz bat in the previous inning.

This will be Shantz' sixth inning of relief and he has handcuffed the Pirate lineup since the third inning."

The announcer looked over at the batter coming out of the Pirates dugout. "Gino Cimoli will pinch hit for Face. Well, Face and Law have given as much as they could in this final game of the 1960 World Series. But it wasn't enough. Looks like their work in the Series is done and that's a good thing for the Yankees."

Mickey was standing in the first base coaching box. He clapped his hands and caught Cimoli's eye at home plate, then he motioned with his right hand to a gap to the left of the second baseman. "OK, Gino. What do you see? Let's go. You're going to be our first base runner."

Shantz threw two pitches and Cimoli laid back on them. The count rose to two balls and zero strikes when Cimoli hit the next pitch just past the second baseman for a leadoff single. The Pirates had their leadoff batter on first base and now Bill Virdon stepped into the batter's box. He readied himself for the pitch from Shantz and what happened next remains one of the most talked about infield ground balls ever hit in World Series history. All hell broke loose.

The Yankee broadcaster used his eyes and his words to set the table for the fans who were at home. "Fans, here in the bottom of the eighth, the Yankees are winning 7-4 and the Pirates have a runner on base with no outs. Bill Virdon, the Bucs' left-fielder, will bat. Virdon's two-run single in the second inning was the last time that Pittsburgh scored. It's been a long dry spell for the Buc hitters and you can give that credit to Bobby Shantz. What a performance. He's been out there for six innings." The announcer paused, then continued. "Cimoli is off the first base bag. He has good speed, so does Virdon. OK, Shantz goes into his stretch and here's the pitch."

Crack!

The Yankee announcer's voice shook for a split-second as he saw the ball jump from Virdon's bat and dart on a beeline to the left side of the infield.

He leaned forward and he spoke into the microphone. "There's a hard smash to shortstop. Kubek comes in on it. Uh Oh! The ball popped up sharply. Hey! The ball hit him! It hit him! Kubek is down on the ground! But where is the ball?"

As everyone in the stadium watched Kubek stretched out on the infield with the ball lying beside him, Richardson came across from the second base side of the bag and picked up the ball. By now there was no chance for a play on either runner and both runners were safe. Pittsburgh now had men on first and second base with no outs.

The ball was secured by Richardson and time was called by the umpire. The radio announcer was still stunned by what he saw and he continued to provide his listeners with the sights and sounds taking place down on the field. Regarding the fallen player, he reported what he saw. "Kubek is withering on the ground and he's holding his throat. He's spitting out blood."

Players for both teams were now out of the dugouts but most stayed off the field and just outside the playing area and watched with quiet concern. The umpire was conferring with the two Managers.

It was more likely that the fans at home listening on the radio or watching on television had a better understanding of what happened on the field than most of the 40,000 fans in the stadium. The radio and TV announcers were getting information from a colleague who was down on the playing field.

The radio announcer continued. "I'm being told that the ball hit something in the dirt and skipped up and struck Kubek in the face or the throat. It's hard to explain exactly what happened. I can't see Tony now that the players and coaches are all surrounding him. He was in obvious pain."

The fans in Forbes Field and the listeners and viewers at home were anxious to learn what happened and what the ruling would be. Was it possible that there was some kind of interference?

What was eventually communicated to everyone was that Virdon's hard hit ground ball deflected off an infield stone and struck Kubek in the Adam's apple. Kubek was treated by doctors on the field, then removed from the field and taken to a nearby hospital. He was hospitalized overnight to monitor his breathing and released the next day and told to eat lightly and to not speak for a few days. The strange play brought to mind a phrase that was often used to explain a twist of fate, plainly, 'that's how the ball bounces.' What soon became clear was that the damage to the Yankees went far beyond Kubek's injury.

Once Kubek was removed from the playing field and transported to the hospital, the game continued.
Now, instead of Virdon hitting into what might have been a possible double play, the Pirates now had runners on first and second and no outs. The "bouncing ball" hit to Kubek became responsible for a two run rally that shortly followed.

Shantz pitched to the next batter, Dick Groat, who hit a single and drove in Gino Cimoli with the Pirates' fifth run. Stengel replaced Shantz with Jim Coates but Coates was unable to stop the Pirates. Bob Skinner laid down a sacrifice bunt that moved Virdon to third and Groat to second. There was one out. Coates was able to get Nelson to hit a fly ball to right field that was too shallow for Virdon to try to score from third base. Now there were two outs. The score was Yankees 7, Pirates 5.

Pittsburgh had runners on second base and third base and one out. The next batter to face Coates was Roberto Clemente who was having a good Series and showing not only his hitting but his speed, fielding, and throwing skills. Clemente already had hits in the six previous Series games. He quickly hit a high chopper to Yankee's first baseman Bill Skowron who stepped towards home plate to field the ball and turned to flip the ball to the pitcher covering the bag, but Coates wasn't there. Coates moved off the mound to field the ball and he was unable to cover the bag so there was no play at first base. Clemente's speed got him to first base and it was ruled a single as Virdon scored the sixth run for Pittsburgh. Coates' failure to cover the first base bag when he came off the mound prevented the Yankees from getting the third out of the inning that would've left the score Yankees 7, Pirates 5 with the Yankees coming to bat in the top of the ninth inning. That out didn't happen and this inning would get even worse for the Yankees.

This crazy, zany, wacky baseball game continued to add to its lion's share of bumps, bruises, and bounces and the Pirates were suddenly within one run, 7-6. Skinner and Clemente were on base and there were two outs when Hal Smith batted for the first time in this game. Smith entered the game as a catcher in the seventh inning when Smokey Burgess was replaced with a pinch-runner.

When Smith stepped into the batter's box, Yankee catcher, Doc Blanchard greeted him with the usual catcher to catcher sign of respect. "Hey, you ugly grunt. Looks like you get a chance to make an out and end this inning?"

"Not yet, Doc." Was Smith's curt reply.

Hal Smith was acquired in December 1959 from the Kansas City Athletics to backup Smokey Burgess behind the plate and to be a right-handed pinch hitter for the club. He had already appeared in three Series games and he was 2 for 7 in his previous plate appearances. Smith had some power in his swing so Coates had to be careful with him. There was a base open and Don Hoak was the on-deck batter.

Stengel decided to let Coates pitch to Smith. The pitcher and the batter were cautious with one another. Smith managed to hold-up his swing on a 1-2 pitch that was called ball two. The count was now two balls and two strikes. The next pitch was critical for the hitter and the pitcher.

With his arms folded, Danny mumbled to himself.

Coates threw his 2 and 2 pitch to home plate and it curved up into the middle of the plate instead of low and away. Smith swung and crushed it and the ball soared towards the left-center field wall to the 406 foot sign. Mantle and Berra both took a few steps toward the wall, then they stopped and watched the ball fly into the stands and dramatically change the score again in this baseball tug of war. Groat and Clemente crossed the plate ahead of Smith and the score was Pirates 9, Yankees 7. Stengel visited the mound and replaced Coates with Ralph Terry but it was one batter too late. Terry got Don Hoak to hit a fly ball for the final out in the eighth inning.

The hometown crowd was ecstatic and the late afternoon sun rose high and seemed ready to play its part in christening the Pirates as the new champions of the baseball world.

Mickey walked over to Danny as the Pirates fielders ran onto the field in the top of the ninth inning. "Danny, I'm really glad I'm on the field for this game. I could never have sat still in the stands."

Chomping on a mouthful of tobacco, Danny agreed with him. "Mick, I already used four packs of chewing tobacco in this one game and I don't remember spitting even once."

Game 7, Yankee ninth inning

Danny sent Bob Friend out to pitch the ninth inning. This was Friend's first appearance in relief during the Series but there was no Game 8 to play, not tomorrow or any day in the future. It was now or never and Friend was given the hard task to stop the Yankees and win the World

Series for Pittsburgh. But Friend fared no better than he did in the two previous games that he started. The first two batters he faced hit the ball sharply and now Yankee runners were on first and second. With Maris and Mantle scheduled to bat next, Murtaugh took the ball from Friend and sent Haddix out to face these two dangerous left-handed hitters. Haddix managed to get Maris to pop out but Mantle hit a single to drive in a run. The Pirate lead was whittled down to a single run, 9-8.

Mantle stood on first and Gil McDougald came in as a pinch runner at third base for Dale Long. The Yankees had one out and one run in. The next batter was Danny's worst nightmare, Yogi Berra. This was almost an identical situation that occurred in the sixth inning of this game when Berra launched an Elroy Face forkball into Forbes Field's upper deck in right field.

Although he was nervous and knew that he should just be quiet, Danny couldn't keep from fussing with the ump when he saw Berra step again into the batter's box. He got the umpire's attention. "Hey Ump. Here comes Yogi again. How many times has he batted today? Check their lineup card. I bet he's batting out of order."

All of the umpires were familiar with Danny's needling and generally let him be playful in his own strategic manner. This time was different. He answered coldly. "I don't count at bats, skipper. I just call balls and strikes."

Danny laughed. "Then just call three strikes and let's get out of here."

This time the umpire laughed, not even looking over at the skipper.

Berra moved up to the plate and concentrated on Haddix out on the mound. Yogi was unaware of what was said between the Danny and the umpire. After taking a few pitches, Berra smashed a wicked fast line drive to the left of first base. Just as the ball hit the dirt in front of him, Nelson lunged for the ball and made a back-handed grab with his glove. He looked to second base but he didn't see anyone covering the bag. He turned and stepped on the first base bag and Berra was out. Mantle who hesitated on the line drive, saw the quick out made at first, and to avoid the sure tag play at second, he decided to turn back from second and slide back into first base since it was now unoccupied. He slid safely under Nelson's late tag. It was an odd sequence and it all unfolded quickly but it was enough for the Yankees' McDougald to score the tying run. The Pirates barely missed executing a double play that would've ended the game, a game that they would've won.

Only now the game was tied, 9-9. Haddix faced slugger Bill Skowron who hit a sharp groundball to Mazeroski to end the inning. The Pirates would have a final opportunity to win the game in regulation but they will have to come from behind again to do it.

Game 7, Home field advantage

Forbes Field remained charged with excitement. The late afternoon sun seemed to have grown even brighter as though it was drawing energy from all the fans, those in the stadium and those at home. Pittsburgh, once the laughing stock of the National League and the negative inspiration for the 1952 baseball film, "Angels in the Outfield", had finally reached the summit of baseball and the city enjoyed every minute of it.

Both teams were playing with all of their energy and heart and they both benefited from ground balls that bounced in their favor. Groat's ground ball in the eighth hit Kubek and prevented a double play that extended a Pittsburgh rally. Berra's smash in the top of the ninth turned Nelson around and likely delayed the double play that would've ended the series with a Pittsburgh win. The two clubs had battled to a draw. If the Pirates scored now, the game would end.

However, the Pirates did have more than hope on their side. They had the best advantage in sports, the home field advantage. Prior to 2003, the two leagues alternated each year as to which league would host the Series, the NL hosted even-numbered years and the AL hosted odd-numbered years. In 1960 it was the National League's turn to host the games. Pittsburgh as the National League pennant winner would play four games at Forbes Field, and play the seventh game in their park, and bat last in the seventh game, if events warranted it.

The cardinal rule in baseball was 'visitors bat first, home teams bat last'. The home field advantage in baseball was the best advantage in all sports. It's an advantage you don't want to give away. Trailing or tied, the home team always gets the last chance to bat, and the visitors don't. So with the score tied, 9–9, the Pirates could score one run and the game was over. The Yankees wouldn't get to bat again. Before the Series began, Fate had given the Pirates this single advantage they had over the Yankees. The Pirates would bat last in the seventh game of the World Series.

The two baseball veterans and lifetime friends took their positions as Yankee pitcher Ralph Terry threw his last warmup pitch. Mickey was in the coach's box at first base and Danny stood like a sentinel at the front of the dugout encouraging his players.

He opened his fifth pack of chewing tobacco but before he placed a wad in his mouth, he called out to the players in the dugout. "C'mon fellas. One run and we win the Series."

The tension in the air was present but it was not stifling, it was energizing to everyone in the stadium. It was nearing 3:30 PM Eastern Standard Time and there was plenty of daylight left for any extra innings that might be added to the 1960 MLB season. It was now or later. Three outs and the game continued, one run now and the game was over. Pirates win.

Game 7, "Hey, Maz, you're up."

"Hey, Maz, you're up." That was the leadership and inspiration Danny provided to Bill Mazeroski and his teammates in the bottom half of the ninth inning, followed by a clear command. "One run. Let's go get it."

Don Hoak was standing near the skipper and yelled out to his teammate as Mazeroski approached home plate. "Look for his fast ball, Maz."

The red, white, and blue bunting and flags were still ruffling in the wind and the sun continued to shine across the ball field. It was still a perfect day for baseball. America's Favorite Pastime thrived on days like this.

Mazeroski stepped into the batters' box at home plate. He set his feet and he readied his bat to be in position for Ralph Terry's first pitch. Only ninety feet away, Terry wrapped the baseball in his glove, then he gripped the ball, and threw a fast ball. It was high, ball one.

That pitch seemed to have turned the sound back on in the stadium as fans rooting for both teams began cheering loudly for their players, The Pirate dugout was filled with sounds of encouragement for Mazeroski.

Danny moved one step higher on the dugout steps. He looked at the scoreboard – he saw the posted score, 9-9, he noted the inning was the 9th and the batter's uniform number was No.9. Suddenly, Danny saw it, so clearly! The memory of last night's dream flashed in his mind, he heard again the ringing phone. He understood now what Unkie was trying to tell him in the dream, and why he woke at 9pm. Can this be possible? Was he really seeing this? He looked to the scoreboard: 9th inning, 9-9, uniform number 9, 9 pm. All 9's. At that moment he looked at home plate just as Terry released the pitch to Mazeroski. Danny felt a light breeze blow by him as Maz swung at the 1-0 pitch. **CRACK!**

The entire stadium and all of Pittsburgh heard the powerful sound of Mazeroski's bat on the ball. Everyone was stunned. All eyes were on the flight of the ball. The entire Pirate team jumped up from the dugout to watch the ball race itself to left field as though it had a date with destiny.

Standing in shock with his hands on the top of his head, Don Hoak screamed at the ball. "C'mon, baby! Get out of here you stinking, rotten, beautiful baseball."

Baseball fans at home shared in the excitement in the stadium as the radio announcer filled the radio waves with his own boyhood wonderment. "There's a long drive to the gap in deep left field. Berra and Mantle are chasing it out near the 406 foot sign." He paused. "Look out now! That ball is going, going, gone! The Pirates win the World Series! Incredible! The Pirates win! The Pirates are World Series Champions!"

One batter. Two pitches. Then a long fly ball into the upper deck. It is still the only game-winning, walk-off home run ever hit in a Game 7 in the World Series. The underdog Pirates won the game and gained their 34th come-from-behind win in 1960. Even though they were outscored by the Yankees 38 to 3 in three games and won four games by less than 2 runs per game, they were the 1960 World Series Champions.

From Mickey's position on the field, he knew the ball was a home run. He moved away from first base as Maz approached the bag so he would not touch or interfere with him, and he pointed emphatically to Maz to step firmly on the first-base bag, reminding Maz to touch all the bases. Mickey didn't want Maz to miss any of the bases during his home run trot. Mazeroski touched the first base bag and the second base bag, then he stepped lightly on third base and he began to jump and dance his way down the third base line towards home plate while the entire Pirate ball club - players, coaches, and field staff - gathered on the field around home plate, leaving only enough room for the umpire to watch Mazeroski step on home plate. As he did so, the umpire signaled that the run scored, and that Game 7 was over. The Pittsburgh Pirates officially won!

Pandemonium broke out on the field and in the stands. Pittsburgh police officers and stadium security personnel were no match for the swarms of fans that stormed the playing field. Unnoticed in this bedlam of celebration was the quiet and solemn exit from the playing field of the mighty New York Yankees including Mantle, Maris, Berra, Ford, and Stengel.

Danny was in the midst of the crush of players and fans. He congratulated Mazeroski, then embraced Mickey and fought back tears. He and Mickey played baseball their whole lives for this moment. Now they walked arm in arm through the crowd of celebrating players and fans.

They looked like they always did when they were together side by side, a misfit pair: one tall and lean, the other short and stocky. That was on the outside. On the inside they were very much alike.

Mickey spoke first. "Thanks, Danny. Thanks for sharing it with me."
"You and me together." Danny gushed. "This is the right way. Nothing will ever feel any better than this, partner."
Just then amid all of the raucous noise and zany celebration, a loud piercing whistle caught Danny's attention. It was a familiar sounding whistle. Danny recognized the tone of it and felt it deep within himself. His eyes and ears strained to search around the stadium for its source but its sound faded away as quickly as it was heard. Danny knew what it was and he whispered under his breath, "Thank you, Unkie."

Game 7, "Let's all go home."

The wild jubilation continued for a long time inside and outside the stadium and throughout Pittsburgh. Kate and Danny finally found one another in the loud, wacky, clubhouse. Standing with their children beside them, they embraced each other tightly and sealed their joy with an out-of-character kiss in public. Coming up for air, Kate spoke softly to Danny. "Danny, I don't think that I've ever seen you so happy."

"Well, hon, I've never been so happy. But as sure as you and I are standing here together, if Bill Mazeroski was standing here with us and somebody told me at this moment that I had to kiss you or Bill, it wouldn't have been you."

Danny's high school sweetheart and lifetime love, laughed. "Today, I don't mind that at all. I know that baseball has always been my biggest competition."

She put her arm around Danny and nudged her children away from the throng of reporters and fans towards the door.
"Now come on, Danny, kids. Let's all go home."

EPILOGUE

"After shocking the baseball world by winning the 1960 World Series, the Pirates dominated the National League well into the 1970s, winning six division titles and two more World Series in 1971 and 1979."
Source- MLB Baseball Hall of Fame, Cooperstown, NY.

Danny, Mickey and the Pirates re-energized the city of Pittsburgh. A bustling city once responsible for providing America with the steel to build the nation, the city had fallen on bad economic times. Now it was the proud home of champions: first in baseball, soon it would be football, and later, hockey. Danny and his Pirates provided a solid and spirited foundation for its citizens who now thrive with new technologies and twenty-first century commerce.

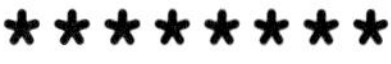

Danny Murtaugh finished his career with these Hall of Fame credentials.

- He managed the Pirates four different times for 15 years between 1958 and 1976.
- He won two World Series, 1960 and 1971 and won five National League pennants.
- He was National League Manager of the Year in 1958, 1960, and 1971.
- He won 1,115 games and finished no lower than 3rd place in 6 of 8 seasons.
- All of this was achieved with a perennial second division franchise in a small market.
- Danny fielded the first all-color starting nine baseball team in the majors on September 1, 1971. In reply to a reporter's question on why he made the decision to field an all-color team of players, he simply said, "I wasn't choosing color, just the best nine players for the game."
- Danny appeared in a total of 2,835 major league games as player and Manager.

Danny and Mickey, Ordinary Heroes

- Danny played in 767 major league games, batting .254, 2942 ABs, 287 walks, 661 hits.
- Danny retired several times after 1960 but returned each time to help Joe Brown and the Pittsburgh Pirates win many more baseball games.
- Danny and his Pirates put the Steel City back on the sports map and set a new standard of excellence for professional sports in Pittsburgh. They led the charge for the rise of the NFL Pittsburgh Steelers and the NHL Pittsburgh Penguins.
- Danny retired from baseball in 1976. Sadly, he suffered a stroke and died at age 59 in 1976.

Mickey Vernon finished his career with these Hall of Fame credentials.

- He won two batting titles: 1946 (.353), 1953 (.337).
- He was voted to play in 7 All-Star games (1946, 1948, 1953, 1954, 1955, 1956. 1958), for three different teams.
- His lifetime batting average was .286 in 2,409 games, 8,731 ABs, 2,495 hits, 172 HRs, 1,311 RBIs
- He holds the MLB record for career double plays at first base (2,044), 4th in career games at first base (2,227), 7th in career putouts (19,754), 9th in career assists (1,444), and fielding chances (21,408).
- His 1st base fielding percentage in 19 years was .990%.
- He was one of only five MLB ballplayers to have batted in four decades through 1960.
- He was the Manager of the Washington Senators from 1961-1963.
- Ted Williams once declared Mickey Vernon to be "the best clutch hitter in baseball"
- Mickey's skills never overshadowed his reputation as "a gentleman".
- A life-long friend said that instead of being a ballplayer, Mickey Vernon should've been President of the United States.
- After a long career as a baseball scout, Mickey died peacefully in September 2008 at age 90.

Kate Murtaugh was at Danny's bedside when he passed away in 1976. She lived quietly surrounded by family and friends, always missing Danny, her personal hero. She never expressed her opinion as to whether Danny was among the best Managers in baseball. She was happy knowing that he was the best husband, father, and friend in her lifetime. Kate died in 2000 at age 82.

Joe E. Brown retired as General Manager of the Pittsburgh Pirates in 1976 at the same time as Danny. This son of funny-man, actor Joe E. Brown, returned to his birthplace in Los Angeles, CA. He died in 2010 at age 91.

Branch Rickey is a member of the Cooperstown MLB Hall of Fame.

- He was General Manager of the Pirates 1950-1955 and resigned in 1955 due to poor health.
- He played, managed and was an executive in major league baseball.
- He was an army Major during the First World War. Baseball Hall of Famers Ty Cobb and Christy Mathewson served under him in the 1st Gas Regiment in France.
- He was General Manager for the 1926, 1931-'32, 1942 World Series champion St. Louis Cardinals and established the minor league farm system with the St. Louis Cardinals
- He was General Manager for the Brooklyn Dodgers, 1946-1949 and was the primary advocate for integrating professional baseball when he recruited Jackie Robinson to play with the Brooklyn Dodgers, and he drafted Roberto Clemente of Puerto Rico for the Pittsburgh Pirates.
- He introduced safety features in baseball such as batting cages, pitching machines, and batting helmets.
- He died while speaking at an awards induction ceremony in December 1965. He was 83 years old.

He made his own observation on the value of sports, once remarking, "A team is where a boy can prove his courage on his own. A gang is where a coward goes to hide."

Danny Murtaugh Hitting Statistics

Source: Baseball-almanac.com

Danny Murtaugh

Danny Murtaugh Hitting Stats

Yr	Age	Team	G	AB	R	H	2B	3B	HR	GRSL	RBI	BB	IBB	SO	SH	SF	HBP	GIDP	AVG	OBP	SLG
1941	24	Phillies	85	347	34	76	8	1	0	0	11	26	0	31	1	-	1	3	.219	.275	.248
1942	25	Phillies	144	506	48	122	16	4	0	0	27	49	2	39	21	-	2	13	.241	.311	.289
1943	26	Phillies	113	451	65	123	17	4	1	0	35	57	0	23	10	-	2	9	.273	.357	.335
1946	29	Phillies	6	19	1	4	1	0	1	0	3	2	0	2	0	-	0	0	.211	.286	.421
1947	30	Braves	3	8	0	1	0	0	0	0	0	1	0	2	0	-	0	0	.125	.222	.125
1948	31	Pirates	146	514	56	149	21	5	1	1	71	60	0	40	4	-	1	8	.290	.365	.356
1949	32	Pirates	75	236	16	48	7	2	2	0	24	29	0	17	3	-	0	2	.203	.291	.275
1950	33	Pirates	118	367	34	108	20	5	2	0	37	47	2	42	1	-	1	8	.294	.376	.392
1951	34	Pirates	77	151	9	30	7	0	1	0	11	16	2	19	2	-	2	6	.199	.284	.265
Career			G	AB	R	H	2B	3B	HR	GRSL	RBI	BB	IBB	SO	SH	SF	HBP	GIDP	AVG	OBP	SLG
9 Years			767	2,599	263	661	97	21	8	1	219	287	6	215	42	-	9	49	.254	.331	.317

Danny Murtaugh Manager Statistics

Danny Murtaugh MLB Managers Statistics

Year	Team	Games	Won	Lost	Win %		
1957	Pirates	51	26	25	0.510	7th	partial
1958	Pirates	154	84	70	0.545	2nd	
1959	Pirates	154	78	76	0.506	4th	
1960	Pirates	154	95	59	0.617	1st	
1961	Pirates	154	75	79	0.487	6th	
1962	Pirates	161	93	68	0.578	4th	
1963	Pirates	162	74	88	0.457	8th	
1964	Pirates	162	80	82	0.494	6th	
1967	Pirates	78	39	39	0.500	6th	partial
1970	Pirates	162	89	73	0.549	1st	
1971	Pirates	161	97	65	0.602	1st	
1973	Pirates	26	13	13	0.500	3rd	partial
1974	Pirates	162	88	74	0.543	1st	
1975	Pirates	161	92	69	0.571	1st	
1976	Pirates	162	92	70	0.568	2nd	
Career	Pirates	**2064**	**1115**	**950**	**0.540**		
MLB			**Wins**		**Win %**		
Rank by %	**>1,000 games**		**50th**		**47th**		
	>2,000 games				**19th**		

Mickey Vernon Hitting Statistics

Source: Baseball-almanac.com

Mickey Vernon

=All Star, shaded = AL Batting title

Mickey Vernon Hitting Statistics

Yr	Age	Team	G	AB	R	H	2B	3B	HR	RBI	BB	SO	SH	HBP	AVG	OBP	SLG
1939	21	Senators	76	276	23	71	15	4	1	30	24	28	9	0	.257	.317	.351
1940	22	Senators	5	19	0	3	0	0	0	0	0	3	0	0	.158	.158	.158
1941	23	Senators	138	531	73	159	27	11	9	93	43	51	7	0	.299	.352	.443
1942	24	Senators	151	621	76	168	34	6	9	86	59	63	2	3	.271	.337	.388
1943	25	Senators	145	553	89	148	29	8	7	70	67	55	8	10	.268	.357	.387
1946	28	Senators#	148	587	88	207	51	8	8	85	49	64	2	0	.353	.403	.508
1947	29	Senators	154	600	77	159	29	12	7	85	49	42	3	0	.265	.320	.388
1948	30	Senators#	150	558	78	135	27	7	3	48	54	43	6	1	.242	.310	.332
1949	31	Indians	153	584	72	170	27	4	18	83	58	51	15	2	.291	.357	.443
1950	32	Indians	28	90	8	17	0	0	0	10	12	10	3	0	.189	.284	.189
1950	32	Senators	90	327	47	100	17	3	9	65	50	29	3	4	.306	.404	.459
1951	33	Senators	141	546	69	160	30	7	9	87	53	45	1	2	.293	.358	.423
1952	34	Senators	154	569	71	143	33	9	10	80	89	66	5	0	.251	.353	.394
1953	35	Senators#	152	608	101	205	43	11	15	115	63	57	4	4	.337	.403	.518
1954	36	Senators#	151	597	90	173	33	14	20	97	61	61	4	5	.290	.357	.492
1955	37	Senators#	150	538	74	162	23	8	14	85	74	50	4	3	.301	.384	.452
1956	38	Red Sox#	119	403	67	125	28	4	15	84	57	40	2	7	.310	.403	.511
1957	39	Red Sox	102	270	36	65	18	1	7	38	41	35	1	5	.241	.350	.393
1958	40	Indians#	119	355	49	104	22	3	8	55	44	56	1	2	.293	.372	.439
1959	41	Braves	74	91	8	20	4	0	3	14	7	20	0	1	.220	.283	.363
1960	42	Pirates WS	9	8	0	1	0	0	0	1	1	0	0	0	.125	.222	.125
Career			G	AB	R	H	2B	3B	HR	RBI	BB	SO	SH	HBP	AVG	OBP	SLG
20 Years			2,409	8,731	1,196	2,495	490	120	172	1,311	955	869	80	49	.286	.359	.428

Source: Baseball Almanac.com

Mickey Vernon MLB Manager Statistics

Year	Team	Games	Won	Lost	Win %	Finish
1961	Senators	161	61	100	.379	9TH
1962	Senators	162	61	101	.370	10TH
1963	Senators	40	14	26	.350	10TH
3 years		363	135	227	.372	

LIST OF PHOTOS

Danny and Mickey, Ordinary Heroes

Danny and Mickey, Ordinary Heroes

30. Chester city, along the Delaware River, pg.236 Chester, Postcard History Series , CHC
31. Ike likes Mickey, 1954, pg.236
32. Joe E. Brown with Danny and Joe L., pg.315
33. Danny and Casey Stengel, 1960, pg.315
34. Maz at the plate, October 13, 1960, pg.315
35. Mazeroski scores the winner, 1960, pg.316
36. Pirates' Cooperstown HOF plaque, pg.316
37. Pittsburgh 'pandemonium', 1960, pg.316
38. Danny Murtaugh Delco plaque, pg.317
39. Danny, Sport's Man of the Year, 1960, pg.317
40. Mickey Vernon statue, Marcus Hook, PA, pg.317
41. Mickey Vernon plaque, MV Park, pg.317
42. Danny and Mickey, 1959, pg.318
43. Mazeroski, Danny, Mickey at home plate, courtesy of Harry Harris, AP, 1960., pg.318

BIBLIOGRAPHY

The Whistling Irishman: Danny Murtaugh Remembered.
Colleen Hroncich, 2010, ISBN 978-1-935592-99-0
Sports Challenge Network Publishing.

Mickey Vernon, the Gentleman First Baseman, Rich Westcott, 2005. ISBN: 0-940-159-94-5. Camino Books, Inc.

1960 Pittsburgh Pirates Day by Day, a Special Season, an Extraordinary World Series. Rick Cushing, 2010.
ISBN 978-1-4349-0498-0. Dorrance Publishing Company.

The Best Game Ever, Pirates vs Yankees, October 13, 1960.
Jim Reisler, 2007. ISBN 13: 978-0-7867-1943-3,
ISBN 10: 0-7867-1943-5. Carroll and Graf Publishers.

Kiss It Good-By, the Mystery, the Mormon, and the Moral of the 1960 Pittsburgh Pirates, John Moody, 2010. Shadow Mountain
Publisher. ISBN 978-1-60641-149-

Baseball's Best Managers, Harold Rosenthal, 1961, Chapter 4,
Sport Magazine Library, Bartholomew House

Ted Williams, Biography of an American Hero, Leigh Montville, Anchor Publishing

Danny Murtaugh Makes History, Luncheon. September 18, 2006.
Video by Bob Allen.

Mickey Vernon, Great Memories of a Great Champion,
Video/ Interviews, Mickey Vernon Sports Museum, 2013.

Danny and Mickey, Ordinary Heroes

Baseball Immortals Caught on Film, Filmed and Narrated by Mickey Vernon, Mickey Vernon Sports Museum.

History of the 97th Infantry Division, www.97thdivision.com

The Story of the 97th Infantry Division, Lonesentry.com

Baseballplayersinwartime.com, Gary Bedingfield

Mickey Vernon Sports Museum, mickeyvernonmuseum.com

Other valuable sources
Baseball-almanac.com
Baseballreference.com
Wikipedia.com

About the Author

RN McLaughlin was born and raised in Chester, PA. He is a graduate of St. James High School and Widener University in Chester, and is a lifelong resident of Delaware County. He currently resides in Ridley Park, PA. He is an avid Philadelphia sports fan who supports all of the local sports teams. He only rooted one time for a team outside the city, that team was the 1960 Pittsburgh Pirates.

Danny and Mickey, Ordinary Heroes
Robert N McLaughlin
2016
Visit *www.dannyandmickey.com*

email: rnm1126@verizon.net

CPSIA information can be obtained
at www.ICGtesting.com
Printed in the USA
FSOW01n0256130916
24882FS